Town House

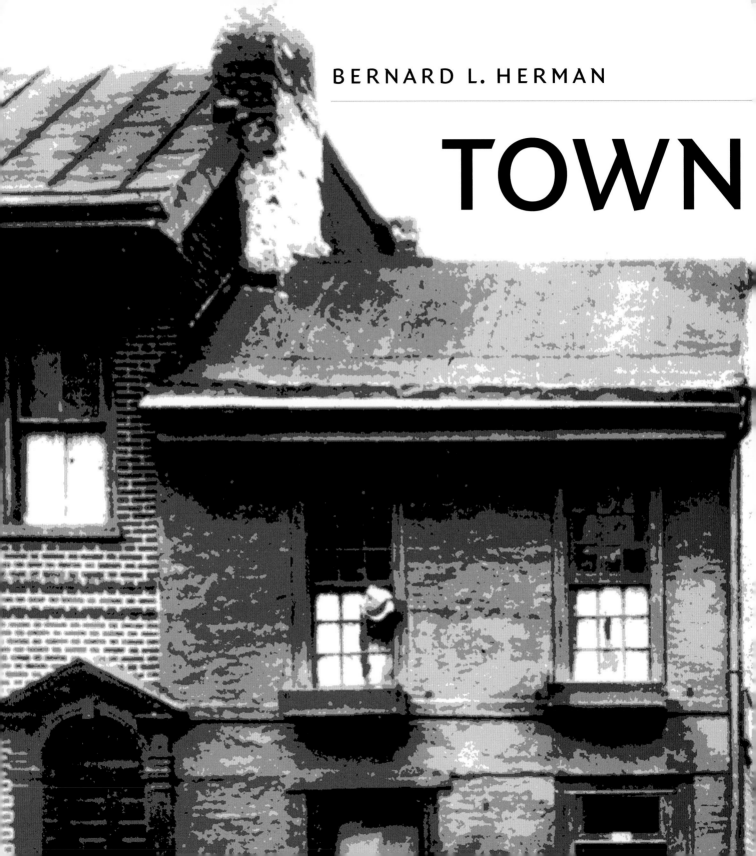

BERNARD L. HERMAN

TOWN

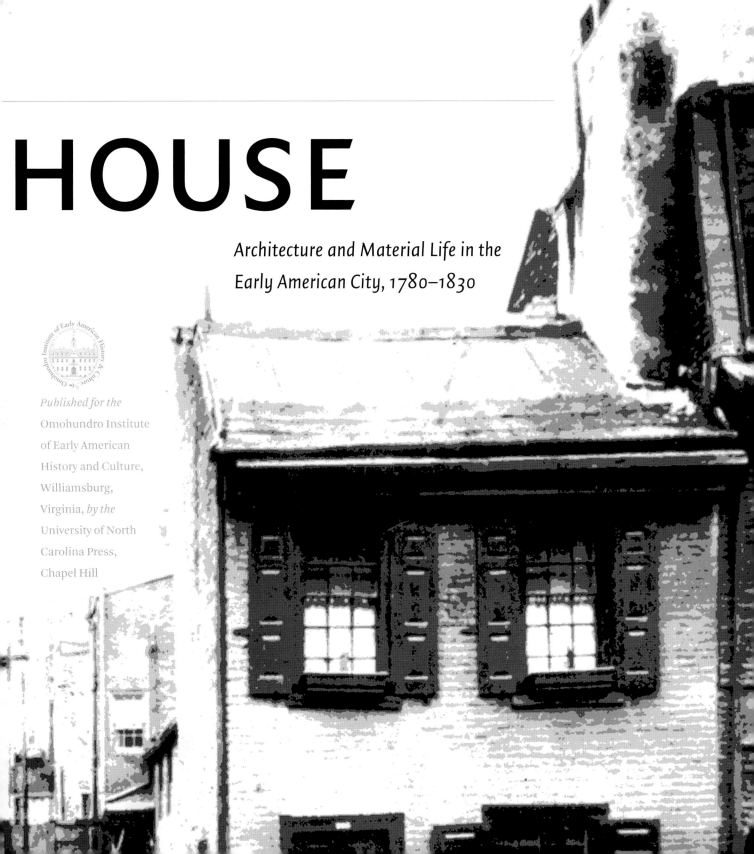

HOUSE

Architecture and Material Life in the
Early American City, 1780–1830

Published *for the*
Omohundro Institute
of Early American
History and Culture,
Williamsburg,
Virginia, *by the*
University of North
Carolina Press,
Chapel Hill

The Omohundro Institute of Early American
History and Culture is sponsored jointly by the
College of William and Mary and the Colonial
Williamsburg Foundation. On November 15, 1996,
the Institute adopted the present name in honor of
a bequest from Malvern H. Omohundro, Jr.

Designed and typeset in Arnhem Blond and Quadraat Sans
by Eric M. Brooks
Manufactured in China

Library of Congress Cataloging-in-Publication Data
Herman, Bernard L., 1951–
Town house: architecture and material life in the early
American city, 1780–1830 / Bernard L. Herman.
p. cm.
Includes bibliographical references and index.
ISBN 0-8078-2991-9 (cloth: alk. paper)
1. Row houses—United States. 2. Architecture—United States—
18th century. 3. Architecture—United States—19th century.
4. Dwellings—Social aspects—United States. I. Omohundro
Institute of Early American History & Culture. II. Title.
NA7206.H47   2005   307.3'3616'097309033—dc22   2005005918

The paper in this book meets the guidelines for permanence
and durability of the Committee on Production Guidelines for
Book Longevity of the Council on Library Resouces.

This book received indirect support from an unrestricted book
publications grant awarded to the Institute by the L. J. Skaggs and
Mary C. Skaggs Foundation of Oakland, California.

09 08 07 06 05   5 4 3 2 1

FOR REBECCA

There was something unpleasant
about the old man, and I turned my
attention away from him to the
discoloured houses squatting side by
side before me in the rain like a row
of morose animals. How eerie and
run-down they all looked! Plumped
down without thought, they stood
there like weeds that had shot up
from the ground.

GUSTAV MEYRINK, *The Golem*

(1915; 1995 translation by Mike Mitchell)

Acknowledgments

This book began when my friend and colleague David Ames directed my energies to the documentation of the now demolished Thomas Mendenhall House in Wilmington, Delaware. The subsequent architectural history and archaeology of the Mendenhall House undertaken with Dean Nelson sparked further explorations into eighteenth-century urban architecture that ultimately inspired this work.

Many individuals and institutions made this book possible. A University of Delaware General University Research award and a grant from the National Endowment for the Humanities enabled me to develop many of the databases that provided a statistical profile for different towns and cities. That work could not have been undertaken without the expertise of Richard Stevens and Rebecca Sheppard. The knowledge, patience, and consideration offered by archivists, librarians, and clerks from Charleston, South Carolina, to Portsmouth, New Hampshire, to the seaport towns of England moved this project forward. I cannot name them all here, but their collective enthusiasm and openness provided information, insight, and humor more times than I can count.

Thanks go to my colleagues at the University of Delaware, J. Ritchie Garrison, Lu Ann De Cunzo, James C. Curtis, Martin Brückner, J. A. Leo Lemay, Damie Stillman, Wayne Craven, Perry Chapman, Wendy Bellion, and

Raymond Nichols. Fellow travelers include Jeffrey Klee, Gabrielle M. Lanier, Amy Henderson, Nancy van Dolsen, Anna Andrzejewski, Eric Gollannek, Jeroen van den Hurk, Zara Anahanslin-Bernhardt, Julie Riesenweber, William Macintire, Amy Johnson, Nancy Ziegler, and Jennifer Barrett. At the Winterthur Museum and Library I benefited from the insights and advice of Gary Kulik, Brock Jobe, Gretchen Buggeln, Neville Thompson, Rich McKinstry, and the great classes of Winterthur Fellows in Early American Culture. Holly Mitchell, Pam Herrick, Phillip Hayden, Thomas Ryan, Rhonda Goodman, Catherine Dann, Ashli White, Laura Stutman, Jennifer van Horne, Dana Byrd, and Bobbye Tigerman all helped me think through elements of the larger project. A National Endowment for the Humanities independent research award funded the time to write the first full draft of this book.

Time spent with friends and colleagues in towns and cities in the United States and England was the best part of this project. I met many wonderful individuals whose collective generosity of spirit made this work possible. I can never thank them enough for all their insights and kindnesses. For their help on Charleston, South Carolina, I am indebted to Martha Zierden of the Charleston Museum and Jonathan Poston and Carter Hudgins of the Historic Charleston Foundation. They along with their staff and Karen Prewitt helped gain access to numerous buildings. Louis Nelson, Gary Stanton, and Carol Lounsbury proved excellent and insightful companions in the field. In Portsmouth, New Hampshire, I turned repeatedly to Richard Candee, Gerald Ward, and Barbara Ward for insight and hospitality. Michael Steinitz introduced me to the richness and subtleties of the seaport towns of Massachusetts Bay. Abbott Lowell Cummings, Myron Stachiw, and Claire Dempsey graciously gave of their rich knowledge of all things New English. In Norfolk I benefited tremendously from the professional expertise of the staff of the Moses and Elizabeth Myers House. Peggy Haile and the staff of the Sergeant Memorial Room at the Kirn Library introduced me to the graphic record of the all-but-vanished eighteenth-century city. Willie Graham generously shared his knowledge of the town house traditions of Petersburg, Virginia. In Lancaster, Pennsylvania, I learned about the borough's early architcture from Thomas Ryan, Tracy Weis, and Patricia Keller. Many friends and colleagues encouraged my work in Philadelphia. Special thanks go to Susan Klepp, Jeffrey Cohen, Susan Garfinkel, Amy Henderson, David Orr, William Bolger, Richard and Miriam Camitta, Beth Richards, Robert Kaufman, and Kenneth Finkel. Ellen Miller always volunteered to make the calls that provided access to a remarkable array of buildings.

In England I turned repeatedly to colleagues in the former Royal Commission on the Historical Monuments of England, English Heritage, and the Survey of London. John and Heather Smith graciously provided the introductions that enabled me to get started on fieldwork in English cities and towns. John's sharp insights provided a framework for questioning the evidence of English urban houses. In London I learned much from Nicholas Cooper, Sarah Pearson, Stephen Croad, Derek Keene, Elizabeth McKellar, Tim Whittaker, Neil Burton, Ann Robey, Richard Bond, John Styles, Amanda Vickery, and Richard Lea. Peter Guillery was a willing partner in multiple architectural adventures. His pointed questions provided a constant and happy reminder about the underlying complexities of London's demotic architecture. His own book on the smaller houses of eighteenth-century London is a powerful contribution to English architectural history. Peter Guillery with Robert Hook introduced me to the towns along the Kentish coast; Roger Leech shared his knowledge of Bristol. Robin Thornes lured me first to the great eighteenth-century port towns of Whitby and Hull and then to Bristol. Robin's thoughtful comments shaped this book in its formative stages. My greatest debt in the United Kingdom is to John and Sarah Bold. Their hospitality never wavered. The conversations John and I shared about how we might profitably interpret the dynamic character of urban landscapes were inspirational.

The extended writing of this book relied on continuing conversations with my beloved friend David Shields. Dell Upton and Cary Carson kindly shared their critical insights on multiple occasions, and Ted Pearson generously weighed in on some niggling questions. As always, I remain particularly indebted to David Orr, Henry Glassie, Don Yoder, and Gerald Pocius, who continue to shape how I think about the world of objects. Colleagues at the Omohundro Institute of Early American History and Culture transformed the manuscript into this book. I am deeply indebted to Fredrika Teute, who asked all the right questions and made this book much better in innumerable ways, and to Becky Wrenn, the indexer. Gil Kelly, Emily Moore, and James Horn at the Institute tamed an unruly manuscript.

My family provided encouragement throughout the research and writing of this book. Thank you, Fredrika and Paul Jacobs, Frederick and Lucy Herman, and Jessica and Nicholas Russanov. Lania Herman helped in the field and offered reminders that cities live. The deepest thanks of all go to Rebecca Herman for her help with everything and always when it matters most.

Contents

Illustrations

Town House

URBAN SETTINGS

HOUSES AND HOUSING IN THE EARLY AMERICAN CITY

This is a study about urban dwellings and the people who built and lived in them, from roughly 1780 to 1830. As a story of buildings and people, this book combines questions and approaches gleaned from the practice of architectural and social history. Writing architectural history, I narrate the experience of city houses and emphasize the ways people anchored their lives in the material world, rather than the design, construction, and style of buildings (although these elements are central to this text). Writing social history, I am mindful that "events take place" and happen in real time and space. Place clearly matters, and occasion always affects experience. Thus, I pursue a material culture approach that draws on both the artifact and its representation in written sources. The goal is to use objects to better understand how and why people acted in particular ways and to assess the larger cultural significances of their actions. Through a material culture approach to history, objects are not relegated to the status of simple illustrations but move to the fore as key elements for deciphering and writing the past.

Each of the chapters in this work begins with an event or vignette and raises questions about its architectural significance. For example, Billy Robinson, on trial for his life in the aftermath of Denmark Vesey's aborted slave insurrection of 1822, in Charleston, South Carolina, mounted an architectural defense in a desperate bid to gain acquittal. Robinson acted on his understanding of how buildings circumscribed his life, and sought to exploit white masters' presumptions of control. Similarly, when Hannah Rand's neighbors came to her Portsmouth, New Hampshire, home to lay out her widow's "third" in the house, she drew on a profound knowledge of the symbolic qualities of domestic space as she negotiated the rooms that would be hers. Houses and housing contained and signified different aspects of city life. They were the physical objects that composed the largest portion of early American urban settings. They are also artifacts that contained and defined the enactment of everyday relationships. In both capacities houses are signifiers that communicate the order (and conflicts) of urban life. Billy Robinson, Hannah Rand, and all the other individuals in these pages knew the signifying power of buildings and the ways in which houses were agents in the business of everyday urban experience. One of our goals is to recover some of what they knew.

I do not retell the stories of the founding of towns and cities of the North Atlantic rim or revisit the histories of economic development, race, and class formation in them. Those investigations have been undertaken with considerable insight and success by others. The same is true for studies of urban form and city plans. Although this book relies on that collected knowledge, its aim is something different. These chapters mount a series of explorations into the ways people employed town houses as symbolic representations of self and community. To begin those explorations requires knowledge of a few words and concepts that provide a working framework for the narration of urban housing as social experience. This introductory chapter defines and illustrates the application of such terms as *presence of place, situation, comportment,* and *circumstance.*[1]

The evocative power of early American urban landscapes arises from a sense that architecture and setting affect our comprehension of city society in particular and immediate ways. As a medium for the assertion of social identity, as settings for the display of gentility and its applications, as sites of power and its negotiation, town houses matter. Architectural settings, however, are employed most often by historians as illustrations for arguments derived from other, typically documentary, sources. Yet, taken together, the physical and documentary evidence of town houses can generate new questions and reframe old ones about urban life and society. Key to this approach is an archaeology of the city that interrogates its very materiality, in this instance through houses and housing. The evidence of urban dwellings provides a social and symbolic sense of the flow and texture of everyday city life and yields what is best understood as the *presence of place*.[2]

Presence of place describes the combination of artifacts and behaviors that lend a locale its distinctive visual and cultural identity. Presence of place is relational; it relies on associations found within the rooms and furnishings of buildings and, in telescopic fashion, on the associations between buildings and their settings on a larger geographical scale. Presence of place recognizes that each late-eighteenth-century American city displayed its own architectural personas—visible identities conveyed in the confluence of regional preference, civic ambition, social customs, economic organization, and individual action and expressed in the details of house plans, construction techniques, siting, and decorative finishes. Presence of place impressed travelers through their perceptions of visual differences between cities. When Charleston resident William Drayton made a northward journey in 1786, he noted the peculiarities of Philadelphia's town houses: The buildings "are chiefly of Brick, of two, three, and a few four stories high; very neatly finished; tho' with some Peculiarity of Style, which I think marks every Country in their Houses." Drayton continued: "These [houses] are generally very narrow, and long; with a Penthouse, wch projects about 2 feet over the first or second Story, and a Deep Cornice over the upper, which has almost the same effect. As they are closely built, and have very little yard-Room, the roofs in general are constructed so flat, as to afford Convenience for drying the Family Linen." To illustrate his point Drayton sketched a Philadelphia town house and labeled it in the "General Style" of the city (see Figure 1.1). Drayton defined the architectural distinctiveness of Philadelphia relative to the town houses that lined the streets of his own Charleston. But Charleston's urban residences excited their own commentary from visitors.[3]

New England traveler Edward Hooker marveled over the city's distinctive appearance: "So many things different from what I had been accustomed to—So many, different from what I expected to find." Hooker continued, describing the appearance of the dwellings in the older, more densely built section of town: "Most of the houses in the city are brick: and a great number of them are covered with a dull looking brownish plaster and chequered, as to resemble stone. Most of them are three stories high." Still, the style of living he saw in these same houses related them to the larger traditions of provincial seaports on both sides of the Atlantic: "It is common custom for those who are in trade to live in the second story, while the lower story is used to trade in." Hooker discovered a measure of familiarity in this verti-

FIGURE 1.1

Typical House in Philadelphia,
Perspective View (circa 1786).
By William Drayton. *Courtesy
South Carolina Historical Society,
Charleston*

General Style of Houses
in Philadelphia.

cal organization of the house, but, like Drayton a generation earlier, he was ultimately drawn to the appearances of difference.[4]

Town houses are markers of social identity, but the symbolic content of any one dwelling is understood only in light of its relationships to its larger environments. Taken together, town houses created urban settings where events happened and objects accrued social meaning through usage and experience. *Situation,* a term employed by eighteenth-century town house builders, best captures this relational and experiential quality. Situation referred in its limited and most specific sense to the location, suitability, and liabilities of a building lot but also carried larger social implications about how individuals should appropriately present themselves in the world. Situation in this expanded sense embraced the relationships between people and their environments and the ways others perceived and valued those relationships. Thus, the interpretation of urban houses and housing needs to address two points: first, the physical nature of the object in terms of design, construction, ornament, and setting; second, the experience of the artifact in terms of use, perception, imagination, and symbol.

Buildings sculpted the contours of urban experience. Eighteenth-century descriptions of early American seaports stressed perceived tensions between urban disorder and regularity. Cities were constant objects of idealization, seen as the outward manifestations of organized, civil society. They were also disparaged as vulnerable to disruptive forces ranging from street demonstrations to the antics of rebellious tenants. Visitors and residents alike assayed the chaotic aspect of cities through the world of the senses: the viscous, clinging muck of muddy streets, the searing stench of rot and sewage, the clattering din of tavern and market, and awkward-looking town houses reflecting shoddy and often flammable construction. In contrast, the regular face of the city celebrated public buildings and civil citizens, the brisk unimpeded flow of trade, and the productivity of craft and industry as well as the fashionable, well-built town houses designed and occupied by people engaged in the material conversations of cosmopolitan tastes that permeated polite society in the North Atlantic rim. Town houses, intimate settings for urban life and action, rendered personal and private experience sensible in the larger situation of urban life; town houses exerted presence of place, communicating and enacting the experiences and meanings of the early American city.[5]

Comportment and *circumstance* help define the ways in which people assessed situation and expressed presence of place. Comportment denotes the visual, spatial, and mental relationships that people perceive, construct, and experience between buildings, settings, objects, and selves. Comportment treats the ways in which people stand in relationship to one another and the worlds they inhabit; it is an evocation of the etiquette of everyday life. The lens of comportment scrutinizes both the exterior and interior domains of the town house. The ways in which the house visually addresses the street or its rooms and bodily relates to them (in placement, importance, architectural decoration, and furnishings) provide material signposts that people use to establish themselves in relationship both to household spaces and to one another. Circumstance, similarly, denotes specific individual and community associations invested in buildings and their settings. Comportment defines a general process centered on the balance of everyday social relationships; circumstance is about how the visible and material world reflects that balance (or imbalance, depending on your perspective). Circumstance refers to the individual design and construction of houses or groups of houses and their subsequent use. Circumstance is where the discovery of context begins.[6]

Artifacts and their settings function as sites for the exchange of symbolic actions, the content of which, reflected in the material world, remains open to negotiation and multiple, intersecting interpretive possibilities. Three brief and very different examples illustrate the layering of circumstance and comportment. North Square in Boston, Massachusetts, provides insight into contexts for individual buildings, their neighborhood and locale, and the place they occupy in the wider topographical and chronological contexts of urban housing and domestic life in the eighteenth-century North Atlantic rim. A portfolio of house plans compiled by New Castle, Delaware, attorney Kensey Johns in the late 1780s, coupled with the house he built on the town's courthouse square, reveals his thought process in architectural design and personal choice. Johns, an affluent and politically connected member of the elite, could afford choices open to few of his fellow citizens. But the range of design options available to him and his family and the ways in which those spaces and appearances architecturally reinforced their public personas were broadly understood in his local community and in the late-eighteenth-century Atlantic world of sociability and gentility. Finally, Caroline Burgwin's memoir of her childhood residence in Bristol, England, introduces the possibilities of an architectural history based on the ways people used and experienced buildings. It is this last framework, an experiential approach to the study of city houses, that guides this book.

North Square in Boston illustrates the ways we can construct multiple contexts or embedded landscapes through the lenses of presence of place, situation, comportment, and circumstance. Although two of the city's oldest extant houses endure as house museums, the physical remains of North Square's colonial and early national housing stock have been swept away. Still, linking buildings to documents is one component of this study; how that practice works can be seen in a reading of North Square.

North Square (formerly Clark's Square) stands in one of the city's oldest and most heavily rebuilt neighborhoods, located a few blocks to the north of the Massachusetts colonial State House. The irregular layout of North Square and the North End at the close of the eighteenth century followed older topographical imperatives based on natural landscape features and property lines dating to the earliest phase of colonial settlement. Formed by the intersection of a spur from Fish Street (the North End's principal wharf-side thoroughfare) and Moon and Garden Court Streets (two block-long lanes opening off Fleet Street), the eighteenth-century streetscape of North Square centered on a spacious, sloping open triangle of ground situated one street in from the city waterfront. The location of a former market, home to a royal governor, and the scene of colonial riots, North Square emerged at the close of the eighteenth century as a neighborhood in transition. Home to artisan, shopkeeper, and merchant families and Boston notables like Paul Revere and the Reverend John Lathrop, North Square and its surrounding streets presented a diverse array of town house designs.[7]

A tax list enumerating the size and appearance of buildings at the close of the eighteenth century presents a first snapshot of North Square, its North End environs, and a sense of the circumstance of the Revere and Pierce-Hichborn Houses. The majority of dwellings were of wood construction, a mode of urban building widely shared with other New England seaport cities, such as Salem and Newburyport, but frowned upon in more distant cities, like Philadelphia, where wood was equated with fire. More than two-thirds of the town houses in the North End were of timber construction; the rest included an equal mix of houses noted as either brick or "wood and brick," the latter likely referring to the practice of building town houses with frame street and backyard elevations and brick walls facing neighboring buildings on either side. The assessors recorded the application of "rough-cast," or stucco, to four of the enumerated wooden houses, a finish that could be scored or pebbled to suggest a higher quality of construction or simply mask the scars of additions and alterations. North End town houses were nearly all either two or three stories tall. Although the numbers of two- and three-story houses were nearly equal, sharp differences emerge in the relationship between building height and material. Only one in three of the frame houses stood three stories high, compared to the three-in-five ratio for brick dwellings. Brick houses, similarly, tended to be larger in area than frame dwellings, averaging 764 square feet on a floor, compared to the 690 square feet of wood and wood-and-brick residences.[8]

Notations on building material, elevation, and area, however, do not fully convey the architectural relationships visible in the North End at the close of the eighteenth century. Although heavily redeveloped in the nineteenth century, the North End retains a handful of the town houses recorded in the 1798 tax. Two of these, the Paul Revere House and the Pierce-Hichborn House, both in North Square, provide a powerful visual sense of the architectural contrasts and tensions found in the North End's oldest extant housing. The task is to understand the two dwellings individually, then relative to each other and, finally, to the larger building traditions that shaped them.

Erected circa 1681, the *L*-shaped Revere House (acquired only at the end of the eighteenth century by the Revere family) replaced an earlier dwelling destroyed by fire in 1679 (see Figure 1.2). Following regional framing traditions identified with early Massachusetts Bay timber construction, the main block of the two-story dwelling consisted of four structural bays demarcated by heavy framing posts that jutted into the room. Overhead, heavy summer beams emphasized the physical structure that defined the single ground-floor room dominated by its chimney bay and adjoining lobby entrance. These and other architectural features ally the Revere House with other colonial New England frame houses documented in a variety of rural and village settings. Other details reveal the building's urban character. Lot limitations and the desire to present the most impressive elevation to the street left the builders with little alternative for service spaces other than behind the house. Although some later-seventeenth-century Boston town houses reportedly made use of separate kitchen buildings, common practice favored service ells like the two-story extension behind the Revere House. The setting of the Revere House also contributed to the installation of double casement windows in the rear elevation; the proximity of the neighbor's dwelling discouraged their more usual placement in the gable.[9]

The overall appearance of the Revere House underscores an almost ambivalent regard for the building's urban identity. Erected in wood as a free-standing structure, the house squandered street frontage with its double-fronted elevation and harked back to the provincial building practices of the Massachusetts Bay region. Timber-frame and lobby-entry-plan houses were the mainstay of Marblehead's early colonial streetscapes. Similar buildings continued to be erected in nearby Salem and Newburyport into the mid-eighteenth century. The colonial architectural context for judging the Revere House was founded in the buildings of other Massachusetts Bay port towns like Ipswich; here, the streets remain populated with seventeenth- and early-eighteenth-century town houses—each built of wood, each standing alone on its lot, each drawing on and reinforcing the decorative vocabulary of its provincial circumstance. Thus, the Revere House was urban by virtue of its setting in Massachusetts's principal colonial seaport, but the use of molded-edge clapboard, front jetty with carved pendants, and interior plas-

FIGURE 1.2
Paul Revere House, North Square, Boston.
As Restored

tered ceilings did not render the appearance of the house so much urban as regionally fashionable in a provincial British-American townscape.[10]

Three stories tall, the brick Pierce-Hichborn House, built about 1711, stood three doors down the square from the Revere House and offered a very different image (see Figure 1.3). The original house plan consisted of a central passage with a single heated room on either side. In this arrangement, the ground-floor front room might have been occupied variously as a shop room, a separate tenant's lodging, or a widow's apartment. With its narrow elevation to the street, facade fronting on a compact private passageway, neat but plain common-bond brickwork, decorative belt courses, and large sash windows, the Pierce-Hichborn House reflected early stirrings of the "provincial renaissance" architecture of colonial Boston. "Provincial renaissance" recognizes both the presence of house-building artisans as carriers of innovative ideas (drawn from a combination of academic and vernacular Anglo-Netherlandish and New England design sources) and the desires of clients, a nascent petite bourgeoisie ranging from government officials to well-to-do shopkeepers with the resources to commission and acquire stylish dwellings.[11]

The architectural language of classicism was readily appropriated into vernacular building strategies through the incorporation of balance and symmetry into the design of street elevations and the installation of decorative trim surrounding doors and windows or elaborating fireplace walls. More problematic were the kinds of spaces that lay behind fashionable appearances. In this context, the Pierce-Hichborn House represents one of many competing architectural alternatives—all centered on dwellings intended for the swelling ranks of an eighteenth-century "middling sort."[12]

A distillation of the larger debate surrounding eighteenth-century urban dwelling choices and informing the design of the Pierce-Hichborn House can be found in the range and variety of modest London residences being erected at the same time. A set of assumptions posited by architectural historian John Summerson continues to shape the interpretation of architectural possibilities for housing London's middling sort from the late seventeenth through the early nineteenth centuries. Summerson grounded the development of Georgian London in the speculative ventures of post-1666 Great Fire entrepreneurs like Nicholas Barbon, whose engagement with the architectural expression of standardization and regularity translated into a conceit for eighteenth-century English society. The house form popularly associated with these concerns was a residence two rooms deep with a side

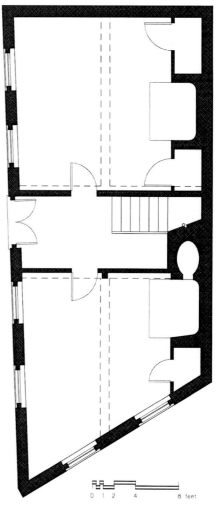

FIGURE 1.3

Pierce-Hichborn House, North Square, Boston

A Before Restoration. *Photograph Historic American Buildings Survey, Library of Congress*

B First-Floor Plan. *After Historic American Buildings Survey, Library of Congress. Drawn by Jeff Klee*

0 1 2   4   8 feet

stair passage and chimneys placed against the lateral walls. Often a third room, or "closet," extended from the rear elevation of the house. Although the precise origins for this dwelling type remain clouded, Netherlandish influences are one likely source for these "Barbon" houses.[13]

In plan, the middling range of seventeenth- and early-eighteenth-century Netherlandish town houses paralleled and anticipated the internal organization of this particular design of English town house even as their exterior appearances expressed a markedly different sense of the urban landscape (see Figure 1.4). Houses one room in width and two or more rooms in depth were a common fixture on the streets of Amsterdam and other Netherlandish cities. Number 13 Rapensburg, Amsterdam, built in 1614 and modified through the eighteenth century, incorporated two rooms placed back-to-back with a side passage extending the full depth of the house. The entry portion of the passage claimed nearly one-half of the area of the front of the house before it met a stairwell and then narrowed dramatically into a corridor leading past the back room to the yard. The house as first built also contained features that would remain foreign to English urban settings. Jambless fireplaces heated the rooms, exposed joists with deeply carved braces jutted from the ceiling, a hoist projected from the attic gable, and enclosed alcoves for beds claimed space in nearly every room. By the eighteenth century the house at 13 Rapensburg had been remodeled with a new emphasis on the creation of more highly ornamented interior spaces. Room uses were more precisely defined and their ornamentation made more elaborate in keeping with their relative importance within the house. Stairs were brought into the open and finished with fine plasterwork, and the back parlor (or *achterhuis*) emerged as a dining room and one of the most beautifully finished rooms in the house. These changes articulated a culture of sociability, accumulation, and display that anticipated and subsequently paralleled urban housing developments across the English Channel.[14]

About the same time London town houses combining Netherlandish and classical design elements were making their debut in the city and its suburbs, hydrographer and chronicler of trades Joseph Moxon published an alternative plan—one that similarly emphasized regularity and standardization in external appearance and fittings but suggested a significantly different internal arrangement, with a central chimney stack dividing the body of the house, a stair placed adjacent to the stack, and a narrow entry running through the house to the back lot (see Figure 1.5). Although the Moxon plan has been deemed a relic of postmedieval London building practices and

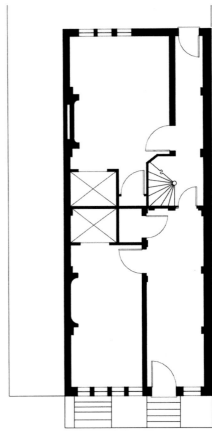

FIGURE 1.4

Number 13 Rapensburg, Amsterdam.
Constructed 1614

A Street View. *Photo by Jeroen van den Hurk*

0 1 2   4   8 feet

B Plan. *After Meischke, Zantkuijl, Raue, and
Rosenberg, Huizen in Nederland: Amsterdam,
212. Drawn by Jeff Klee*

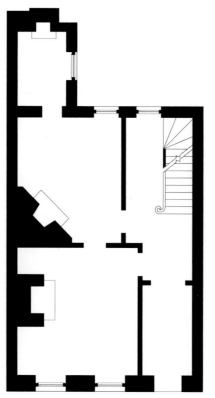

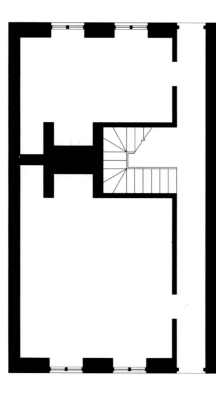

0 1 2   4   8 feet

held in counterpoint to the Barbon house, surviving buildings suggest that these houses remained popular through the eighteenth century. London town house plans recorded from the 1690s through the 1720s show the presence and variety of these center-chimney houses as they stood throughout the city (see Figure 1.6).[15]

London builders also drew on other design options. Two of these alternatives, which probably enjoyed only modest use in London, gained broader circulation in eighteenth- and early-nineteenth-century American urban settings. The first of these options included dwellings that placed the stair between the partition wall dividing the rooms and the jamb of the back chimney (see Figure 1.7). This compact arrangement appears to have been favored in circumstances where flexibility in the use of ground-floor spaces was an important consideration. Several of these houses stand in Deptford

FIGURE 1.5

House Plans, London

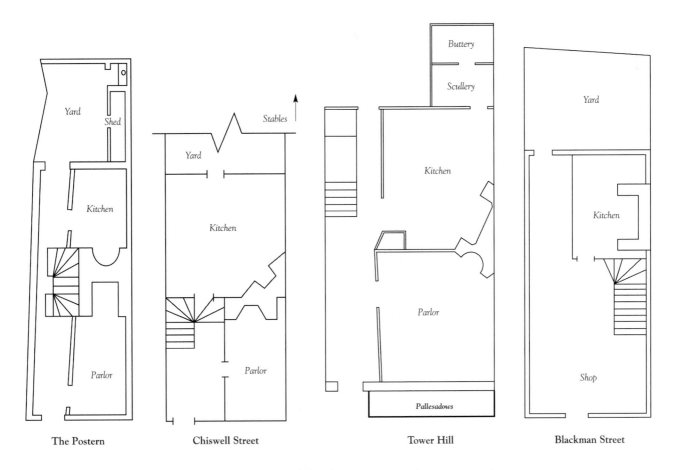

| The Postern | Chiswell Street | Tower Hill | Blackman Street |

High Street on the south side of the Thames, east of the city center. In each example, the house suggests a pattern of use that included a ground-floor shop and upper-story living quarters. Although the influence of this arrangement on the town houses of Boston and other northern New England seaport towns appears minimal, it did emerge as one of the dominant house forms of Philadelphia, Baltimore, and other mid-Atlantic cities.[16]

More immediate to understanding the Pierce-Hichborn House is a second family of dwellings located throughout greater London that placed the stair in the center of the house between the front and rear rooms (see Figure 1.8). In the majority of recorded examples, an interior passage extended past the front room to the stair in the middle of the house. The stair hall itself took one of two forms; it either reached all the way back to the party wall or was brought forward to create space for an unheated room or closet behind

FIGURE 1.6

Four House Plans after Original Surveys in "City Lands and Bridge House Properties" (1680–1720), London Record Office.

Drawn by Rebecca Y. Herman

FIGURE 1.7

Goddard's Pie Shop, 203
Deptford High Street, London

the stair. Although the most commonly recorded variants of this arrangement incorporated an internal entry, others made use of external passages or walkways that extend from the street. The builders of the Pierce-Hichborn House clearly embraced a version of this option, as did designers and clients in other eighteenth- and early-nineteenth-century American towns, including not only those of northern New England but also those of Charleston, South Carolina.[17]

The four alternatives exhibit strikingly different modes of access between interior and exterior spaces. The Moxon plans reveal a much more segmented quality that clearly divided the front and back of the house. One advantage in this segmented division was the possibility of dividing the Moxon house into front and back tenements. The Barbon plan, on the other hand, offered the option of using the rooms on a single floor en suite, an arrangement that facilitated acting out the increasingly popular rituals of polite sociability. The flow of space in houses where the stair was tucked into the back room was more open and public and was part of an arrangement that simplified movement between rooms on each floor but rendered access between stories more awkward. Finally, central-stair plans of the type exemplified by the Pierce-Hichborn House offered a house where front and back spaces were divided by an entry, such that the front room could lend itself for use as a shop or private parlor.[18]

The builders of the Pierce-Hichborn House took the same approach as many of their London contemporaries and erected a house that looked to a variety of possibilities and then drew on the one that best answered the demands of situation and circumstance. Their solution endures, not as an example of a house "type," but as artifactual evidence documenting a dynamic process of architectural design. The theme of circumstance complicates the interior of the Pierce-Hichborn House and its visual relationship to the Revere House. In their comportment, the two dwellings exhibit very different building sensibilities that describe two divergent worldviews forced into convergence by circumstance. While the Revere House draws on traditions of timber-frame construction, siting, and house plan closely identified with seventeenth-century New England villages and rural settlements, the Pierce-Hichborn House responds to building patterns associated with eighteenth-century English cities and towns and, specifically, the rise of a well-to-do merchant and artisan society.

If the Revere House cued itself to the visual culture of the provincial hinterlands of the Massachusetts Bay colony, the Pierce-Hichborn House was connected to a community defined, not by locality, but by "middling" urban sensibilities caught up in the exchange relations of the North Atlantic rim. Both houses, however, stood in contrast to their neighbors just up Garden Court Street. The Foster-Hutchinson and Clark-Frankland Houses presented classically inspired symmetrical elevations to the street, and to their neighbors and passersby in North Square (see Figure 1.9). The double-pile Foster-Hutchinson House, with its massive pilasters capped with Ionic

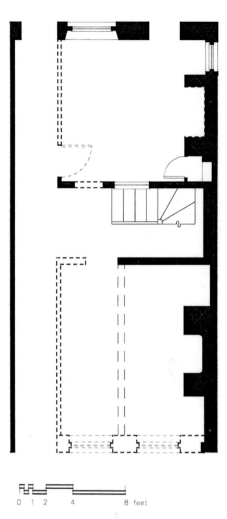

FIGURE 1.8

94 Mile End Road, Mile End Town, London, Reconstructed First-Floor Plan. *Drawn by Jeff Klee*

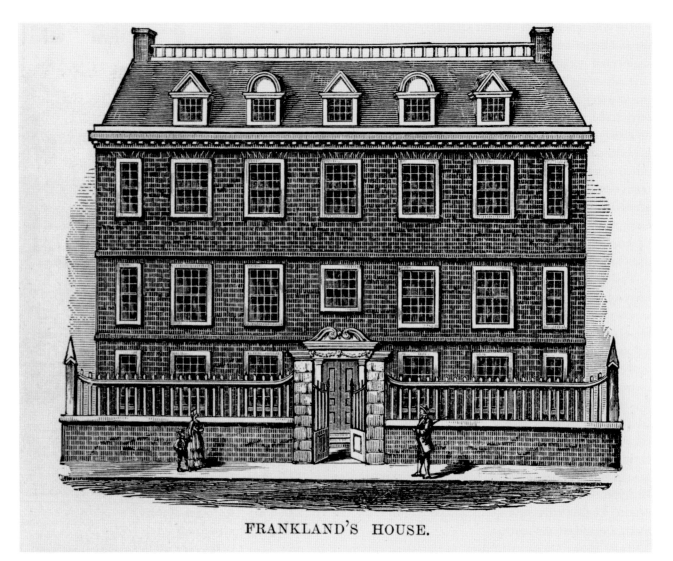

FRANKLAND'S HOUSE.

FIGURE 1.9

Houses, Garden Street Court, Boston.
Nineteenth-Century Views. *From Samuel Adams
Drake,* Around the Hub: A Boy's Book about
Boston *(Boston, 1882), 151, 152*

A Clark-Frankland House, North Square and
   Garden Court Street

capitals, included a balustraded cornice and second-floor balcony centered
on an arched opening leading into either an upper-story salon or a drawing room. The Clark-Frankland House asserted its stylish identity through
devices such as plat bands separating the stories, a scrolled pediment entry,
chimney closets with windows, and a row of alternating pedimented and
segmentally arched dormer windows. Like the Foster-Hutchinson House,
the Clark-Frankland mansion announced its double-pile, center-passage

THE HUTCHINSON MANSION.

B Foster-Hutchinson House,
Garden Court Street

plan to the street. Self-assuredly stylish and aggressively elite, these houses found their singular counterparts in every eighteenth-century English provincial seaport and market town on both sides of the Atlantic, from the shipbuilding center of Whitby on the Yorkshire coast to the lowcountry entrepôt of Charleston, South Carolina.[19]

The Pierce-Hichborn and Revere Houses paled in scale and finish compared to the great mansions that stood at the top of North Square and extended up Garden Court Street just as they dominated the two small frame town houses that separated them. Similarly, the architectural vista on the opposite side of the square from the perspective of the Revere House, Pierce-Hichborn House, and their neighbors comprehended backyards, work yards, and tenements associated with commercial premises lining Fish Street and fronting the city's wharves. Thus, the visual juxtapositions that defined North Square in the late 1700s were vivid. At one end of the scale stood the Reverend John Lathrop's three-story, 2,000-square-foot, brick-and-frame house. Occupying the site of the old "church of the Mathers," it overlooked the square and Eliza Phillis's modest two-story, 294-square-foot dwelling sandwiched between the Revere and Pierce-Hichborn Houses. By the 1820s, however, the impact of those distinctions diminished; North Square town houses grew more uniform through alterations and changing uses such as increasingly down-scale and subdivided shops and tenements. The Revere House was raised a full story, and its interior arrangements were updated; the Pierce-Hichborn House received a new, two-story brick kitchen and more fashionable finishes for its old interiors. Meanwhile, the heirs to the middling artisans, well-to-do merchants, and urban elites who occupied North Square through the eighteenth century sought housing elsewhere. The wealthiest relocated to Beacon Hill terraces; those of more modest means found new accommodations suited to social expectations and financial realities in Boston's dramatically growing southern and western suburbs. In the emerging city landscape of early-nineteenth-century Boston, architectural comportment assumed neighborhood proportions as urban settings grew increasingly segmented and distinct.[20]

The houses of North Square, standing and vanished, yield multiple insights into the eighteenth-century urban landscape. First, they provide a cross section of the domestic buildings crowding one city's colonial waterfront. North Square's architectural mix ranged from small frame cottages tucked into surrounding lanes and alleys to some of Boston's grandest town houses fronting the streets leading into the square. Second, the houses recorded in and around North Square suggest the mixed planning options individuals pursued in compact situations. Third, the range of houses in terms of material, size, and elevation indicates the dramatic variation of streetscapes in a small area and through the larger city. Finally, in their absence, both the smallest town house and largest mansion inform us of how little we actually know about the urban environment and the ways it acted on perception, action, and imagination. *Comportment* and *circumstance,* the visual and spatial relationships between buildings and their settings, describe the substance and significance of those processes.

The houses of Garden Court Street and North Square, however, were visually and experientially linked through their urban circumstances. All of the buildings stood in view of one another just as they stood in sight of the back lots of the houses overlooking Fish Street and the harbor with its boatyards, docks, and floating city of ships. What we discern in those visual relationships are nested sets of larger contexts. The houses define an environment where both difference and familiarity reign. As distinct as these buildings are from one another, they are also united in their shaping of a particular cityscape defined by qualities of juxtaposition. These houses interact with one another. The Clark-Frankland House echoes the sensibilities of the Foster-Hutchinson House even as it diminishes the visual impact of the Revere House. The Pierce-Hichborn House cleaves to the Revere House in the sense that both houses document the material position of a successful and influential artisan community. But they fracture along the lines of artisans' representation of self. The older Revere House draws its visual and spatial associations from local practice and significance; the Pierce-Hichborn House connects with an architectural vision linked to notions of urban identity more than of place.[21]

The relationships between the houses of North Square underscore two problems in thinking about town houses. First is the question of process. How did builders design a house? The second is one of experience. How did people encounter and know these buildings in the course of everyday life? The examples of Kensey Johns and Caroline Burgwin offer insight into these difficulties.

Recognizing the interplay between regional traditions and transatlantic metropolitan values in late-eighteenth- and early-nineteenth-century buildings erected in cities throughout the North Atlantic rim suggests a strategy that looks at individual buildings as options exercised by people making and communicating a sense of self and their environment. Whatever the physical and economic constraints on the planning and construction of actual dwellings, town house builders chose their solutions within an identifiable range of options. The idea of choice—the selection of options from that array of possibilities—stresses the myriad ways in which people conceived of, erected, used, and attached meaning to the places they lived, visited, and saw. Choice does not require an encyclopedic knowledge of town house types, but a familiarity with how the parts of houses work toward varying

FIGURE 1.10

Kensey Johns House, New Castle,
Delaware (circa 1789)

A Exterior

social and functional purposes. Choice softens the hard edge of type and reveals the suppleness of designers' minds negotiating the variables of client, artisan, function, site, and situation.[22]

While some town houses clearly document the triumph of one set of possibilities and their associated cultural values over another, most fall somewhere in between and reflect a process characterized by choice and constraint. Clients and builders drew on a range of design options, modifying them to suit both their expressive needs and the limitations imposed by cost, site, craft, and community perception. Nowhere is this more apparent than in the 1789 town house overlooking the public square in New Castle, Delaware, that Kensey Johns, attorney and state chancellor, designed for his family and legal practice (see Figure 1.10). Johns's design choices were exceptional. As members of the wealthy elite, he and his family enjoyed the means to undertake a house far beyond the expectations of the vast majority of city residents anywhere in the late-eighteenth-century United States. Johns's atypical choices are bound to broader town house design processes by the fact that every builder made choices about housing. Unfortunately, the more usual range of choices is documented only in rare instances.[23]

When Johns decided to contract for his new town house, he communicated his intentions to carpenter Peter Justis, who resided in nearby Wilmington. In his reply, Justis sympathized with his prospective client about obtaining a suitable lot in the old colonial capital, which still retained the county's legislative functions. He concluded, "Sir when you Sute yourself with a Lot forward mee with a line if you Pleas and I will Draw a Plan and Bill of Scantling agreeable to the Situation and your Desire." Although Justis died before he concluded a building contract with Johns, his solicitation for information on "situation" and "desire" initiated a design process shaped through negotiation, codified by contract, and realized in brick and timber. Following Justis's death, Johns concluded his town house contract with other builders after providing them with a contract and a plan of the proposed dwelling. Acting as his own architect, a practice common among late-eighteenth-century educated individuals, Johns developed at least eight plans for his house before settling on one. Because the surviving drawings are unnumbered, a progression from one concept to the next cannot be established. Still, grouping the plans by the ways in which they organize rooms, we can tentatively reconstruct Johns's thoughts on design as he refined the form his house would take.[24]

With a single exception, all the plans Johns considered incorporated a primary entry via an unheated passage containing an open staircase and access to a suite of first-floor rooms. The one exception offered a three-room arrangement with a detached kitchen and provided direct entry into a primary living area with a stair and the largest fireplace in the main body of the dwelling (see Figure 1.11). The three-room arrangement reflected a well-established regional building type (as did the Revere House) associated with millowners, tavernkeepers, wealthy landholders, and other individuals who desired a house that incorporated a large public room. The significance of Johns's consideration of this particular design reveals a dilemma in pur-

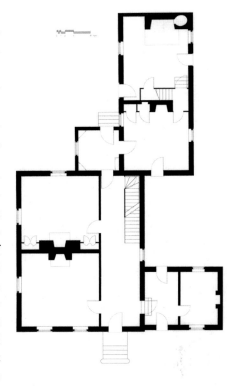

B First-Floor Plan. Including Kitchen Wing Added Shortly after House Was Completed. *After Historic American Buildings Survey, Library of Congress. Drawn by Jeff Klee*

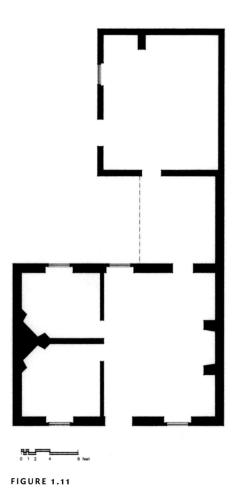

Kensey Johns House, Proposed Three-Room Plan, with Kitchen Wing. *After original drawings in the Historical Society of Delaware, Wilmington. Drawn by Jeff Klee*

pose. Intended for a corner lot fronting the green and looking past the courthouse square to the town waterfront, Johns's house was a carefully formulated presentation of self that asserted his place in a community standing at the threshold between an agricultural hinterland and the late-eighteenth-century Atlantic world. His problem lay in the intended audience this choice would address and the associations evoked. As a preferred dwelling type for a rural elite, Johns's plan architecturally bound him to the immediate contexts of local culture—but satisfied neither his situation nor desire.

The remaining drafts prepared for Kensey Johns's town house can be divided into two groups: center-passage and side-passage options. Two center-passage proposals reflect the abandonment of the "open" form of the three-room plan in favor of a double-fronted town house that employed an unheated entry as a reception area and social buffer. The more detailed proposal presented an L-shaped house with the main block containing a parlor, an entry with a staircase, and common room (see Figure 1.12A). A gable extension and rear ell added a lodging room and kitchen on the ground floor. The proposed elevation offered a symmetrical, five-bay gable front to the street in a style reminiscent of a handful of early Georgian plantation houses associated with other Delaware elites. In his alternative center-passage plan, Johns sketched a twenty-eight-by-forty-foot house with a broad entry flanked on the right by a parlor and an office, and on the left by a common room and lodging room offering access to a kitchen wing (see Figure 1.12B). The accompanying site plan identified additional buildings and spaces, including a smokehouse, granary, office, backbuildings, well, yard, garden, and private alley leading to the street. Together, Johns's plans display a significant shift in the architectural persona he wanted to project in the public sphere. The two-story, five-bay house with its pedimented gable front presented an impressive image. The incorporation of service separated from the main house by the lodging room rejected the practice of segregating service from the house in an outbuilding sited across an open or shedded yard. The introduction of an entry and stair hall ritualized and directed access into the house in ways that effected social distance and enhanced spatial control.[25]

The remaining five drawings produced the final design for the house. One of them presents a balanced, three-bay front to the street with a centrally placed door that opens into a ten-by-sixteen-foot entry dominated by a grand stair (see Figure 1.12C). The largest room in the house stood behind the entry, and a pair of thirteen-by-fourteen-foot rooms occupied the gable end of the house. A door located under the stair landing led into an

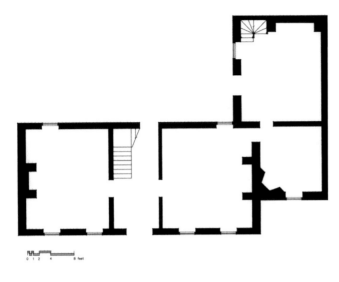

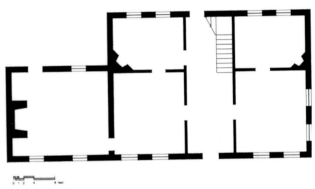

A L-Shape with Parlor, Entry with Staircase, and Common Room

B Two-Rooms Deep, with Entry, Parlor, Office, Common Room, and Lodging Room

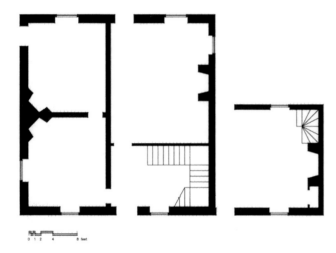

C Corner Entry and Stair Hall

FIGURE 1.12
Kensey Johns House, Proposals for Entries
with Stairs. *After original drawings in the Historical
Society of Delaware, Wilmington. Drawn by Jeff Klee*

eighteen-foot-square wing attached to the opposite gable. This design continued Johns's engagement with a plan that extended two rooms in depth and emphasized the entry and stair hall as the primary axis for the house. Before Johns completely abandoned this option, he apparently toyed with an alternative possibility addressing some of its liabilities. First, he turned the house away from the public square so that it fronted the street that led from the public wharves, past the courthouse, and into the town's agricultural hinterland. The new orientation led Johns to design a new front elevation that included two symmetrically placed entries with the one nearest the corner opening into a formal stair hall and the other yielding separate access into a twelve-by-seventeen-foot office heated by a corner fireplace. The new design pushed the most formal social spaces to the rear; the dining room behind the stair overlooked the public green across the street, and the parlor was oriented toward the back garden. The plan then placed cooking and service functions in a back ell, buffered from the main body of the house by a six-foot passage. The placement of interior doorways, however, reveals the still unsatisfactory traffic flow in this proposal. Access between dining room and parlor required passage under the stair and through the entry. Movement between kitchen and parlor was even more segmented. A servant's journey might begin at the cooking hearth, proceed across the kitchen passage, traverse the dining room, turn through the entry, and conclude in the parlor. As a workable solution, the plan failed.

Johns resolved his indecision in the last three drafts in his portfolio. Narrowing their options, the Johns family settled on a ground-floor plan composed of a ten-foot-wide passage running the full thirty-two-foot depth of the house and providing direct entry into a front parlor and slightly smaller back room, likely intended as a dining room (see Figure 1.12D). Three windows illuminated the front parlor, against two provided for the back room. The rooms' slight difference in size, the placement of one behind the other, and the number of windows in each signaled their relative status—a status that Johns's joiners would gloss with decorative paneling and molding. This rendering of the Johns House exhibited two additional features: interior gable end chimneys and a cellar kitchen placed under the dining room at the back of the house. Although this plan answered almost all of Johns's design concerns, he continued to tinker with the layout.

The last two plans are variations of the same solution. In both, Johns retained his selection of a side-passage plan that included a broad stair hall, a front parlor, a back dining room on the ground floor, and provision for a

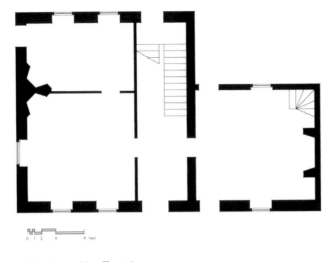

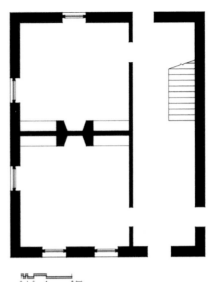

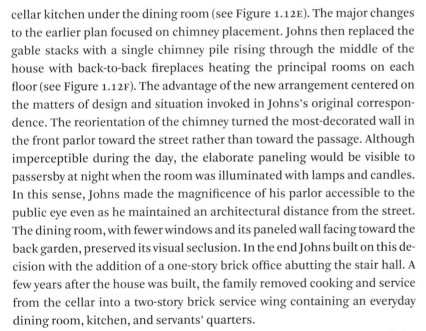

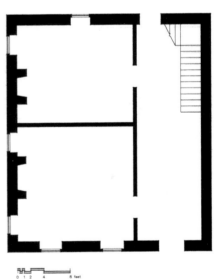

D Side Entry with Office Wing

E Side Entry with Central Chimney

F Side Entry with Gable Chimney

cellar kitchen under the dining room (see Figure 1.12E). The major changes to the earlier plan focused on chimney placement. Johns then replaced the gable stacks with a single chimney pile rising through the middle of the house with back-to-back fireplaces heating the principal rooms on each floor (see Figure 1.12F). The advantage of the new arrangement centered on the matters of design and situation invoked in Johns's original correspondence. The reorientation of the chimney turned the most-decorated wall in the front parlor toward the street rather than toward the passage. Although imperceptible during the day, the elaborate paneling would be visible to passersby at night when the room was illuminated with lamps and candles. In this sense, Johns made the magnificence of his parlor accessible to the public eye even as he maintained an architectural distance from the street. The dining room, with fewer windows and its paneled wall facing toward the back garden, preserved its visual seclusion. In the end Johns built on this decision with the addition of a one-story brick office abutting the stair hall. A few years after the house was built, the family removed cooking and service from the cellar into a two-story brick service wing containing an everyday dining room, kitchen, and servants' quarters.

The significance of the Johns family's New Castle town house rests in its reflection of a design process marked by the consideration, rejection, and acceptance of multiple possibilities. At its heart stood the issues of desire and situation first introduced by Johns's builders. Desire captured the expressive intention behind the design. How could and should their house function in a society where public and private worlds intersected on so many levels? The basic spaces they considered varied little across the range of options considered: entry, parlor, dining room, kitchen, chambers, and office. But what did vary was the assembly of these spaces into an arrangement that satisfied a desire shaped by domestic, social, and public concerns. As the Johnses winnowed their options, they implicitly recognized different constituencies that their house would address. Situation represented the Johnses' other concern. In its most literal sense, situation intended siting and placement of the building—its projected physical circumstance. It also implied the limitations that tempered desire, such as financial constraints or the perception of how the community would receive the building. The plan of the Kensey Johns House vividly illustrates choice as a design process where a client works through a series of options. But the story of the house lacks a sense of how the dwelling contained and shaped the lives and relationships of its occupants.

The experiential quality of a house is reflected in a second narrative, the memoirs of Caroline Burgwin Clitherall, compiled from her childhood journals, written in the years prior to the American Revolution. The story she tells is set in Bristol, England, where she lived with her aunt and uncle in their Georgian town house. The house (see Figure 1.13), located on King Square, was likely one of a group of new dwellings touted in a 1762 sale advertisement:

> A very neat Strong-built House, in the New Square, with two large Arch cellars, two Handsom Parlours, and a large Dining-Room, all neatly wainscotted and ornamented with enriched Cornishes, two curious Marble Chimney-Pieces, with Pattern Tile, and the Entrance panell'd.[26]

Typical of the King Square houses (and the alterations they have endured over time) is Number 5, a three-story brick building with stone trim around the windows and doors. The ground-floor arrangement includes an entry, stair hall, a large front parlor, and smaller back dining room. Upstairs, the best parlor occupies the entire front of the house. The "enriched Cornishes" mentioned in the advertisement are of cast plaster with modillion blocks, rosettes, and an egg-and-dart molding.

The magnificence of the King Square houses impressed young Caroline Burgwin: "The House in Kings Square was huge and elegantly furnish'd," but it was also the site of childhood amusements such as "working in my

FIGURE 1.13

King Square, Bristol, England,
End Building with Side Street Entry
(circa 1760)

own Portion of [the] Garden . . . keeping School for about twenty or more rag Dolls—whom I arrang'd at the head of the great-stair case," or secreting herself "in a small garret-room, hidden, and reading intently." Burgwin reserved her most elaborate picture of the house and its rooms, however, for her narrative recounting her beloved aunt's death, where the close quarters and immediacy of the King Square house are laid bare.

In the first scene, Burgwin remembers her aunt's last sufferings—her body consumed with cancer, her pain and lucidity dulled with opiates—and a group of physicians attempting to surgically excise the malignancy:

> I was accustom'd to see the Physician attend every morning, and wou'd often listen to the suppress'd groans, scarcely audible which came from my Aunt's room during the last week of her illness.—This wou'd call forth floods of anguish from myself—One morning, whilst seated in a window recess in the drawing room, which had a door communicating with her chamber, I was surpris'd to see four physicians enter, and after talking in a low voice, go into my Aunt's room—I had been in the habit (after learning from Augusta) the name of the disease) of *studying,* those pages of "Buchan's "domestic medicine"—which treated "of Cancer" I could not tell, *why so many* doctors had come, and applied to Augusta, who said "an operation was to be perform'd—" I knew enough, that surgery employ'd a knife, and throwing Buchan upon the seat in the recess, ran off to my own room.

She depicts the flow of traffic in and out of the second-story rooms during an extraordinary event. Occupying a window seat in the formal front room, she could both see and hear the progress of her aunt's illness. The doctors arrived in the entry below and ascended to the drawing room before entering the adjoining chamber. As a child, Caroline Burgwin possessed something of the transparency of servants in the sense that she witnessed the physicians' whispered consultation while they remained seemingly oblivious to her presence. The horror of surgery routed Caroline Burgwin from her window seat, up the great stair, past the place of her dolls' school on the landing, to her own chamber in the story above. Here she secluded herself in anguished prayer. Finally, she left her chamber and descended "slowly down stairs" to the entry, where the housemaid Augusta brought her cloak and the housekeeper, Mrs. Vardy, dispatched her to Uncle King's house.

Burgwin returned to King Square after her aunt's death. In her depiction of a grieving household she walks us through the King Street residence one last time:

> Glad as I was to return to my Home, my heart was chill'd as I past thro' the silent rooms—I left my Uncle seated in the little breakfast Parlor—and went in search of Mrs. Vardy—I found her in the House Keeper's room with Augusta, both were weeping and my entrance added to their tears. . . . I went into the Servant's-Hall, and saw that all were sad—Fury and old Peg, recognis'd and fawn'd and jump'd around me—Augusta accompanied me up stairs—I enter'd the drawing-room, and going to the recess,

saw "Buchan" just where I had thrown it—The door to my Aunt's room was partly open,—The only light admitted thro' the drawing room door. . . . The furniture just as then—The dressing table and toilet the same.—at the foot of the Bed were two wooden stools—"what are these." I ask'd Augusta—Your Aunt's Coffin rested upon them and they have never been remov'd, forgotten I suppose.

Finally, Caroline Burgwin ascended to her own chamber:

I went up stairs to my own little room, opening into that of Mrs. Vardy—There in one corner, was my baby-house, furnished by Mrs. Pearith, during my period of the measles—a small book-case, containing my own volumes—A flower pot of Geranium and another of some Plant—I had nurs'd as my own—Yet *here* was no longer *my* room.

Upstairs and downstairs, from cellar kitchen to best chamber, Burgwin's recitation maps the interior of the town house through its relationships with household residents. The breakfast room behind the ground-floor parlor and her aunt's chamber behind the second-floor parlor define the core of the remembered house and confirm their connections with the heads of household. The divided world of servants in the cellar kitchen and upper-story chambers speaks to the segmented experience of those employed in the service of others. And what of the changes in young Caroline Burgwin's town house experiences following her aunt's death? Her upper-story room adjacent to the housekeeper's lodgings still contained her possessions but no longer represented her space. Access to her portion of the garden and the dolls' school on the stair landing now existed in the past.

Burgwin's narrative charts a transformation in the ways that she knew and experienced her aunt and uncle's town house. As a girl her movements between the worlds of service and authority reflected a child's ability to step outside spatial and social boundaries; coming of age with her aunt's death heralded the end of her claim on those spaces as her own and marked her final departure from the house in King Square. Burgwin's vivid account tacitly recognizes the relationships between individual experiences and architecture; it describes the circumstance and comportment of spatial occurrences, associates them with individuals, and maps the ways in which the house charted and acted on her experience. Burgwin's farewell walk through the King Square house was neither accidental nor incidental. It framed a larger set of relationships that reflected dramatic changes in her own life and enables us to descry larger, more personal patterns in urban life from an intimate perspective.

The town house is both setting and agent for experience. Presence of place and comportment depend on human movement and the engagement of all the senses. As organizing ideas, they describe processes centered on the ways in which individuals ordered and made sense of the environments they occupied, no matter how fleeting the occasion. Only through the archaeology of life inside the urban residence can we begin to discern the presence of place at the many points where artifacts and experiences connect. The material flow of everyday life in the early American city propels us in an exploration of town house experiences. Caroline Burgwin's leave-taking is our invitation.[27]

THE MERCHANT FAMILY'S HOUSE

We can imagine Elizabeth Myers sitting in the parlor of her new house (built in 1797) in Norfolk, Virginia, thumbing down the corner of her worn copy of Elizabeth Raffald's *Experienced English House-Keeper,* a combination cookbook and guide to household management and entertaining. Always a source of inspiration, Raffald's tiny volume contained detailed directions for fancy recipes and novel table settings—culinary arts for the merchant family's house. The particular item that engaged Elizabeth Myers's imagination described an intricate and fragile table ornament of sugar spun into multiple edible globes. As a translucent centerpiece, it provided a visual focus for conversation, but its gustatory appreciation was consummated only when the guests broke it into pieces and devoured its shards as part of the dessert course. The seduction of eye and palate heightened temptation.

To make a Desert of Spun Sugar.

Spin two large webs, and turn one upon the other to form a globe, and put in the inside of them a few sprigs of small flowers or myrtle, and spin a little more round to bind them together, and set them covered close up before the fire, then spin two more on a lesser bowl and put in a sprig of myrtle, and a few small flowers, and bind them as before, set them by, and spin two more less than the last, and put in a few flowers, bind them and set them by, then spin twelve couple[s] on tea-cups of three different sizes in proportion to the globes, to represent baskets, and bind them two and two as the globes with spun sugar; set the globes on a silver salver, one upon another, the largest at the bottom, and smallest at the top; when you have fixed the globes, run two small wires through the middle of the largest globes across each other: then take a large darning needle and silk, and run it through the middle of the largest baskets, cross it at the bottom and bring it up to the top and make a loop to hang them on the wire, and do so with the rest of your baskets, hang the largest baskets on the wires, then put two more wires, a little shorter across, through the middle of the second globes, and put the ends of the wires out betwixt the baskets, and hang on the four middle ones, then run two more wires shorter than the last, through the middle of the top globes and bring the baskets over the lowest; stick a sprig of myrtle on the top of your globes, and set it on the middle of the table. . . . You may make the baskets a silver, and the globes a gold colour if you choose them.—It is a pretty dessert for a grand table.[1]

The instructions for constructing spun-sugar globes from molten sugar for a table decoration, along with directions for concocting punches, building jellied bird's nests, and fabricating other tabletop exotica, come from the Moses and Elizabeth Myers family papers. Elizabeth Myers, her daughters, daughters-in-law, or housekeepers dog-eared the pages of recipes in Mrs. Myers's copy of *The Experienced English House-Keeper.* Other recipes they copied in longhand from printed sources or in the course of conversation. The site of their culinary labors was the Myers kitchen, a space furnished with little more than an open hearth, one or two worktables, a few worn chairs, and cooking utensils. The Myers dining room was the seat for presentation and judgment, the place where guests enjoyed these productions first as ornament and then as a literal part of the meal.

What unifies the Myers recipes, either marked in cookbooks or copied by hand, is their exceptional, ephemeral, and labor-intensive production. The Myers recipe for light white bread required not only the regulation of time and temperature for its production but also an oven that could be fired to a sufficient temperature. The detailed sequence of mixing, rising, kneading, proofing, and baking followed the clock over the course of two days and demanded vigilance.

Recipes also record how food as artifact could define the architectural experience of formal dining. Household spaces acquired their meanings in the theater of the everyday. The plan of the house and its ornamentation provided a series of settings, connected through a variety of activities and perspectives ranging from the casual to the formal. The physical circumstances of those activities gave substance to the relationships they contained. In an elite household like the Myers residence, the array of objects that defined space in terms of circumstance and comportment extended beyond the specifics of plan and ornament to include even the most fleeting productions seen and experienced by family, guests, and servants. Their dining room was defined as much by the artifacts they brought to bear on the occasion as by furniture and architectural ornament. The presentation of food like spun-sugar table decorations elaborated the significance of architectural spaces in the instant of their consumption by the senses, beginning with sight and concluding with taste.

Both in preparation and consumption, the fine loaf and the sugar ornament mapped a complex array of relationships that captured the architectural interplay between cosmopolitan and provincial cultures and the ways in which town house furnishings and their uses shaped and directed the experience of urban living. The intensive labor, expensive ingredients, supervision required to prepare such food, and complexity of behaviors surrounding the consumption of the final product convey a sense of the command of the human and material resources required to produce it. As in most affluent early-nineteenth-century Chesapeake households, cooking in the Myers dwelling was performed by servants or slaves who knelt, crouched, and stooped before the fire or stood and worked at tables. The mistress (or her designee, a housekeeper) supervised from a position of managerial authority. The mistress planned meals with particular attention to special events. In the case of the Myerses, this household task included drawing up shopping lists and menus. Servants were assigned particular tasks that included cooking, cleaning, waiting, and shopping in the city markets.[2]

The spun-sugar globes and baskets, along with visual delicacies such as gum-paste dessert baskets, Chinese temples and obelisks of fine flour and sugar, and jellied fish ponds, placed the meal, the table, the room, and the house at the intersection of local practice, cosmopolitan performance, and a tradition of elite display. The origins of spun-sugar ornaments and other confections doubling as decoration and dessert extended deep into the formation of the early modern world. The rising availability of sugar in sixteenth-century Europe inspired confectioners in the art of spun-sugar ornaments, or "subtleties," for noble tables. Fashioned in the forms of objects, animals, and buildings, subtleties crowned the ephemeral artifice of the table with their desirability and expense—only to be admired and consumed. Elizabeth Myers's spun-sugar centerpiece continued an aristocratic European tradition by providing a focal point for the dining room table that displayed not only sophistication but also a kind of feminine authority. The dining table was a landscape under her dominion, and its magnificent ornamentation displayed her mastery of the arts of household management and entertainment.[3]

Sugar globes were doomed productions. Guests savored their flavor, texture, and appearance, a connoisseurship that required the social knowledge of genteel dining. The shimmer of candlelight in the slightly sticky myrtle-filled gold and silver sugar globes at the table's center offered visual and tactile sensations that gained their fullest appreciation in the literal consumption of the centerpiece that concluded the meal. Exceptional constructions, they served their greatest purpose over the span of a few hours, and then their ruined remains were consigned as snacks for cooks who would never sit at the table or discarded in the kitchen yard for the pleasure of chickens and guinea fowl. Their purpose was inextricably grounded in time and place. Time, measured out not so much in the passage of days and years as in the staging of events, bracketed episodes of household experience ranging from the daily trips to the city markets to dining room extravaganzas. Place provided the appropriate setting for events that engaged architecture and furnishings as agents in the presentation and negotiation of elite town house life. Ornamental desserts are significant for their reflection, testing, and reinforcement of a complex array of urban encounters; objects, ranging from a sugar centerpiece to a merchant family's house, provided social and cultural maps intimately charting the comportment of an elite merchant family's social and economic aspirations.[4]

In the fluid economic and social settings of the early American merchant city, elites claimed privilege and authority through the accumulation of wealth and the material display of social knowledge that money (and credit) made possible. The label "elite" carries a world of social freight. The measure of elite status lay in the ways in which magnificent houses, sumptuous dinners, and fashionable furnishings were social capital. Put into play on formal and informal occasions, the material culture of genteel ambition demanded the display of social knowledge through polite conversation and the complex rituals of sociability. It shaped and was shaped by behaviors that both brought people together and created distinctions that divided them. The elite social identity of the Myerses and their peers stems from *exclusivity* and *agency*. Exclusivity carries two implications. First, it implies a social identity defined by difference, and, second, it conveys the idea of social separation. In myriad and complex ways, elites communicated that they were not just different from other social groups: they were better. Their expression of exclusivity could be conspicuous and highly visible, or subtle and inaccessible to those outside the group. Exclusivity created divisions within the elite community as well as the larger society.[5]

Agency comprehends an association between elite status and the means, ability, and inclination for elites, singly or in concert, to act in ways that affect their larger community and perpetuate their own economic power, social authority, and individual identity. The categorization of elites depends on the presence of groups identified as nonelites within the larger social system. Inherently competitive and directed toward the acquisition of authority, elites operated from contexts defined by the tensions between group and individual interest. In this sense, elite identity depends on other groups as a key part of the audience for displays of superiority and distinctiveness. The crux of these points lies in the recognition that elites consolidate their own status by distinguishing themselves from other individuals and groups. Elite status relies on action; thus, it is competitive and porous. Because their expression depended on circumstance and setting, elite behaviors in the early American city were grounded in the material life of acquisitiveness, display, competitiveness, and consumption—all attributes of a larger culture of eighteenth-century Atlantic mercantilism where mutual interests in commerce, politics, and recreation coalesced around fashionable social rituals.[6]

Norfolk's circles of elite society to which the Myerses belonged centered on groups of individuals with the means, knowledge, and power to advertise and perpetuate their status. Their ranks included merchants, planters, government officials, international delegates, and visiting dignitaries. The rites of assembly, played out around dining room tables and in the dances of the salon, bound these disparate individuals together—and kept them in tension. An observer of the Norfolk scene in the early nineteenth century noted: "The chief boast of the place must be its inhabitants . . . their manners, (those of the better sort I mean,) are at once easy and polite; familiar, and yet sufficiently elegant. The style of intercourse is generally frank and sociable, without those contests of vanity and ambition which embitter society in larger places." Presumably, the author was included in rather than excluded from the society of Norfolk elites.[7]

Several cautions temper an understanding of society and social life in the merchant family's town house in the early national period: first, the danger inherent in creating absolute social divisions based on occupation and wealth; second, the instability of those categories; and, third, the need to perceive the intimacy of the Atlantic world of the late 1700s. Merchant society in the United States after the Revolution lacked a precise social identity. Rather, there was a continuum with the wealthiest merchants at one end and poorer traders at the other. Individuals across this spectrum were unified by their engagement with an ideology of acquisitiveness and competitiveness set in a context of national and international exchange. Key elements in this culture were the role of the family as a corporate unit and the ways in which seemingly private domestic spaces served broader exchange relations. The corporate sense of the merchant family—where husband, wife, and children, not just the merchant as the nominal head of household and business, formed the basic unit of social and economic action—is underscored in the Myers House by Elizabeth Myers's table ornaments and the family's reputed skill at staging musicales for their guests.[8]

Wealth did not determine status; it purchased opportunity. Many successful merchant families saw themselves as epitomes of a cosmopolitan urban elite culture and as the willing, avid bearers of its traditions. Philadelphians, Charlestonians, Bristolians, and urban merchant families grown rich in trade and residing around the greater compass of the North Atlantic rim coalesced into multiple groups bound by various forms of social behavior, including membership in clubs and professional societies, involvement in public service and elected office, and the sociability of dining room and parlor. The physical sites in which they performed their identity constituted part of this extended urban fabric. Simply, their social identity depended on their material world for its expression. Because the elite merchant household relied on an expressive culture that was both affirming and divisive, they needed to convey both social difference and a sense of community. The exclusivity they cultivated also required rules of inclusivity, typically in the form of polite rituals that connected social life to the world of trade. Thus, the unifying traits of the transatlantic merchant community at the end of the eighteenth century were social and economic; they were located in an arena of competitiveness and mobility linking the countinghouse to the town house.[9]

Elizabeth and Moses Myers's house still stands in Norfolk, where it has weathered waves of catastrophe, prosperity, and a particularly brutal interlude of urban renewal (see Figure 2.1). Preserved as a house museum complete with family furnishings, the dwelling, surrounded first by parking lots and then modern commercial development, endures as an evocation of a bustling, grimy, worldly early American seaport. The Myers House, erected in 1797 and dramatically enlarged in two phases in the early nineteenth century, illuminates the context of the merchant family household. In the present, its physical isolation in a landscape of urban renewal tends to emphasize the cultural and social connections that define a past community in terms of mentalité rather than place. Regrettably unencumbered by the neighboring buildings and gardens that once surrounded the house, we find ourselves free to reconstruct other sets of relationships and communities that transcend locale. In the instance of the Myers House we turn to a community of merchant interests rooted in an elite world of exchange relations: commerce, conversation, gaming, music, etiquette, and a host of other social performances Norfolk merchant households employed to define themselves and others.[10]

The artifact most central to meeting these performances was the house, not only in its appearance and appointments but also in its uses. The merchant family's town house, the most visible outward expression of its status and identity, had to function successfully in multiple overlapping situations. The exterior of the structure, its scale, construction, and ornament, reinforced local distinctions between the occupants and their neighbors in similar or less grand houses. In this sense the house functioned locally, establishing its competitive frame of reference relative to a specific place. The interior of the house operated differently. In addition to the segmented experiences of the individuals who composed the household (ranging from slaves to master and mistress), the interior of the house, through its room uses, decorative appointments, and fashionable furnishings, engaged social relationships that transcended place and were defined in the competitive culture of Atlantic cosmopolitanism. From the start it is easiest to conceive of the merchant family's house with a local exterior and a transatlantic interior, but with the caveat that the distinction is one of emphasis in settings where access, audience, and event shaped the textures of experience.

Built and insured in 1797, Moses and Elizabeth Myers's house at Catherine and Freemason Streets was a thirty-six-by-forty-two, two-story, gable-front mansion (see Figure 2.2). The main floor of the house contained three

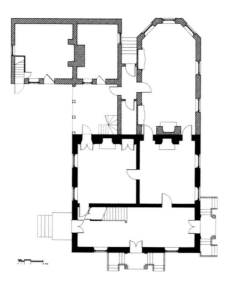

FIGURE 2.2

Myers House, First-Floor Plan. The black
areas represent the first phase (circa 1797);
the gray areas reflect the additions made
before 1816. The area connecting the original
dining room to the service yard was remodeled
extensively in later renovations. *Plan courtesy
Mark R. Wenger and Willie Graham, Colonial
Williamsburg Foundation. Drawn by Jeff Klee*

principal rooms: a broad passage running the full length of the Catherine
Street elevation and two smaller heated rooms behind. Three exterior doors
led into the passage, which doubled as a salon and was finished with a
decoratively stuccoed ceiling executed in the latest neoclassical fashion.
The two rooms behind the passage were a parlor and a dining room, both
finished with mantels elaborated with applied composition ornament,
including classically inspired floral elements, urns, and "harvest" figures
(see Figure 2.3). The dining room, with its own exterior entry onto the
kitchen dooryard, occupied the corner of the house directly above the cellar kitchen and looked over the Myers private garden. Traffic in and out of
the kitchen either came through this dooryard or up a flight of stairs located
beneath the main stair in the passage. Upstairs, the Myers House continued
the plan of the ground floor, with the best room located above the parlor.

The builders created an additional unheated space by partitioning the end of the second-floor landing that fronted the intersection of Catherine and Freemason Streets below. Like their first-floor counterparts, these rooms were similarly enhanced with delicate neoclassical finishes (see Figure 2.4). The attic rooms were plainly plastered and likely served as servants' quarters in an allocation of household space common to elite late-eighteenth-century town houses throughout the North Atlantic rim.[11]

The organization of the house around avenues of movement describes

left:

FIGURE 2.3

Myers House, First-Floor Parlor Mantel and Chimney Breast

right:

FIGURE 2.4

Myers House, Second-Floor Parlor Chamber Mantel and Chimney Breast

an urban dwelling where symbolic action and the presentation of self were essential elements in everyday life. Through the skillful placement of doors in the house design, Moses and Elizabeth Myers organized the traffic flow through their dwelling in a way that maintained the segregation of cooking and service from both the more refined and public activities of the salon and dining room and the private ones of the second-floor quarters. Domestic movement for those who set and waited the tables led up cellar stairs and under the main stair into the dining room, or from cellar to dooryard to the dining room back entry. The pattern of formal movement in the original plan of the Myers House progressed from passage to parlor to dining room. Even as the Myerses and their dinner guests moved horizontally from entry to parlor to dining room, their servants moved continually up and down. These two planes of action converged at the table where diners sat and servants stood. The inversion of status was complete. The individuals at the top of the domestic hierarchy sat beneath their subordinates who stood attentively waiting on their master, mistress, and guests, even as their kitchen colleagues sweated over the cooking fires below. In the merchant family's house and the dwellings of other urban elites, such as well-to-do attorneys or planters, the relationships between architecture and society, food and furnishings, and entertainment and commerce were thoroughly intermixed in a complex and subtle system of signs. This symbolic system was linked and reinforced not only through the commentary it offered on the family but also in the ways it connected them to a larger society steeped in a transatlantic world of competitiveness and acquisitiveness—a world defined by a modern culture of exchange.

Still, the Myerses remained architecturally unsatisfied. By 1816 they had enlarged their mansion (already one of the largest and best appointed in the city) first with a two-story brick combination porch, kitchen, washhouse, and quarter in the yard behind the old dining room, and then with a two-story brick dining room wing. The new dining room with its octagonal end doubled the depth of the house along Freemason Street and provided the setting for larger dinners than the old arrangement it replaced. A pair of arched alcoves equipped with notched baseboards accommodated the back legs of custom-built sideboards. The Myerses also purchased and installed an imported marble mantel in the new space. Such architectural details reinforced the room's purpose as a grand space for entertainment (see Figure 2.5). Scale and finish set this room apart. The location of the new dining room also made it more public than the room it replaced. Now the

FIGURE 2.5

Myers House, First-Floor Interior,
Dining Room Addition

left:

A Mantel and Chimney Breast

right:

B Compass-Arched Sideboard Alcove

range of public rooms—salon, parlor, and dining room—wrapped the corner of Catherine and Freemason Streets. The former dining room declined in status in its new use as a secondary sitting room and occasional music room. The new kitchen building similarly changed the Myers House. The old vertical arrangement of a cellar kitchen and adjoining sculleries and servants' hall long familiar in other urban settings, including London and Philadelphia, gave way to a strategy steeped in local practice that placed cooking and servant quarters in an outbuilding in the yard (see Figure 2.6).

FIGURE 2.6

Myers House, Kitchen (early nineteenth century).
The construction of this building moved cooking
functions out of the cellar of the main house

The remodeled Myers House was no less elegant in its second appearance, but it was decidedly more regional in the architectural organization of the kitchen and related service spaces. Although cellar kitchens continued to appear in some houses, local custom increasingly led to the placement of service spaces in freestanding outbuildings. This practice was consistent with the organization of plantation domestic complexes throughout the Chesapeake Bay countryside.[12]

The Myers House in both of its early phases occupied the architectural pinnacle of genteel Norfolk society. Other Norfolk families made wealthy through trade and the harvests of backcountry plantations erected their own urban mansions, several of which adhered to the gable-fronted design of the Myers House. In 1796 merchant Conway Whittle insured his new two-story frame house and outbuildings west of Granberry Street. The dimensions of the thirty-six-by-fifty-five-foot structure and its siting, narrow end to the street, suggest that it followed the architectural fashion of gable-fronted Federal period houses consisting of a formal front passage that also served as a salon. Whittle's mansion was flanked on either side by sixteen-foot-square dependencies, one of which functioned as a kitchen, the other as a rental property for a Norfolk surgeon. Conway Whittle's new mansion represented an improvement over the house he formerly rented. Described four years earlier, the house was advertised as "32 feet square, two story high, with two rooms and a passage below, elegantly finished, and three above, with an extensive garden and an elegant yard, with all the necessary out houses situated on the main street."[13]

A decade later the Taylor family erected their two-story brick house (later known as the Taylor-Whittle House) on the corner of Duke and Freemason Streets several blocks west of the Myers residence (see Figure 2.7). Although the Taylors' house lacked a salonlike passage on the ground floor, the overall plan echoed the first phase of the Myers House. The ground floor included a square entry and stair hall placed in the corner nearest the street intersection outside. Three rooms, each outfitted with composition ornament mantels and other neoclassical detailing, completed the plan (see Figure 2.8). As originally designed, the house included a cellar kitchen and storage spaces, and, like the Myers House, the Taylor dwelling presented an impressive front, complete with a pedimented gable enframing a large lunette lighting the attic rooms. The rooms behind the entry salon included a parlor and dining room. Whittle's house, insured at eight thousand dollars, represented one of the most valuable in a city where the average stood at just under two thousand dollars—a group representing the best dwellings in Norfolk. The houses of the merchant elite occupied a desirable and, for the majority of Norfolk's householders and renters, unattainable apex of local architecture. More typical were frame houses, most uninsured, standing one story tall, containing one or two rooms, and sometimes supplemented by a kitchen in the yard (see Figure 2.9).[14]

While they dominated the local landscape in a distinctive manner, the gable-fronted mansions of Moses and Elizabeth Myers and their contemporaries were not the only housing options for Norfolk's merchant elite. Other residents commissioned houses two rooms deep with a side passage and stair hall in an arrangement familiar in cities from Boston to Savannah

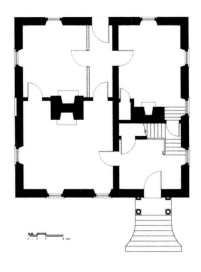
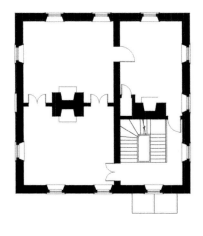

FIGURE 2.7
Taylor-Whittle House, Duke and Freemason
Streets, Norfolk (early nineteenth century)
opposite:
A Elevation
left:
B First- and Second-Floor Plan. *After Historic
American Buildings Survey, Library of Congress,
and Hansbury, Evans, Wright, Vlattas, Architects.
Drawn by Jeff Klee*

(see Figure 2.10). "FOR SALE," advertised Charles Miles in 1793, "a large two story House, containing two rooms and a passage on the first floor, three bed-chambers and a garret above, with two large cellars." Miles's town lot was organized around a jostling multitude of outbuildings. The "stable, kitchen, smoakhouse, two lofts, and a pump, together with a spacious yard and garden," visually connected this urban "plantation" to its tidewater hinterland. In other instances Norfolk's merchant town houses followed urban precedents that placed commercial and domestic service on the ground floor and residential functions in the upper stories. William Bland, rector of the Episcopal church, advertised this division in the sale of his "large and Commodious" house on Main Street: "On the first floor, there is a very convenient room for a Store and a Counting Room, and an exceeding good kitchen; on the next floor a large Passage, thirty feet long and twelve wide, with two elegant Rooms well finished." Built singly, in pairs, or short rows, these houses with their commercial spaces and their outbuildings were a common fixture in the Norfolk cityscape.[15]

Anne Ritson, an English woman, lampooned a shed-roofed variation of such a dwelling (along with outbuildings and yard) that she rented with her merchant husband in the early 1800s:

And instantly we will repair
To our new house, for change of air,
Which we went in, I will remember,

FIGURE 2.8
Taylor-Whittle House,
First-Floor Dining Room Mantel

Brewer street.

FIGURE 2.9

House in Brewer Street, Norfolk (circa 1835).
From "Description of Real Estate Held by the Virginia Bank, circa 1833–1856," Sergeant Memorial Room, Kirn Memorial Library, Norfolk

The beginning of November.
The house, they said, was very good,
And built of right well season'd wood;
Two large rooms were on the ground floor,
Above the front a chamber o'er;
A staircase to th' apartment led,
With a small room, would hold a bed;
O'er the back room that was below,
Nothing except the roof did go;
The negro kitchen stood before
The entrance to the parlour-door;
A smoke-house near the kitchen stood,
Those buildings generally are wood;
A piece of ground, that made a show,
Tho' nothing did within it grow,
But grass so high, so coarse and strong,
'Twas difficult to get along.

S. Tuckers.

Catharine street.

cost $4500.

FIGURE 2.10

Houses in Catherine Street, Norfolk (circa 1835).
*From "Description of Real Estate Held by the Virginia
Bank, circa 1833–1856," Sergeant Memorial Room,
Kirn Memorial Library, Norfolk*

For this small mansion in repair,
Distant from the obnoxious air
Of Norfolk's stink, we ev'ry year
Paid full two hundred dollars clear.

Although Ritson's depiction of the quality of Norfolk rental housing in the
early 1800s is less than flattering, it is accurate. Insurance surveys from the
late 1790s through the 1820s place the Ritson house in the context of an
urban landscape where individual wooden houses occupied open lots with
a kitchen and smokehouse standing behind or to the side of the dwelling.
Other local builders (and their tenants) opted for urban mansions that reflected the style of the plantation countryside—freestanding houses often

House and 10 acres of land called Sycamores near Norfolk
Cost 1200 $ sold to J Bonny for $800 cash

FIGURE 2.11

The Sycamores, Norfolk (circa 1835).

From "Description of Real Estate Held by the Virginia Bank, circa 1833–1856," Sergeant Memorial Room, Kirn Memorial Library, Norfolk

built of wood, clad with beaded weatherboard, and designed around a centrally placed entry and stair (see Figure 2.11).[16]

When lawyer William Wirt and his wife Elizabeth relocated to Norfolk in 1803, they rented what he described as "the best [house] in the town," and continued, "altho built for a private family, has until lately been occupied by the bank of Norfolk." He wrote back to his wife, who was preparing to join him:

As to the house which I have taken, it is a spacious brick house—it had originally three rooms on the lower floor; but when it came [to be] occupied by the bank and its directors, they knocked down one of the partitions and turned two rooms into one. This large room I shall occupy as an office; and this is separated from the dining room by a fine airy passage. A mahogany stair case leads to the second story. *There* is an elegant drawing room which is separated by another passage from two bed chambers with fire places for wood.—The cellar floor is divided into six or seven apartments among them two kitchens, a cellar for liquor, a room for coal, another for wood etc.

The Wirts' town house contained familiar elements despite its alteration into a bank. The drawing room on the second floor, the dining room screened from rooms converted to banking needs (an alteration William Wirt intended to preserve for his own legal work), and the placement of service functions in the cellar represent a general arrangement associated with elite town houses on both sides of the Atlantic.[17]

On at least one occasion a local sea captain and merchant attempted to break with the prevailing traditions of elite housing with a mansion designed by visiting English architect Benjamin Henry Latrobe in 1796. The client, Captain William Pennock, challenged Latrobe, known for his arrogance, to design a town house "which should have only 41 feet front; which should contain on the Ground floor, 3 Rooms, a principal Staircase, and backstairs; and, which was the essential requisite, the front door of which should be in the Center." The wager-winning result was a monumental brick pile, capped with a hipped roof and vertically divided by successive belt courses and variably proportioned windows. Latrobe's plans and elevations called for a three-story mansion that introduced a new and innovative design vocabulary to Norfolk elites (see Figure 2.12). The five-bay, center-door front masked a plan that incorporated a lofty entry dominated by an open stair that swept elegantly upward; a series of regularly spaced doorways that opened individually into a front office, back parlor, and large dining room terminating in an octagonal bay; and a segregated service passage and stair that connected the formal rooms in the house to their working precincts. With its bold massing, intricate avenues for internal movement, and landscaped lot that placed the house away from the street and bracketed its entry with a pair of dependencies, the Pennock mansion raised the stakes in the city's contest of architectural show.[18]

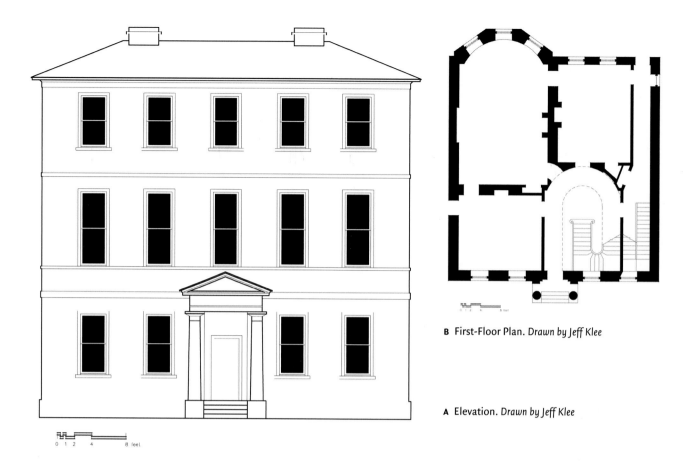

B First-Floor Plan. *Drawn by Jeff Klee*

A Elevation. *Drawn by Jeff Klee*

FIGURE 2.12

William Pennock House, Main Street, Norfolk
(circa 1796). *After Benjamin Henry Latrobe, in Cohen
and Brownell, eds.,* The Architectural Drawings of
Latrobe

Unfortunately, the design exceeded the abilities of local builders and
failed to satisfy the sensibility of the client's family. Latrobe never intended
that his design be executed, and news of the attempt to build the house
came as a shock:

> I dined at the Eagle tavern in Richmond, where . . . [a table companion]
> related that some time ago, a frenchman was at Norfolk, who had given
> Captn. Pennock the most preposterous design, which he had ever seen;
> that Captn. Pennock had been mad enough to attempt to execute it, and
> that having carried up part of the Walls he was now perfectly at a stand, as
> none of the Workmen knew how to proceed.

Latrobe realized that he was the "frenchman" in question and hastened
to contact Pennock. Returning to Norfolk, he found his design completely

botched in its execution and did his best to resolve the many problems created by Pennock and his builders in their attempts to raise this "preposterous" house. In retrospect Latrobe commented:

> It was my intention to have built the house upon a small rise in the Garden, and to have occupied the street by two small, and ornamental stores, which would have yielded a very good rent. On this account, I have arranged all the communications along the entrance front; whereas, had I known how much interest would be taken in what is going forward in the street, I should have given the ladies a good room in front, at least upstairs. . . .
>
> The Walls are built of very bad bricks. The front is faced with red Philadelphia bricks, which being thinner than the others are badly bonded, and the wall has given way, and is bulged about four inches. The woodwork in general is indifferently performed, excepting that executed by Gracie which includes the staircase. The cornices which I designed, were deemed too plain, and Mr. Ferguson was employed to furnish such as were *tastier,* and *finer.*[19]

The debacle of the Pennock house gets at several issues essential to the interpretation of elite houses in the early American city. Like the mansions of the Myers and Taylor families, the Pennocks' town house was intended by its builders from the start as an outward show of attainment and taste. Pedestaled on a low rise set back from the street, framed by its "ornamental stores," constructed with finer-quality brick, planned with elaborated, almost sculptural interiors, designed around a plan that placed dining and reception in more private situations away from the street, the Pennocks projected a house that embraced a transatlantic cosmopolitan standard of architectural sophistication and identified them as its chief proponents. But the Pennocks could not escape their local selves. The mix of bricks from different sources produced a precarious facade that failed upon completion. The local joiner and plasterer performed adequately, but the Pennocks interceded with their own aesthetic sensibilities and altered the design and character of the interior in ways they found *"tastier,* and *finer."* Most telling, though, was the Pennocks' dissatisfaction with the functional placement of rooms. Too late, Latrobe realized that the theater of the street was all-important in the everyday lives of the Pennock household. The ladies did not seek privacy so much as they wanted a voyeur's distance from "the dust, the noise, and the smells of a seaport" and the society it superintended. A plan that placed the house closer to the street and the best room on the second floor overlooking the action below acceded to those wishes and accorded with local practice and a desire to see and to be seen in an elevated situation.[20]

Buildings with a range of uses lined the street that the Pennock ladies longed to oversee. Main Street ran parallel to the waterfront and was the setting for at least a dozen merchant dwellings in 1801. The Pennock House visually anchored a street of town houses that reflected a variety of building practices and traditions. Merchant Luke Wheeler rented the brick house that stood ten feet to the west, separated from the Pennocks by a private lane. Leased from one of Norfolk's numerous women property holders, Wheeler's house presented an imposing image with its thirty-eight-foot-square footprint and three-story elevation. The presence of a cellar kitchen, like the one in the original phase of the Myers House, reflected a tactic for housing domestic service familiar in other Atlantic seaport cities. Extending beyond Luke Wheeler's leased house were four freestanding town houses owned by Ann Livingston. The largest of the dwellings was a two-story, forty-eight-by-thirty-eight-foot frame residence, enlarged with an eighteen-foot lean-to and built with brick gables in a style long practiced in the Chesapeake Bay backcountry. The remaining three buildings, each standing roughly twenty feet from its neighbor, also followed local precedent with their long elevations to the street and their separate one-room kitchens placed in the yard behind the house. Like the Pennock and Wheeler houses, these dwellings were home to merchants and sea captains.[21]

Near Main Street ranged the maritime world of the wharves, warehouses, and countinghouses. The core of the commercial district was the public Commerce Street Wharf ascending from its Elizabeth River landing to the central Market Square. Of the eighty-two individual merchants or merchant firms, fully one-third gave addresses on the town docks and commercial square. Another one-quarter gave addresses on the city's many privately owned wharves that adjoined the public anchorage. Intermixed with merchants' premises were the shops of ship chandlers, artisans working in maritime-related trades, and other retail stores. For example, the five frame buildings Paul Loyall insured on his wharf in 1796 included his own two-story, twenty-by-fifty-foot warehouse and other structures rented to, among others, a blockmaker and blacksmith. Loyall's own two-story brick house (one of the largest in town) stood around the corner on Main Street, sandwiched between a one-story frame barber shop and the brick walls of a house burnt almost twenty years earlier during the Revolution.[22]

Leading away from the Elizabeth River and into the local backcountry was Catherine Street, which, like Freemason Street that intersected it four long blocks away from the river, was home to another eight merchants. The streets themselves formed the avenues of a processional landscape not unlike those associated with Virginia's tidewater plantations. They were the thoroughfares that led from the hub of commerce to the seats of social power. The streets' early-nineteenth-century appearance, however, undermined their symbolic function. "I am sorry to say that all isn't quite so handsome when you get into the town," one chronicler wrote in a letter to a friend: "The streets are surely a little too crooked for beauty, as even Hogarth, with all his passion for the 'waving line,' must have confessed; and besides this, are in some parts intolerably dirty, that is, where they haven't yet been paved. The principal ones, however, are kept clean, and handsomely lighted." A decade later in 1828 Ann Royall noted a marked improvement: "I expected to have seen an old, dirty-looking, gloomy, clownish town, inhabited by barbarous tuckyhoes: on the contrary the houses looked fresh, and the citizens polite and hospitable; on the score of refinement and taste, it has more than any town in Virginia; in this respect, it resembles Boston."[23]

Among the Myerses, Whittles, and Pennocks we discern the tensions that defined the town houses of merchant society. The recipes that established the transatlantic society of the table also recognized the regional culture of the kitchen; the houses that asserted architectural status in their exterior appearance acknowledged the discomfiture encountered between traditional practice and cosmopolitan aspirations. Both the recipes and the houses are facets of a shared ambivalence centered on how a particular group of individuals sought to present themselves and test the social and business acumen of others in a world that presented both local and transatlantic identities. The interplay between local and global geographies distinguishes the merchant family's house and is apparent in the ways in which different types of tables—dining, card, and tea—functioned as maps in a mental landscape defined by presentation and exchange. While the town houses of the Pennocks, their neighbors, and peers reinforced an outward impression of merchant society as one that often lacked visual cohesion, their interiors suggest a different story.

Inventories of household goods provide the starting point for understanding how merchant families organized the interiors of their houses. When the Myers House was inventoried in 1820, the court-appointed surveyors found the house pretty much as it survives today. The ground-floor arrangement consisted of the long dining room, drawing room, passage, parlor, and a porch connecting the house to the separate kitchen. The Myers dining room, like many of its elite counterparts, was furnished in a manner that suggested extensive entertaining. Multiple dining tables, a pair of sideboards, a dozen chairs, china, glassware, cutlery, and table ornaments constituted the contents of a room designed for the social performance of formal dining. The adjacent drawing room held an array of seating furniture, including ten chairs and two settees. The five family portraits hanging on the walls defined the proprietorial nature of a room dedicated to conversation. The passage that doubled as a salon contained nine more chairs, an additional settee, and a pair of card tables. In the warmer months, cross breezes admitted through its multiple exterior doors provided an additional space for conversation and gaming. The ability to fold card tables and pull them back against the walls with the seating enabled the Myerses to employ this large open room for other entertainments, such as dances and musicales. Finally, the parlor (the room devised as the dining room in the original plan) with its chairs and sofa provided another site for seating and conversation. Upstairs, the passage, which opened onto the principal chambers and looked out over the street below, contained two tea tables, a pair of card tables, eleven stuffed chairs, and a sideboard that likely housed the accoutrements for playing cards and taking tea.[24]

The Myers House, with all its many chairs, settees, sofas, and tables for tea, cards, and dining, was furnished for the rites and rituals of sociability. The ground floor defined a house with many public faces for the invited and socially initiated where social knowledge held sway. It was not enough for aspiring elites to occupy a fashionable house with stylish furnishings—they had to know how to use those objects to communicate their ability to act in appropriate ways. To own a porcelain-and-silver tea set indicated wealth; to decant and serve the tea and converse demonstrated the capacity to utilize this social capital. Thus, the greater value in tea tables, card tables, portraits, and settees lay in hosts' and guests' proper employment of them. In a highly competitive society of conversation, gaming, dining, and dancing, performance was everything. Poor performance could lead to embarrassment and diminished social standing. The furnishings of the Myers House upstairs passage also reflect Latrobe's observation about the ladies of the

Pennock household a generation earlier. Positioned above the intersection of Freemason and Catherine Streets, this space with its stuffed chairs and tea and card tables provided the occupants of the house with a commanding view of what was "going forward in the street," an inexhaustible fountain of local news and speculation. (Missing from the Myers inventory, though, are objects related to their Jewish identity. Like Jewish families in other early-nineteenth-century American cities, the Myers family kept their artifacts of faith as private heirlooms.)[25]

The plan and furnishings of the Myers House are unique only in their details. Conway Whittle's house, inventoried in 1817, identified a similar "Saloon and Passage," outfitted with a harpsichord, eleven windsor chairs, two sofas, cabinet, and portable desk. An oilcloth covered the floor; pictures graced the walls. The extensive seating furniture and harpsichord suggest that this was a performance space where family and friends were entertained with music and conversation. "Down Stairs Room No. 1" appears from its furnishings to have been a formal dining room. The primary objects here included two "Mahogany Tables and Ends," mahogany breakfast table, dining table, and a set of eight mahogany chairs with "hair bottoms and check Covers." The floor was laid with a "Turkey" carpet. The dark and exotic tropical woods of the furniture staged an opulent visual background for the glittering array of silver, glassware, and china stored and displayed in Whittle's cupboards. As in the Myers House, the Whittle family enjoyed the competitive sociability of dining, tea, and card tables. Like many Norfolk elites, the Whittle household was supported by the labor of enslaved servants who worked in the detached kitchen, where cooks bent before the fire and waiting servants prepared to make the ten-yard dash across the intervening garden that divided the realms of domestic work and polite sociability.[26]

Other Norfolk elites occupied more modestly scaled but similarly finished and furnished town houses. Wholesale merchant Phineas Dana's family lived in 1808 in one of a pair of three-story brick town houses he owned on Main Street, away from the city's commercial center. In plan, the Dana residence followed the convention of a side-passage plan, two rooms in depth, made familiar in eighteenth-century London and Philadelphia. When first insured in 1802, the house likely included a cellar kitchen that was similar to the original arrangement of the Myers and Taylor-Whittle Houses. With fewer and somewhat less elaborate rooms packed into the eighteen-by-twenty-five-foot perimeter of their dwelling, the Danas still managed to possess and display the material culture of sociability. The passage held an overflow of chairs, but its apparent narrowness precluded its use as a salon in the style of the Myerses and Whittles. The front room displayed both the artifacts of tea and conversation and the secretary that held Phineas Dana's books and personal papers. Discreetly removed from the eyes of the street, the dining room stood behind the front parlor. Looking out over the family garden populated with chickens, a cow, a pair of horses, and miscellaneous outbuildings, the dining room contained two tables, one-half dozen chairs (in addition to the fourteen lining the passage), a sideboard with a china press, mahogany stands, and the requisite sets of china and glassware.

Because of its relatively compressed size, the Dana residence could not contain the culture of sociability on the ground floor in the style of the Myers or Whittle Houses. Thus, the resulting furnishing strategy for the Dana residence produced a house spatially organized and furnished in a different way but one that matched the physical circumstances of the dwelling. The Danas' largest room, likely their best, occupied the full length of the second-floor front of the house. Furnished as the best chamber with a curtained bed, a crib, washstand, and secretary, this was a private space where the family also stored their stock of silver tea and dinner services. All the remaining rooms on the second and third stories of the house were similarly furnished, and each defined the domain of private family lives. The third-floor front room represented the single exception. Ascending the stairs that wound upward through the house, the Danas and their guests entered a less formal entertainment space, equipped with a pair of card tables and a dining table. These objects' position at the top of the house renders it unlikely that they were simply stored there, awaiting a summons for downstairs use. Instead, the Danas created a private upstairs salon for selected guests and friends. The chairs in the ground-floor entry could almost as easily be carried upstairs to this space as inserted into the dining room. For all its differences in scale and organization, the Dana family's house paralleled its larger neighbors in the balancing of private lives and public spaces.[27]

Similar in plan and furnishing were the town houses of Robert Hayes and James Maxwell. Both dwellings were designed around a formal entry and the stair hall and a pair of ground-floor rooms outfitted for sociability. In the Hayes House the front room on the ground floor was clearly the best furnished, with its mahogany chairs, card tables, and full array of objects for tea service, including table, caddy, tray, and a set of "Nankeen tea china." Sixteen Hogarth prints and another one of a view of Gibraltar enlivened the walls and complemented the material culture of conversation. The Max-wells' somewhat more modestly furnished residence interpreted the same plan with a ground-floor front parlor and back dining room. The Dana, Hayes, and Maxwell Houses shared characteristics with the Myers and Whittle mansions despite obvious physical and organizational differences. In all of these houses, social display and performance intersected with the trading world of wharf, countinghouse, and merchant society (not just of Norfolk but of the Atlantic trading world) and defined the intersection of different forms of social knowledge encoded in artifacts ranging from town houses to the spun-sugar ornaments on Elizabeth Myers's dining room table.[28]

How did the houses, furnishings, and social behaviors of Moses and Elizabeth Myers and their Norfolk neighbors fit into a larger Atlantic culture steeped in acquisition, display, and exchange and dependent on both competitive and ameliorative behaviors? Merchants could not have succeeded without mutual support, cooperation, and trust. Similarly, they could not have achieved their goals without a degree of ruthlessness and ostentation. Sociability neatly brokered these tensions. Conversation, cards, and dining effectively brought people together and enabled them to set themselves apart. Every American and English seaport city and inland market town of the eighteenth and early nineteenth centuries possessed its own monuments to the attainment of individual wealth and status. Significantly, the material culture framework that the Myerses were exposed to in the early 1800s had been well established in older English and American towns for at least a century.[29]

Commissioned by wine merchant Henry Peckham, the Pallant House (circa 1710–1713) in Chichester on the south coast of England epitomized the town houses of newly minted merchant elites who visibly asserted their wealth and status in English provincial towns (see Figure 2.13). Elevated slightly above the street, Peckham's residence comprised three parts; two bays flanked a slightly projecting central unit. Decorative brickwork, including rubbed-brick quoins at the corners, engaged-brick pilasters defining the central element, and finely gauged and scalloped-brick flat arches above the first- and second-story windows enhanced the arrangement. A parapet outfitted with blind windows, a classically inspired doorway framed with Corinthian pilasters, and an almost comic pair of carved-stone ostriches mounted on brick, monogramed gateposts put the exterior of the house in a category of idiosyncratic excess.

The interior was no less impressive. Peckham's town house followed a

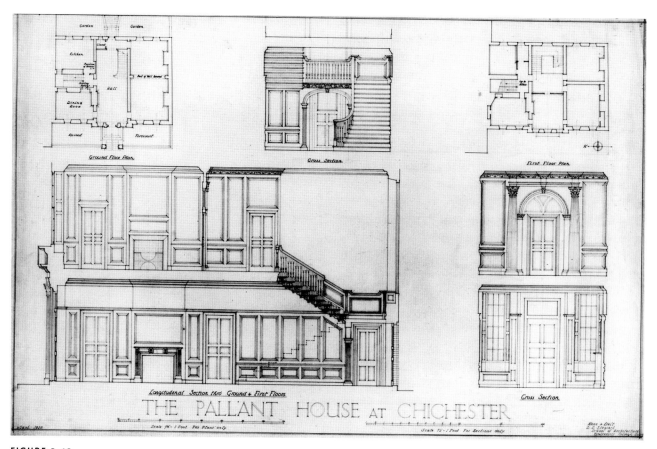

FIGURE 2.13

Pallant House, Chichester, England.

From L. W., "Wren's House and Pallant House,
Chichester" (1912)

variation of a double-pile, center-passage plan favored by urban and rural elites on both sides of the Atlantic. The path from the street carried the visitor up the outside steps, past the birds' ossified stare, and under Peckham's monogram. Admission to the house was gained through the imposing doorway and into an entry and stair hall that took up nearly one-third of the ground floor. To one side stood a double drawing room; on the other were the dining room, service stair, and kitchen. The first floor of Peckham's town house was geared almost exclusively toward reception, entertainment, and service. The upstairs chambers, plainer in finish and more intimately scaled, defined the family's quarters with the exception of the room located above the entry. The position and architectural detail of this room continued the same motifs of the hall below and tied the second-floor room to the ground-floor culture of sociability and display. As a private parlor overlook-

A Blaydes House, High Street, Hull, England, First-Floor Reception Room

B 19 Grape Lane, Whitby, England, Second-Floor Front Room

ing the street, Peckham's second-floor room anticipated the private parlor with a public view that the Pennock family longed for nearly a century later and an ocean away.[30]

Houses like the Peckham mansion were a common urban fixture in an uncommon way. Every American and English seaport city and market town possessed its share of these pretentious, assertive, urban mansions that continued to be built through the eighteenth and early nineteenth centuries, but each one was an exceptional private production. In the mideighteenth century, the Blaydes House in Hull and 19 Grape Lane in Whitby projected similar statements of exterior authority through displays of symmetry and architectural fashion (see Figure 2.14). Like the Peckham and Myers Houses, they addressed the circumstances of their local settings by external appearances, even as they contained and communicated the style of transatlantic merchant society through their interior spaces and decora-

FIGURE 2.14
Mantels

FIGURE 2.15

Wentworth-Gardner House, Mechanic Street,
Portsmouth, New Hampshire (circa 1760)

A Exterior

tion. The interiors of these houses and their early American counterparts, embellished through architectural details (like carved woodwork and ornamental plaster), furnishings, and use, were linked by an evolving common language of fashion.[31]

In Portsmouth, New Hampshire, the Wentworth-Gardner House erected in the 1760s perpetuated the same design concerns that drove the design of

Peckham's mansion and its many eighteenth-century parallels (see Figure 2.15). The two-story, boxlike dwelling with its rusticated wood front held to a plan centered on a spacious central passage with a carved stair enframed by a classical arch. The ground-floor parlor to the left of the entry exerted its authority with a view of the family's wharves and warehouses across Mechanic Street. The manner in which the Wentworth-Gardner House dominated its environs resonated not just with other urban merchant houses but also with the mansions of the wealthiest Virginia and Maryland planters in very different landscapes. In all these settings the houses dominated as symbolic nodes for social and economic authority. They drew the public gaze to their magnificence. These private monuments also provided a vantage point to preside over the surrounding landscape, whether urban waterfront or plantation countryside. The gaze outward was proprietorial, representing a visual claim on the environment.[32]

The interior of the Wentworth-Gardner House featured a paneled fireplace wall with flattened and engaged classical pilasters and a richly ornamented mantelpiece. The carved floral elements of the mantelpiece were a recurring motif in elite Portsmouth houses of the mid-eighteenth century, but their location relative to the overall plan of the dwelling varied. In the Chase House similar carved elements appear in a back parlor; in the Manning House the carved swags of the mantel accented both a front ground-floor reception room and the second-floor best chamber (see Figure 2.16). This shared design element of the best rooms of Portsmouth eighteenth-century elite town houses consistently defined a category of refined space and the patterns of behavior and admittance associated with these rooms, regardless of their position in the dwelling. Thus, the location of the best room within the overall plan varied from house to house, but the architectural ornament and furnishings that announced their relative importance remained constant. More to the point, these interiors sent a dynamic message that was stated and received between householder and the guest privileged to enter the best room. Through the connoisseurship and knowledgeable reading of visual cues, the invitation and its acceptance were a point of congruence between privileged status and privileged recognition.[33]

Furnishings completed the physical topography of Portsmouth parlors, dining rooms, and drawing rooms in the same manner as in the houses of Norfolk's merchant elite. The house of Margaret and Thomas Manning in 1819 incorporated architectural elements that reflected both local preference and cosmopolitan taste. The exterior of the Manning House adhered

B First-Floor Front "Best" Room

FIGURE 2.16

Manning House, Manning Street, Portsmouth (mid-eighteenth century; demolished). *Photos Courtesy Collection of Strawbery Banke Museum*

A Exterior

more closely to the precedent set by other local merchant mansions raised in the late colonial period. The plain clapboard exterior, orientation to the street and nearby waterfront, and the center-passage plan of the Manning House followed local practice. The interior rooms included a parlor furnished with a heavily carved mantel highlighted with carved floral festoons, entry with open stair, and paneled dining room and kitchen fireplace walls (see Figure 2.17). The parlor furnishings included carpeting, card tables, gilded mirror, ten chairs, two settees, and a sofa. Branched candlesticks, chimney ornaments, brass andirons, and other decorative items completed the parlor setting. Although architecturally less elaborate, the dining room continued the material display of wealth and sociability. A secretary and worktable stood alongside a sideboard, a Pembroke table, a set of ten leather-bottom chairs, and an extensive display of china and glassware, ranging from a japanned knife tray to a silver-edged coconut cup. Designed in a culture driven by an exchange ethic, the Manning House competed successfully in both local and transatlantic circumstances. The regionally distinctive northern New England exterior of the town house contained an interior complete with architectural finishes and furnishings that provided a familiar setting for guests and associates steeped in the same social traditions.[34]

No early American seaport city differed more dramatically from Portsmouth in exterior appearances than Charleston, South Carolina. Despite the seeming peculiarities of its town house designs, the interior landscape of Charleston's town houses unfolded in a manner reminiscent of other port cities. The most formal room of late-eighteenth-century Charleston town houses was the drawing room, also known as the parlor or best room. The location of this best room (identified through a close examination of internal finishes) followed one of two primary choices: on either the first or second floor, but always in the front, or street side, of the house. The choice related directly to the overall functions of the house and its outbuildings and its location in the city. The houses that combined residential and commercial uses generally placed the drawing room on the second floor and over a ground-floor office or shop that could be entered directly from the street. Sociability, literally and symbolically, occupied a space above commercial endeavor. The pattern of placing the best room on the second floor echoed through the architectural culture of the North Atlantic rim seaport cities and was expressed in a variety of regionally and even locally identifiable house plans and styles.

The second favored placement of the best room was on the first-, or ground-, floor front of the house. In eighteenth-century Charleston, the single houses where this option was most commonly exercised stood away from the commercial center of the city and along its predominantly residential fringe. On Orange and Legare Streets, builders of houses without commercial functions brought the best room down into a more intimate relationship with the street—a choice that speaks to the possibility of early neighborhoods defined by shared status rather than by a topographical proximity to trade or work.[35]

The three dwellings of 90, 92, and 94 Church Street provide a glimpse at the appearance and placement of the parlor within the single house from the mid-eighteenth through the early nineteenth century (see Figure 2.18). Two of the town houses (the Legare dwelling at 90 and the Cooper residence

B First-Floor Parlor

C Second-Floor Parlor Chamber

A Entry

B Dining Room

C Kitchen

FIGURE 2.17

Manning House Interior.

Photos Courtesy Strawbery Banke Museum

at 94) were constructed in 1759 and 1760, respectively, as three-and-one-half-story, center-passage-plan dwellings with ground-floor, front commercial rooms entered directly from the street. The mid-eighteenth-century lot arrangement at 90 Church Street included a two-story quarter-kitchen, a domestic-service building typically containing a kitchen and washhouse on the ground floor and a number of slave apartments upstairs. The lot at 94 Church Street included a narrow passage behind the house with access to the neighbors' back buildings on the interior of the block. Although neither building individually retains all of its first-period interior finishes, together they provide an overall impression of the decorative and functional consideration of early single houses.

The Legare House at 90 Church Street contained a fully paneled, heated office or counting room. The stair in both buildings was an open-string arrangement, and the Cooper House stair was finished with heavily turned balusters, paneled soffits, and elaborately carved cornice. In the progression of spaces from the street to the outbuildings in the yard, the paneled dining rooms that stood between the entry passage and the house and kitchen's shared rear dooryard were the plainest ground-floor spaces in the main block of both houses. On the second floor, the hierarchy of rooms ran from

FIGURE 2.18

Legare House, 90 Church Street, Charleston,
South Carolina (1759–1760)

A Elevation

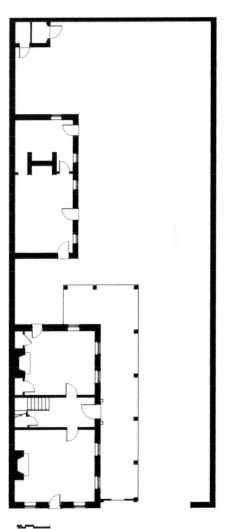

the front, best parlor overlooking the street below (and, as in the Cooper House, provided with a small wrought iron balcony), the passage and stair, and to a dining room looking out onto the back buildings, service yard, and garden. The third floor, considerably less finished than those floors below, contained two secondary sleeping chambers. A spatial and functional hierarchy combining commerce, social life, and domestic operations into a functionally and symbolically effective building bound houses like the three on Church Street together in a larger urban landscape.[36]

The parlor, or drawing room, in the Church Street houses reflected the

B Reconstructed Eighteenth-Century House and
Lot Plan. *By Jeff Klee and Gabrielle M. Lanier*

FIGURE 2.19
Legare House, First-Floor Front Room
Mantel and Chimney Breast

greatest decorative investment in an interior hierarchy of finishes that visually conveyed the relative importance of individual rooms. In the Charleston single house, the placement of the parlor, or drawing room, at the front juxtaposed the most formal room with the public world of the street, but access invariably mediated that juxtaposition. For single houses where the best room occupied the second-floor front, access could be gained only by entering the house through a formal entrance facing the street, passing down the piazza and through a second formal entry into the stair passage, and ascending the stairs to the upper floor. In dwellings where the best room occupied the ground floor, a route that led from street to piazza to entry to parlor regulated access. Both routes required either familiarity or the privilege of invitation. Within the house, the best room defined one extreme of a spatial hierarchy glossed with ornament and articulated only through the visual relationships between rooms. No visitor could easily mistake the best room for a front office, chamber, or everyday back dining room (see Figure 2.19). The quality of detailing in the best rooms might differ from house to house, but within each house the hierarchy of detail clearly communicated a decorative and social progression.[37]

A generation later, the Christie family commissioned the construction of their town house (circa 1805) between the Cooper and Legare dwellings. Although identical to its older neighbors in plan and the functional placement of rooms, the Christie House reflected the newer, more delicate taste of neoclassicism (see Figure 2.20). Changes in fashion, however, did not alter the basic intended use of architectural ornament as signposts that reassured guests with a shared vocabulary and access to social rites but excluded the ignorant. Decorative plasterwork and composition ornament communicated an established hierarchy of rooms associated with the single house, but the visual culture underlying the particulars of what was being said had changed.

The heavy moldings and classical entablatures that distinguished the rooms in earlier houses on the basis of complexity and density yielded to a more narrative iconography (see Figure 2.21). Music rooms announced their purpose with cornices embellished with stringed instruments; chambers extolled felicity with composition-ornament mantelpieces depicting birds fluttering about fledglings in their nest; dining rooms and libraries (often conflated into a single room) signified their position as seats of knowledge and conversation with decorative elements drawn from Aesop's fables, classical mythology, and the picturesque. The relationship of neoclassical

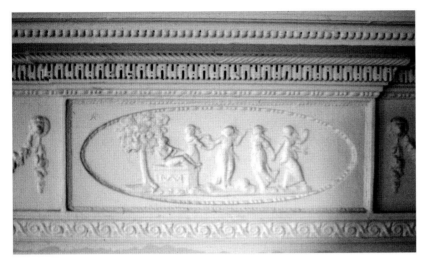

iconography to room use in Charleston town houses was neither exact nor uniform but still evoked a strong sense of associations. Moreover, the stock quality of neoclassical ornament lent itself readily to all sorts of interior situations. Identical decorative elements appear in Charleston houses based on a variety of plans; their consistency erases differences in the larger design of the town house while visually reinforcing the comparable spaces they shared. A parlor was a parlor regardless of plan and placement. In use, that parlor served the same functions of display and sociability as the props and furnishings found not just in other Charleston town houses but in urban residences around the North Atlantic rim.

The use of composition (or stucco) ornament in late-eighteenth- and early-nineteenth-century Charleston parlors finds precise analogues in comparable parlors in other, even distant cities. Composed of a mixture of resin, glue, linseed oil, and whiting that was steamed, beaten into a stiff paste, and pressed in molds, composition ornament was applied to woodwork ranging from door casings to mantels. Mantels in the Christie house, ornamented with classically draped figures flinging themselves about the tableaux of a harvest dance or with still-life urns sprouting vines, flowers, and fruit, linked this parlor to the interior fixtures of the Myers and Taylor Houses in Norfolk, the terrace houses of Parliament Street in Hull, the Haven family mansions in Portsmouth, New Hampshire, and the new residences of Grafton Way in Bloomsbury, London. The effect is dizzying; the interiors emerge as artifacts of both local society (defined by location and class) and a more diffuse

A 54 Montagu Street (circa 1806),
First-Floor Parlor

B Blake Tenement, 4 Courthouse Alley
(circa 1760–1772; remodeled early nineteenth
century), Second-Floor Front Room

FIGURE 2.21
Composition Ornament Details, Charleston

Atlantic community (defined by exchange relations, emulation, mutuality, and the knowledge of manners). Charleston town houses, like their contemporaries in other seaport cities, referenced two geographies where local outsides and global insides defined social landscapes embedded in the genteel residences of the Atlantic world.[38]

The furnishings of the Charleston drawing room or parlor reflect the same archaeology of etiquette witnessed in other urban settings that revolved around competitive and convivial exchange relations, often regulated by the rules of polite discourse. Francis Simmons's estate inventory for his house on Legare Street lists the furnishings of the second-floor drawing room: card tables, tea table, fourteen cane-bottom chairs, three settees, carpet, and accents such as "elegant" chimney ornaments. Angus Bethune's front parlor overlooking Broad Street held fourteen mahogany chairs, two card tables, tea tables, and a sofa. At least one painting graced the wall, while plated candlesticks and chimney ornaments attested to the affectations of a culture of refinement. Card tables, however, were not just objects of polite discourse—they were an arena for the complex competitive world of trade and social rank in a society where the distance between countinghouse and dining table was minimal. Whether card games were based on partnerships or on individual play, they brought people together in a simultaneously sociable and competitive activity. No one wanted to lose, but more important than the desire to win was the ability to sustain loss with grace. Visitors and residents knew the rules of the game on multiple levels, and they understood the visual and material world that often encoded those rules.[39]

Merchants in other early American cities furnished their parlors similarly. Joseph Spear, a Baltimore merchant who specialized in provisioning ships with "navy Bread," lived in a three-story row house two rooms deep and entered by a side stair hall. The designation of this room as "Front Room Down Stairs" reflected his intention of using this space as the formal heart of the house. In his parlor he placed a dozen mahogany chairs, two card tables, a tea table, and a sofa along with other lesser objects. Michael Gundacher, a Lancaster, Pennsylvania, merchant, occupied a three-story brick town house on the city's main thoroughfare. A two-story brick back building extended the living spaces contained in the twenty-nine-by-thirty-five-foot house deep into Gundacher's urban lot, which also contained his stable and store. Gundacher's residence consisted of a ground-floor arrangement including a front room, back chamber, and stair hall with kitchen, washhouse, and back dining room in the sixteen-by-sixty-four-foot ell. As in the town houses of Norfolk, Charleston, Portsmouth, and Baltimore merchants, Gundacher's dwelling provided a suitable vehicle for material display. Although somewhat reorganized for Gundacher's final illness, the ground-floor rooms contained the predictable array of dining table, card table, and extensive seating furniture. Gundacher's residence also reflected a strong regional sensibility, in this case Pennsylvania-German, marked by the installation of ten-plate cast-iron stoves. The principal second-story room in the Gundacher house doubled as chamber and sitting room, with beds interspersed among the family's best "stuff bottom" chairs and sofas, tea service, mahogany card tables, and sideboard. The Gundachers' household furnishings describe three modes of social discourse: card playing, tea drinking, and conversation situated in rooms that housed both the public and private life of an elite merchant family. Philadelphians Stephen and Mary Collins provided for display and performance with a best room located on the second floor at the front of their house and furnished with the same materials for competitive entertainment and conversation: card tables, mahogany chairs, sofa, and ornaments such as glass candlesticks and "Chinese Jars." The Collins, Gundacher, and Spear households followed a similar furnishing pattern of card tables, seating, and appropriately tasteful decoration, steeped in the visual language of polite fashion.[40]

Larger social continuities suggested by the furnishing strategies echo in the architectural detail of town houses like the Norfolk mansion of Moses and Elizabeth Myers. Dining room and parlor offered an important venue for face-to-face negotiations, where the competitive culture of trade coincided with hospitality. The Myers dining room table, crowned with Elizabeth Myers's spun-sugar centerpiece, established an arena for one aspect of these competitive exchanges; the tabletop could function metaphorically as a representation of the city itself. As prescribed in the popular culture of genteel society, the dining table offered a regular rectangular or oval field, free from irregular topography and previous constructions that marred the city proper (see Figure 2.22). The table was divided into place settings equally distributed around its perimeter. Public points defined by serving dishes, candlesticks, and centerpieces provided intersections for individual place settings. The host and hostess occupied opposing ends of the table, and their company (often all men) was placed between them. In theory, all the guests enjoyed equal access to the commerce of the table and the transactions associated with conversation and etiquette. In practice, preferred

FIGURE 2.22

Plan for a Dining Room Table Setting
(circa 1825). *From Thomas Cosnett, The Footman's
Directory and Butler's Remembrancer. Courtesy
Winterthur Library: Rare Book Collection*

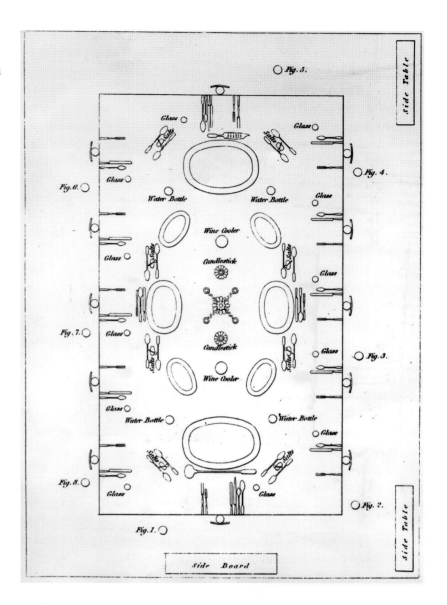

seating (expressed, for example, in proximity to the host's seat of power)
defined a topography of unequal access and authority.[41]

    The dining table, like the city plan, was a scene for exchange. Both were
settings where objects were set in social motion. How individuals comported themselves in parlor, dining room, or countinghouse depended on
a thorough knowledge of the rules of material as well as verbal discourse.

Success was determined by the diners' ability to negotiate and conclude trade in an arena of competitive display that embraced domestic objects ranging from chairs to ceramics. Once seated at the table, or once standing in the countinghouse or on the vendue range, the ability to perform socially and commercially (and the two were not very far apart in the mind of the eighteenth-century Atlantic world) distinguished the players and provided the means to ascendancy or downfall. The flow of conversation along the lines of acceptable topics, the use of wit without resorting to insult or crassness, and the ability to substantively inform and amuse nurtured and sustained a competitive culture. Similarly, an awareness of how to eat properly—using the soupspoon for soup, accepting service, and even chewing—further defined the place of the individual in a competitive setting that required knowledge and ability. The rituals of the dinner table mirrored the negotiation of the world of trade. Success in trade arose in part from the able negotiation of advantage, which drew on an extensive and intimate firsthand knowledge of markets, profits, competitors, and etiquette. Success at the dining table reflected a similar competitive desire for gaining social advantage, but here the mannered skills and subtleties of sociability superseded knowledge of the marketplace. As two elements in an embedded landscape, the architecture and actions of trade and table informed and reinforced each other.

The connections suggested between tabletop and the plan of the mercantile city extend to tea and gaming tables. The connection between dining table, countinghouse, and card table is easy to establish (see Figure 2.23). The players sit symmetrically around the perimeter of the card table and play either individually or in partnerships. The language of bidding, betting, bluffing, counting, and winning or losing is associated with the language and practice of trade. Unlike the dining table with its hierarchy of seating, the card table provides equal access to a field of competitive action where attention is focused more on the transactions of gaming and less on the niceties of etiquette and conversation.[42]

Tea table topography was a different terrain. No less competitive and requiring considerable prior knowledge and the ability to perform, the tea table was represented in the popular culture of prints and literature as the domain of women (see Figure 2.24). The conspicuous asymmetry and social imbalance of the tea table distinguished its use. The circular table provided a pedestal for the display of teapot, creamer, sugar bowl, tea canister, cups, saucers, sugar tongs, and spoons for admiration. Their placement, while

FIGURE 2.23

Card Table Set for Play. *Elias Hasket Derby House Museum, Salem National Historical Park, Salem, Massachusetts*

artful, did not provide equal access for all participants. Tea drinkers did not sit around the tea table in the same way that guests occupied their places at a dining table or in the manner that players faced each other across a card table. Instead, the hostess occupied a chair placed slightly askew to the center of the table and served her guests from a very different attitude of resident authority. Guests sometimes occupied chairs near the tea table or sat on chairs and settees around the room. The overall effect was of studied

FIGURE 2.24
Tea Table Set for Tea, Best Chamber,
Myers House

casualness where the culture of the salon prevailed. In the world of urban exchange relations, the tea table and its fragile array provided a field for competitive trade in conversational intimacy and guarded informality. The emphasis on casual display by both hostess and guests relied on a sensibility that reified etiquette and social knowledge. Like gaming and dining, taking tea tended to occur in an architecturally constant setting defined by the best rooms in the house. The interior detailing of the parlor, drawing room, and dining room possessed the quality of a landscape where major topographical features remained the constant setting for shifting forms of architectural and social experience.[43]

The material differences between the organization, appearance, and placement of tea, card, and dining tables posit social and functional distinctions. Each offered a different terrain demanding different performance skills; the larger significance of each table was realized only when those skills were brought into play and made visible for the pleasure and judgment of all. Still, the sociology of use remains unresolved. Tea taking as social behavior changed over the course of the eighteenth century. Largely the province of women in the colonial period, the domain of the tea table opened to men in the early national period. But, even as men increasingly participated in taking tea, the seat of authority remained feminine. Card playing in the home provided a considerably less gendered field for the display of social knowledge. Women competed with men as equals. Formal dining also changed in the post-Revolutionary decades, and dinners where women conversed shoulder-to-shoulder with men became more common. Variation and change in the sociology of tea, card, and dining tables suggest larger changes in early American urban landscapes where social life might not have been so rigidly divided.[44]

The desire to translate the profits of mercantilism into the architecture of status saturated the merchant family's house—and the senses. The Myers family, always meticulous record keepers, maintained a running diary of groceries bought in the Norfolk public market. From these purchase lists, we can reconstruct not only a sense of diet but also one of display where regional foods and cosmopolitan cuisine jostled for culinary attention. Food was an instrumental vehicle for polite interaction. A table set with fine silver and china does not convey the same message as one graced with roast fowl, asparagus, Madeira, and sugar sculpture. The delicacies served were as important as the platters on which they were presented and the cutlery with which they were cut, speared, and eaten. Similarly, the music performed by the family in the salon and heard by guests seated on settees and mahogany chairs, or the gambling games played on mahogany card tables in neighboring merchants' houses, defined both the competitiveness and sociability at the heart of mercantilism.[45]

Their dishes cleared away, the Myers guests concluded their repast by breaking off bits of Elizabeth Myers's spun-sugar centerpiece and consuming the sweet and fragrant morsels of the culture that defined them all.

THE BURGHER'S DILEMMA

Carl and Catherine Reisinger planned the renovations they wished to make to their one-story brick house. Situated on King Street, just two blocks east of the courthouse and market located in the central square of Lancaster, Pennsylvania, their old house measured eighteen by thirty feet. It extended two rooms in depth with a large front room facing the street and a smaller one in back. Although the front of the Reisingers' dwelling contained a fireplace, the back room was either warmed by a cast-iron stove or simply left unheated. With direct entry into a heated room that served as kitchen, dining room, and everyday gathering space and an unheated inner room removed from the casual everyday traffic of the street, the Reisinger town house followed rural building traditions closely associated with the locally dominant Pennsylvania-German culture. The Reisingers' remodeling project, however, eschewed local practice in favor of a British-American urban image.

The Reisingers' remodeled town house stood in contrast to the earlier dwelling, transformed by 1815 into a two-story brick structure, enlarged further by the addition of a rear ell measuring twenty-six by fourteen feet (see Figure 3.1). The Reisingers' dramatic remodeling campaign not only raised and extended the building but also transformed its interior arrangement. The front room, originally the family's principal living quarters, entered di-

FIGURE 3.1
Carl and Catherine Reisinger House,
King Street, Lancaster, Pennsylvania
(circa 1790)

A Elevation

rectly from the outside, found a new use as a downstairs sitting room, buffered from the street by the introduction of a four-foot-wide entry hall that led back to the old stair passage. Upstairs, the Reisingers installed a more formal parlor with a fully paneled fireplace wall. Cooking and domestic functions formerly housed in the main body of the dwelling were relegated to the new ell that contained a ground-floor kitchen and its own outside entry opening into a narrow yard connected to an alleylike passage to the street. The entry into the ell provided a buffer between the more formal front of the house and its kitchen filled with the sounds, smells, and heat of everyday domestic work.[1]

Tax lists compiled in 1798 and 1815 enumerated Lancaster's houses by building material, size, and value. In 1798, roughly one-quarter of the borough's town houses were of brick construction. In assessed value, the Reisingers' old dwelling, valued at $505, stood below the town average of $730. That figure, however, is deceptive in a city where a handful of houses valued between $3,000 and $5,000 skewed the average. More representative is the fact that within the total range of house values from $103 to $5,000, the Reisingers' residence stood at the exact center. In 1815, the assessed value of the remodeled and significantly enlarged house still occupied the middle ground. But, in a city where the proportion of brick houses had grown to one-third of all dwellings, the reworked residence was valued at nearly one-half more than the average. In short, the Reisingers' renovations significantly improved their architectural standing among the city's total architectural fabric and left them comfortably ensconced in the middling ranks of the owners of Lancaster's brick houses.[2]

The Reisingers' dilemma is reflected in the architectural fabric and plan of their house. The remodeling resulted in a larger, visibly and experientially different dwelling. Their choices were made in the context of an urban environment that incorporated simultaneously a strong local Pennsylvania-German identity and an equally strong presence as an economic and social center connected to state and national politics and trade. Exemplified by the Reisinger House, the negotiation of a regional culture in Lancaster town houses in the early nineteenth century was far from uniform. Individual identity, cultural preference, economic means, and social circumstance all contributed to the architectural choices made by individuals in this German-speaking city. For the Reisingers and many of their bourgeois contemporaries, the choice boiled down to the resolution of the tension between traditional practice and contemporary cosmopolitan aesthetics.[3]

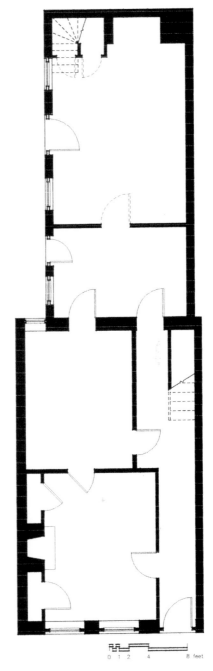

B First-Floor Plan. *Drawn by Jeff Klee*

What distinguished Lancaster's streetscapes at the turn of the nineteenth century was the strong visual presence of the city's Pennsylvania-German origins and its reflection of cultural preference in a city where vital and distinctive provincial ethnic traditions infused every aspect of urban life. Although English was the official language and culture of government and commerce, German words and ways made the city distinct. The point of interest is how individual owners and builders negotiated the intersection of regional and metropolitan values in the form, construction, and ornament of the buildings they erected. The Reisingers clearly contracted with builders to make the desired alterations in their dwelling, and in a sense the authorship of the finished building was theirs. Still, the Reisingers answered to the material circumstances of their lives. The availability of craftsmen able to design and execute the extensive renovations represented one set of constraints. Multiple architectural consensuses defined by ethnic and class identity in Lancaster also informed and shaped the outcome of the Reisingers' endeavors. In short, the Reisingers' town house was the product of multiple hands and minds and reflected larger changes in the city fabric. In Lancaster, the state capital at the turn of the nineteenth century, the tension between local and cosmopolitan cultures meant unending negotiation on many levels. Thus, the importance of the Reisinger house is twofold. First, the plan and finishes of the dwelling document one household's response to that tension. Second, the Reisingers' actions hold implications for a larger understanding of how urban housing in other late-eighteenth- and early-nineteenth-century American cities negotiated parallel architectural identities. The first step to making sense of these processes resides in understanding how the Reisingers' remodeled house fitted into Lancaster's early 1800s streetscapes.

Established as a market town in Lancaster County, the Borough of Lancaster emerged at the end of the eighteenth century as county seat, state capital, and contender for the seat of federal government. The plan of the landlocked town centered on a public square defined by the intersecting thoroughfares of King and Queen Streets (see Figure 3.2). Lancaster's Center Square and its immediate environs provided the setting for courthouse, market, churches, taverns, and primary merchant establishments. The classically inspired courthouse, in the middle of Center Square, drew on the same classical design traditions that informed the plan and appearance of public buildings in England and America. Oriented on axis with the intersecting streets, the Lancaster courthouse effectively announced the center of town and presented a symmetrical face to all comers. John Pearson, a

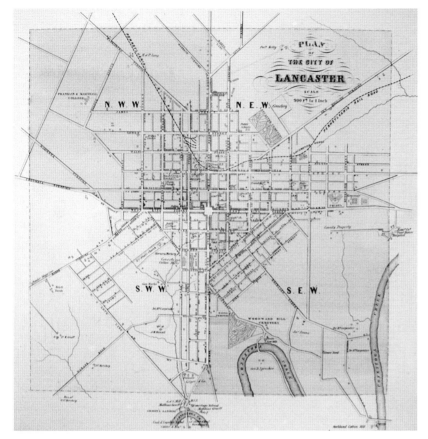

FIGURE 3.2

Plan of Lancaster (circa 1864). The areas set at diagonals to the central square are the later-eighteenth-century additions of Mussertown and Adamstown. H. F. *Bridgens*, Bridgens' Atlas of Lancaster Co., Penna, from Actual Surveys *(Lancaster, 1864). Plan courtesy Lancaster County Historical Society*

Quaker of English descent and newly elected state senator from near Philadelphia, described the courthouse in the winter of 1801 as "a handsome building about sixty feet square, two stories high and built with brick. . . . The rooms are large commodious and pleasant, from the Senate Chamber you have a fine view of the three streets issuing as it were from the building." Benjamin Henry Latrobe recorded the building in a watercolor sketch that depicted its larger setting (see Figure 3.3).[4]

Extending down the street, a range of two-and-one-half-story brick town houses equipped with shallow pent roofs sheltering ground-floor entries and shop fronts echoed similar streetscapes in Philadelphia. A three-story building standing on the adjacent street displayed a ground-floor elevation opening into commercial premises with its doors and windows framed by pedimented surrounds. Next door, a low, one-story town house squatted ad-

FIGURE 3.3

Center Square, Lancaster (circa 1796). By Benjamin Henry Latrobe. *Courtesy The Maryland Historical Society, Baltimore, Maryland*

jacent to a row of three dwellings of two stories that likely contained shops. The courthouse and its neighbors, painted by Latrobe, contrasted even more sharply with the Pennsylvania-German dwellings lining streets just two blocks from the city center, as Pearson observed:

> You see excellent three story brick two story stone and the old fashioned ones composed of wood and brick, some of frame only, some are of black limestone procured from the neighboring high grounds. . . . The roofs are generally of oak, some of cedar and some of white pine, many of them painted; tile is rarely seen. In the principal streets and near the center and most valuable parts of the town are many very mean houses of a single story but perhaps half the houses are of one story, some of the wealthy citizens to this hour build houses of that kind, four rooms on a floor and apparently well finished, by which it appears that their opinion

is favorable to one story houses. You will observe many of the genuine German kind a frame bricked with a great number of ties and studs the studs frequently lean and often are hewed crooked I suppose for ornament and stand in almost every direction.

Pearson's view is selective and judgmental. He makes distinctions between excellence and meanness, provincial and cosmopolitan, and (implicitly) backward and fashionable, locating those differences in his perceptions of Pennsylvania-German architectural practice. But—whose city was it?[5]

Pearson's perceptions of Lancaster are decidedly Anglocentric. Philadelphia was his frame of reference, and the standards of his assessment of Lancaster's dwellings reflected that bias. Pearson and many of his contemporaries also made the assumption that Pennsylvania-Germans were essentially a society of farmers, but, in fact, it was a socially, occupationally, and economically diverse society. Pennsylvania-German artisan households like the Reisingers' were common in Lancaster and defined an urban culture of the middling sort. Moreover, Pennsylvania-German town culture was not without Continental antecedents and parallels. The petite bourgeoisie *(Kleinbürger)* of eighteenth-century German cities presented much the same architectural image as their distant American cousins. The combination of Anglocentric and stereotypical perspectives resulted in descriptions like Pearson's that could make sense of Lancaster's visual culture only by casting it in a different context. The frailty of his reading (and ours) is further confused by the material and visual relationships between the surrounding Pennsylvania-German landscape and Lancaster's civic and visual center.[6]

Students of the urban landscape often draw on an interpretive approach that defines a city core and its periphery. The core comprehended the hub of urban activity centered on trade, politics, and public culture. The periphery surrounded the core and spread out along the framework of major streets connecting the greater city and the neighboring countryside. No hard boundary existed between core and periphery. Even as market squares, churches, and civic buildings occupied the core, less desirable public functions, such as almshouses and prisons, were typically relegated to the edge of the city. Similarly, domestic buildings, including town houses and their outbuildings, remained common fixtures at the very city center. Thus, the perceived relationships between the urban core and its peripheral landscapes are less about a functionally segmented physical landscape and more about a way of describing the dynamic interaction between cities in terms of a city's constituent environments. The recognition of core and periphery in Lancaster provides a means for looking at the architectural consciousness of the early-nineteenth-century city and helps us shape a broader understanding of the Reisingers' town house in its overlapping and competing contexts.[7]

The Catherine and Carl Reisinger House reveals a series of choices made by the couple to reconcile differing urban and backcountry building traditions. The Reisingers' remodeled town house drew on a plan familiar to artisan, shopkeeper, and minor merchant households from Baden, in Germany, to London's Spitalfields to Philadelphia's Society Hill to Charleston's wharfside neighborhoods. A narrow entry opened into the ground-floor front room and led to the upper-story rooms, which included the best parlor; an exterior covered passage that ran between the Reisingers' house and their neighbors opened onto the kitchen and back dooryard. The second-story parlor, stylishly paneled, stretched the full length of the house in a manner common to both freestanding dwellings and row houses in other cities from Charleston to Bristol to Portsmouth. The back entry and stair modified and applied the tradition of a Philadelphia-style piazza—the placement of the stair in a smaller room between the front and back parts of the house—in a Pennsylvania-German town house setting. The front rooms in the first and second stories of the Reisinger House possessed open fireplaces, a feature that the back rooms lacked, as did the adjoining first- and second-story rooms of the rear ell containing the kitchen at its farthest end. The absence of fireplaces in the house's middle rooms does not suggest that they were unheated but rather that they were heated by other means, specifically with cast-iron stoves vented through stove pipes feeding into masonry flues in the uppermost reaches of the house.

The lack of fireplaces and the presence of stoves in the Reisinger residence, more than any other detail, speak to the heart of the cultural traditions that shaped the form and appearance of their remodeled house. Cast-iron stoves were a hallmark of eighteenth-century Pennsylvania-German dwellings in both the city and the countryside. The Reisingers incorporated their heating preference in the design of their town house, setting aside the back rooms of the house as stove rooms. The presence of stove rooms in Lancaster town houses like the Reisingers' provides a relatively sensitive measure of how city residents situated themselves between what they saw as German and English ways. In the neighborhood of Mussertown that began a block south of the Reisinger House, Lancaster builders pursued town house forms that bore little resemblance to Anglo-American urban dwellings found in other towns and cities. Local preferences for plan types and construction techniques distinguished much of the cityscape in the same way that single houses and urban plantation compounds magnified Charleston's regional identity. Two Lancaster houses in the Mussertown neighborhood make the case.[8]

A one-story house on Front (now Church) Street follows a three-room plan common to the eighteenth-century Pennsylvania-German countryside (see Figure 3.4). Built of logs laid up with dovetail corner notching and clad with beaded weatherboard, the house presented an asymmetrical, four-bay front to the street. The door opened into a room thirteen feet wide that extended the sixteen-foot depth of the house. The kitchen *(Küche)* contained the stair to the finished loft and a large cooking fireplace (removed in the early twentieth century). The kitchen with its open hearth was the working heart of the building. The stove room *(Stube)* stood adjacent to the kitchen in the front of the house. The two windows that pierced the front of the house afforded both light and a view of the activity on the street. A jamb stove radiated heat from the corner behind the kitchen chimney. Behind the stove room, the *Kammer* was a long narrow room suitable for a downstairs sleeping chamber or storeroom. Although later-nineteenth-century repairs replaced the back wall of the log house with brick, the dwelling continued to present a public face of the decidedly rural Pennsylvania-German character that Pearson found so striking.[9]

Susannah Dietrich's house occupied a lot on Middle Street (now Howard Avenue) behind Front (see Figure 3.5). Built in the last decade of the eighteenth century, the Dietrich house was erected with half-timber construction, where the framing members of the house were filled with brick and left exposed as exterior decoration. The roughly twenty-seven-by-twenty-two-foot house enumerated in tax lists for 1798 and 1815 was described as a one-story frame house. The building, valued at $190 in 1798 (placing it in the lowest quarter of assessed properties), was one of only a handful of Lancaster town houses illuminated by casement windows. When Phillip Metzger, a prosperous butcher, acquired and remodeled the house in the 1820s, he erased much of the building's visible German character. A veneer of brick masked the old-fashioned, half-timber walls, and new sash windows replaced the old leaded casements. The three-room arrangement of kitchen, stove room, and *Kammer* was reworked into a side-passage plan with all-new interior woodwork. Metzger left the old kitchen largely intact, but opened up the stove room and *Kammer* as a single stove-heated room. A

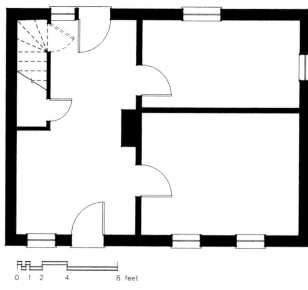

B First-Floor Plan (with chimney removed in the nineteenth century). *Drawn by Jeff Klee*

A Elevation

FIGURE 3.4

Ulrich Lamparter House, 429 Church Street, Lancaster (late eighteenth century)

shed addition across the back of the house compensated for the loss of the old *Kammer*. Metzger left elements of the older house intact only in out-of-the-way places. The half-timber rear wall survived under the shed and later applications of plaster; the half-timbered gables disappeared from view, concealed at first with weatherboard and later by neighboring houses; out of sight, the stove room cellar below with its infilled ceiling was forgotten. Like the Reisingers, Metzger attempted to bridge two cultures. Even as he eradicated the most visible outward signs of the dwelling's Pennsylvania-German origins, he retained a modified version of its earlier plan, where a stove-heated parlor remained a desirable feature.[10]

Other Pennsylvania-German town houses, both those surviving and those described in local records, reflect the same architectural preferences for three-room plans, stove rooms, log, stone, half-timber construction, and distinctive decorative details. The Dellow-Mellinger house accommodated a three-room plan that also included a full cellar entered at street level and a symmetrical, five-bay front with a centrally placed doorway (see Figure 3.6).

FIGURE 3.5
Susannah Dietrich House, 125 Howard Avenue,
Lancaster (late eighteenth century; remodeled
and cased with brick after 1822)

Like their counterparts, these houses underwent significant nineteenth-century changes. The owners of the Dellow-Mellinger House demolished the old central chimney pile and converted their town house into a plan with a central hall containing an open stair to the upper story. Their old stove room received a new corner fireplace befitting a parlor in the English style but retained its position abutting the still unheated *Kammer*. Like Reisinger and Metzger, the remodelers of the Dellow-Mellinger House were negotiating cultures, creating dwellings that embraced modern fashion and preserved customary spaces.[11]

Complicating the picture is the fact that Lancaster's Pennsylvania-German character was surely influenced by eighteenth-century German urban building traditions. German town houses associated with the petite bourgeoisie both paralleled and differed from the Reisingers' prerenovation residence (see Figure 3.7). Eighteenth-century town houses in Baden placed the primary (and most formal) living space to the street, with the kitchen and downstairs sleeping chamber oriented to the yard behind the house. By the later eighteenth century the practical organization of the ground floor was altered. Although the old ground-floor divisions remained preserved, the rooms adjacent to the passage were no longer used as dwelling spaces. The result was a town house that placed domestic functions in the upper stories.[12]

In Mainz, local practice placed the kitchen in the front of the house adjacent to the entry and stair in an arrangement reminiscent of the Reisingers' house. In multistory buildings where each floor defined a household, the uppermost stories sandwiched the kitchen between front and back rooms. This arrangement required the use of internal windows in partitions between rooms to borrow both light and air from the adjoining spaces fronting street and yard. Regardless of kitchen placement, builders of multistory dwellings in both places embraced a division that set the ground floor aside for commerce and shop work while the stories above contained parlors, kitchens, and sleeping chambers. Although the foundations of the Reisingers' house and those of their German contemporaries offered geometrical similarities, actual local practice took distinct routes. Thus, the Reisingers kept the kitchen on the ground floor while the residents of contemporary German town houses placed cooking and related household functions in the upper stories, freeing their ground-floor rooms for craft and commercial purposes.[13]

Other Lancaster individuals and families (both English and German) who commissioned new houses or had their old residences remodeled embraced town house designs that engaged a more cosmopolitan sensibility. Attorney and merchant William Montgomery, one of the city's wealthiest early-nineteenth-century citizens, commissioned a three-story town house on Queen Street in the first block below Center Square (see Figure 3.8). Erected in the first decade of the nineteenth century, Montgomery's house was notable for its scale, plan, and details. The thirty-three-by-forty-eight-

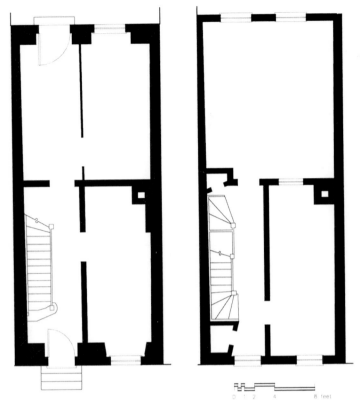

A 14 Liebfrauenstrasse, Mainz, Germany,
First- and Second-Floor Plans. *After Stephan,*
Das Bürgerhaus in Mainz, 98

B 11 Lupfenstrasse, Baden, Germany, First-Floor
Plan. *After Ossenberg, Das Bürgerhaus in Baden,*
194. Drawn by Jeff Klee

FIGURE 3.7

Kleinbürger Houses

foot building incorporated a ten-foot-wide apsidal-ended passage that terminated in an open stair winding up to the second- and third-floor rooms. A bow window projecting from the rear walls of the elliptical first- and second-story back rooms provided a view of the household's private gardens. The Flemish-bond brickwork elaborated with decorative jack arches above the doors and windows asserted an architectural identity that had little in common with the design traditions and construction practices of the Lancaster County hinterland.[14]

The earlier Ellicott-Sehner House on nearby Prince Street presented a plan and finishes comparable in quality to those of the Montgomerys' house (see Figure 3.9). Constructed in the late 1700s, the dwelling made use of a

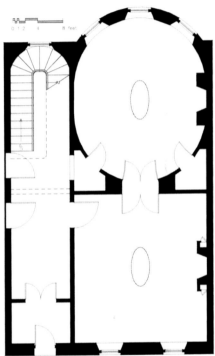

B Reconstructed First-Floor Plan.
Courtesy Jeff Klee. Drawn by Jeff Klee

side-passage, double-pile plan, augmented with extensive back buildings containing the kitchen, domestic work spaces, and supplementary chambers. The best room in the house occupied the second floor and overlooked the street. With its raised panel finishes utilizing classical elements, the Ellicott-Sehner House displayed a greater affinity with its Philadelphia contemporaries than it did with its Lancaster neighbors. Still, as the 1815 inventory for merchant Michael Gundacker shows, members of Lancaster's

wealthy elite maintained customary features, such as the general use of stoves, even in the town houses that seemingly repudiated Pennsylvania-German ways.[15]

The town houses of William Montgomery and Susannah Dietrich represent two points in an architectural continuum: the former rejected nearly every visible vestige of local practice while the latter adhered to the most traditional Pennsylvania-German building details. Most of Lancaster's residents, German or English, occupied town houses somewhere in between, houses that blurred ethnic lines as clients and builders made choices that

merged vernacular building traditions and the developing class consciousness of the middling sort. The Reisinger House reflected just this sensibility.
Even so, the Reisingers' remodeled dwelling with its two-story elevation and
side-passage plan represented the best of the city's middling houses. Two
other houses yield a better sense of what more mainstream Lancaster town
houses looked like by the 1820s and provide insight into the decisions the
Reisingers made in reworking their eighteenth-century town house.[16]

A one-and-one-half-story town house on Middle Street (now Howard Avenue) stands as one of a pair of early-nineteenth-century brick town houses
created by dividing a larger dwelling into two smaller ones (see Figure
3.10). Behind its street elevation, the house retains evidence of an earlier
eighteenth-century Pennsylvania-German town house. The first house followed a three-room Pennsylvania-German arrangement with entry into a
heated kitchen backing onto a stove room and *Kammer*. The first house also
made use of the same building techniques Pearson found noteworthy. The
half-timbered exterior offered the decorative placement of structural members to the public eye, and on the interior the builders installed clay- and
straw-wrapped insulation, wattle-and-daub partitions, and a heavy summer
beam with one end planted in the masonry of the central chimney stack.
The remodelers kept only elements essential to the structural integrity of
the building and those that could be masked with new finishes. Like the Reisingers just three blocks to the northeast, the owners of the Middle Street
house transformed their town house out of one culture and into another.

Other Lancaster builders commissioned new houses that incorporated
plan elements and finishes similar to the Middle Street house and reminiscent of the Reisingers' original dwelling. The Bindery on Water Street, for
example, integrated a number of features into a pair of matching one-and-
one-half-story town houses (see Figure 3.11). Erected around 1830, the double house was composed of two separate residences, each based on a plan
centered on a large front room that lent itself to commercial and domestic
purposes. Behind the main room stood a smaller room heated with a cast-
iron stove and opening directly into a kitchen ell. Running beside the back
dining room, a compact passage connected the front room directly to the
service wing and contained the stairs to both garret and cellar. The plastered
interior surfaces, plain mantel, and door and window trim would have been
unremarkable features to visitors from other urban places, but the single-
story elevation for town houses standing only a block distant from the city's
central square and the presence of a stove room would have excited com-

FIGURE 3.10
Town Houses, Middle Street (now Howard
Avenue), Lancaster (late eighteenth century;
remodeled circa 1825)

ment that touched on the very core of town house design and urban identity. The image of urban regularity and standardized building techniques presented by buildings like the Water Street houses or the remodeled tenements on Middle Street only halfheartedly embraced the sense of space that connected bourgeoisie in different cities with a spatial sense of class that transcended place. Equally important to Lancaster builders was the sense of place rooted in the backcountry of Pennsylvania-German hinterland and Old World building traditions.[17]

Like town houses in other cities, the Reisinger House derived its meaning from the place it occupied in the physical and perceived circumstances of the larger urban landscape. The Reisinger House stood on the northern edge of the eighteenth-century borough's southeastern ward, an area bordered by King Street to the north and Queen Street to the east. The city's central square, occupied by the courthouse, defined the element of the grid from which the city radiated. Center Square was clearly visible from the street in front of the Reisingers' house. In the southeastern ward, however, new streets violated the original grid and sustained the geographical identity of two discrete neighborhoods known as Mussertown and Adamstown, both characterized by the distinctive Pennsylvania-German building traditions observed by Pearson. The leading edge of Mussertown began one block behind the Reisingers' lot. The location of the Reisinger House literally placed it between two worlds: the metropolitan face of King Street (the road that literally led to Philadelphia) and Lancaster's Center Square and the provincial face of Mussertown and the Pennsylvania-German backcountry that informed its architectural character. Again, the Reisingers' town house found its significance in a larger context of architectural choice that was as much public as it was personal.

It would be a mistake to interpret town houses like the Reisingers' King Street dwelling as the product of a declining folk culture overrun by the irresistible forces of a metropolitan world steeped in British colonial traditions. We would also err in lionizing the distinctive features of Lancaster's town houses as emblems of cultural resistance to English ways or the result of cultural accommodation. These houses speak more directly to the many ways in which residents of early American cities negotiated their architectural identities to suit their own needs and aspirations. As symbols, their houses assert individual values in a larger, more conflicted urban setting. The Reisingers' dilemma lay in negotiating private values in the public sphere of the street. The options they drew upon and those they chose were accessible

FIGURE 3.11

Bindery, Water Street, Lancaster (circa 1830)

A Elevation

to all with the ability to build and furnish houses. The choices made about street elevation, location and finish of the second floor parlor, installation of stove rooms, and relegation of cooking and domestic work into a service ell enabled the Reisingers to situate themselves at a point on an architectural continuum represented at its extremes by the grand architectural gesture of William Montgomery's Queen Street mansion and Susannah Dietrich's half-timbered Middle Street dwelling. As the early nineteenth century unfolded, the majority of Lancaster builders who shared the ranks of the middling sort with Catherine and Carl Reisinger continued to work toward architectural solutions that synthesized local and cosmopolitan identities.[18]

The negotiation of urban architectural and cultural identity took place up and down the eastern seaboard. The town houses in the environs of Charleston's Civic Square, like those lining King and Queen Streets around Lancaster's Center Square, occupied an urban landscape dominated by the architecture of provincial, civic, and ecclesiastical power: statehouse, courthouse, city hall, and church. In Charleston, the bold architecture of British imperial rule measured out in the stiffly symmetrical authority of the province's colonial statehouse resonated in the soaring authority of church and state symbolized in the arcaded elevations and triumphant steeple of Saint Michaels (see Figure 3.12). More subtle in its assertion of power, the neoclassical detailing of city hall (originally intended as a branch of the Bank of the United States) rendered the structure of public finance and governance delicate. The congregation of eighteenth- and early-nineteenth-century public buildings in Civic Square provided one terminus for the larger ensemble of buildings that lined the first blocks of Broad Street. Anchored on the Cooper River waterfront by the great Georgian bulk of the Exchange, the stretch from East Bay to Meeting Street, with its noisy blend of residential and commercial uses, presented a familiar face to any traveler in the North Atlantic rim in the late eighteenth and early nineteenth centuries. The streets leading into Broad and East Bay, however, offered a locally distinctive aspect with rows of wood and brick "single houses" sited gable end to the street on long narrow lots and supported by clusters of outbuildings, including kitchens, washhouses, and quarters for enslaved servants.[19]

The same spatial tension between Lancaster's Center Square and its surrounding neighborhoods is equally apparent in Charleston, but with the city's own local flavor. This tension assumed two guises. First, there was the tension between the type and appearance of buildings at the town or city core and those sited farther away nearer the urban periphery. In both instances, core and periphery existed as mental landscapes as much as physical spaces. The urban spatial imagination easily rendered the short physical distance of one or two blocks into a much greater perceptive distance. Those distances are clearly reflected in the Reisingers' house (both old and remodeled). Second, there is a tension between local construction and design traditions and ideas of architectural form and use steeped in the larger

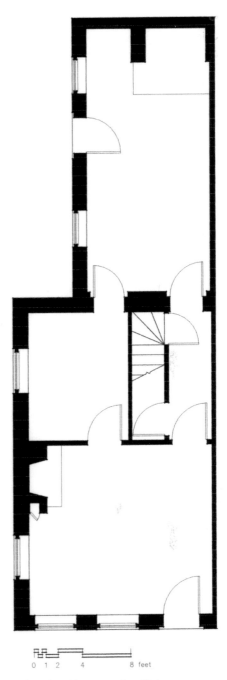

B First-Floor Plan. *Drawn by Jeff Klee*

exchange culture of the North Atlantic rim in the late eighteenth and early nineteenth centuries. In Lancaster and Charleston, the urban center was defined by public and commercial uses familiar to most travelers on both sides of the Atlantic at the close of the eighteenth century. Familiarity of form, however, did not obscure the peculiarities of local appearance. Thus, while the architecture of commerce and sociability remained accessible, the visible details of construction and ornament communicated local preferences. The turn-of-the-nineteenth-century interplay between these tensions and their resolution remains visible in the streets connecting Charleston's Cooper River waterfront to its civic center.[20]

In the first blocks of early-nineteenth-century Broad Street, which runs from East Bay Street to Meeting Street, merchants occupied fully one-third of the premises that lined the street, often devoting the ground floor to commercial activities and the upper stories to residential functions in a manner observed in every contemporary American port city and market town. The architectural strategy of street-level premises and upper-story dwellings also served the artisans and shopkeepers who registered Broad Street addresses. These functions were housed in a variety of building types, ranging from freestanding dwellings to rows of two or three buildings sharing party walls. Late-eighteenth-century plats for three properties in the first blocks of Broad Street illustrate overlapping solutions for the integration of home and business. In each of these settings, the accommodations for enslaved servants and laborers played a key role in the organization of the house.

The property survey for merchant James Gregorie's house at 28 Broad Street shows a complicated site plan with a three-story brick house fronting the street and an array of outbuildings and work yards leading back to a roughly forty-five-by-eighty-five-foot formal garden (see Figure 3.13). The legend for the 1797 survey notes that the "lower story" of the slate-roofed house "is occupied as a Store and Counting room." The house presented a large, unheated front room to the street. A centrally placed doorway, likely flanked by windows, aligned with a second doorway in a partition that screened the heated counting room from the shop area. The stair to the second- and third-story living quarters rose in a compact entry that could be entered from the back counting room or through an exterior door opening from a narrow outside passage just wide enough to admit a small carriage. The side entry served two purposes; it gave the family private access to their living quarters and enabled the proprietor to work with his inventory in the two brick stores located in the work yard. The larger storehouse with cellar was built of brick, covered with slate, and fronted the stable yard. The smaller store of similar construction was actually an element in a longer range of domestic work spaces that included a pantry, washroom, kitchen, carriage house, and stable. Following Charleston practice, slaves occupied the second-story rooms above the working buildings in the compound.[21]

Plats for merchant Benjamin Smith's house drawn at the turn of the

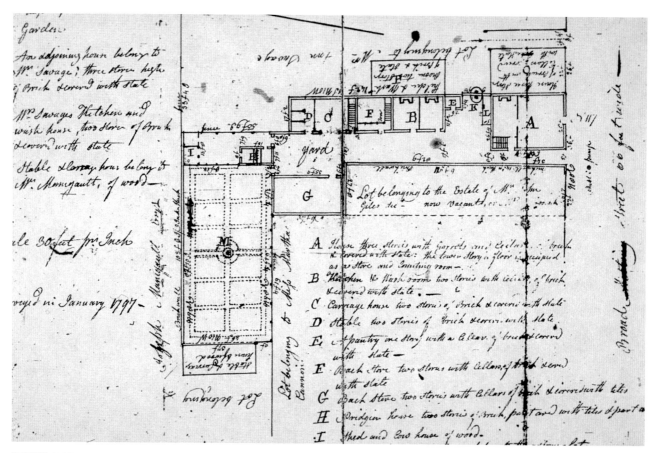

FIGURE 3.13

Plan of James Gregorie's House and Lot, 28 Broad Street, Charleston. *After McCrady Plat #503, Charleston County Register of Mesne and Conveyances (CCRMC)*

nineteenth century show the square footprint of the house that occupied the southwest corner of Broad and Church Streets (see Figure 3.14). An 1816 newspaper ad described the arrangement as "THAT well known, large and commodious Dwelling HOUSE and STORES. . . . On the ground floor is the Store and two Counting-rooms; on the second there are four Rooms adapted for a Drawing-room, Dining-room, etc. and a Bed-chamber at the end of the Balcony; on the third are four Chambers and a Dressing-room; a dry Cellar, the whole length and width of the House." Built with a centrally located doorway in its symmetrical, five-bay Broad Street elevation, the house incorporated a plan that placed a large, open, commercial room in the ground-floor front with a range of two rooms and a center stair taking up the back of the house. A series of three doors placed in the partition wall that divided

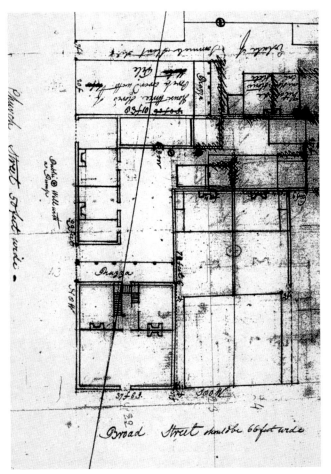

the house provided access into the building's private spaces. The stair, the entry located behind the commercial room, and a full-length piazza buffered this access in a manner consistent with Gregorie's smaller premises at 28 Broad Street.[22]

Also similar to 28 Broad was the overall disposition of the back lot, advertised as containing "two Kitchens and a Pantry; two very convenient Stores and Cellars; a Stable for two horses; and a Carriage house in Church-street—all of brick and tile or slate—the large Back Store, fireproof. In the yard, there is also a large Cistern and Bathing house." The property surveys illustrate the *L*-shaped lot behind both the Smith house and its Broad Street neighbor, a three-story brick double tenement. A narrow passage between the rear piazza and a two-story brick outbuilding, likely serving as kitchen, washhouse, and slave quarters, opened onto a paved yard that contained a well and pump and was surrounded by additional outbuildings and a brick wall that screened Smith's property from his neighbors. Standing within the walled, almost fortified compound of Benjamin Smith's premises were two brick warehouses and two smaller unidentified outbuildings. When the property was resurveyed in 1837, the plat legend still identified the main building as a "Brick Dwelling and Store."[23]

The back lot, however, was largely reorganized. The kitchen now occupied the warehouse that stood at the back of the property and had been extended with a two-story brick addition that filled in the open space in the *L*. The small brick buildings and second warehouse had been demolished and replaced with a three-story brick building extending into the extremity of the paved yard. Still, all the ingredients for a back building complex that worked with the house in the integration of domestic and commercial functions remained apparent. Why the change? The new configuration coupled all the outbuildings in a continuous train that backed onto adjacent yards furnished with similar buildings. The new arrangement met the needs both of emerging nineteenth-century domestic sensibilities that placed a premium on consolidation and compartmentalization and of the lingering antebellum insecurities white Charlestonians harbored in the churning wake of Denmark Vesey's plotted African-American insurrection of 1822.[24]

The Blake Tenements in Courthouse Square illustrate the common Broad Street practice of building town houses in pairs with party walls (see Figure 3.15). Built in the 1760s, the Blake Tenements were the first installment of a larger speculative building venture completed with the construction of a terrace of four similar town houses and outbuilding complexes facing Meeting Street. A detailed 1788 survey for the earlier State House Alley properties shows a pair of houses with their kitchens, yards, and shared garden and privies. Standing on a raised basement separated by a passage leading from the street to their backyards, each of the two three-story, Flemish-bond houses presented a symmetrical, three-bay, center-passage front. Their identical ground-floor plans, which lent themselves to both residential and business uses, consisted of a large front room outfitted with paneled cupboards or bookcases and entered directly from a raised porch. A second door at the back of the front room opened into a centrally located stair. The back of the house included a narrow passage along the party wall and a smaller heated room with storage closets and doorways onto both

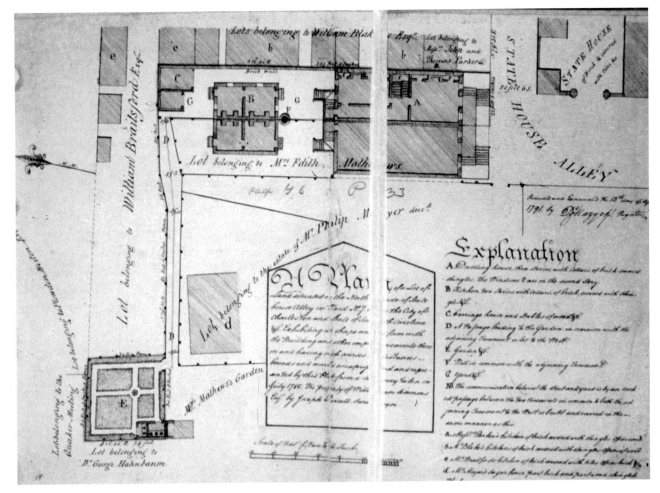

FIGURE 3.15

Blake Tenements, 4 Courthouse Square,
Charleston (circa 1760–1772), Plan of Houses
and Lots. *Charleston County Deed Book, G-6, p. 33,
CCRMC*

the stair and the entry at the back door. The stair to the upper stories of the
house provided access to the best parlor and family chambers; the passage
to the rear door opened onto a narrow flight of porch steps descending to
the work yard, kitchen, and quarters and down a fenced, five-foot-wide path-
way to a formal garden roughly 110 feet distant. Recorded in the 1803 street
directory as the premises for attorneys, factors, merchants, and a physician,
the Blake Tenements and their Meeting Street counterparts addressed the
same functional considerations observed in the Gregorie and Smith dwellings. The ground-floor plans offered commercial spaces and offices at the
front of the house, interior access to the householder's rooms, back rooms

A Elevation

that lent themselves to different uses ranging from dining to business, and yards furnished with outbuildings. Unlike Gregorie's and Smith's back lots, the Blake Tenements lacked stores and warehouses—a clear indication of businesses that did not require the architectural infrastructure necessary for merchandising or craftwork.[25]

The synthesis of local practice and cosmopolitan ideas distinguished the houses in the precincts of Charleston's core just as it did the dwellings in and around Lancaster's Center Square. In both urban settings, residents and builders strove for designs that integrated commercial and residential functions through strategies that accommodated the particulars of their social landscapes. In Charleston, the details of the urban landscape were profoundly influenced by the organization of the house around the presence and labor of enslaved servants. Back lots furnished with freestanding domestic work buildings and enslaved servants' quarters visually and architecturally linked Charleston's urban houses to its plantation hinterland. The resulting cityscape perfected the concept and reality of the urban plantation. At the same time, elite Charleston town house interiors containing withdrawing rooms, salons, and best parlors became the sites of cosmopolitan exchange even as their exteriors increasingly asserted the unmistakable regional identity that characterized the antebellum city's architectural culture.[26]

Town houses with ground-floor premises and upper-story dwellings were not limited to Broad Street. The Alexander Perronneau Tenement at 141 Church Street, for example, was erected on a plan that incorporated a ground-floor front shop with back living quarters (see Figure 3.16). Built with the ground floor of Bermuda stone and the second of brick, the two-story structure possessed a full cellar for storage and a finished garret. The stair that wound up through the house occupied a space in the back room between the fireplace and partition wall. The overall arrangement included a series of doorways aligned against the south wall and a narrow exterior passage along the north elevation. The front door opened from Church Street into the commercial room, the door in the partition led from the public space of the shop and into the private world of the household, and the door in the back wall opened onto a small work yard or possibly a kitchen. The narrow exterior passage led from Church Street past the house and into the work yard behind the building.

The arrangement of rooms and their different functions in the Perronneau Tenement resonates throughout the late-eighteenth-century Atlantic urban world. Similar buildings lined the streets of Petersburg, Virginia,

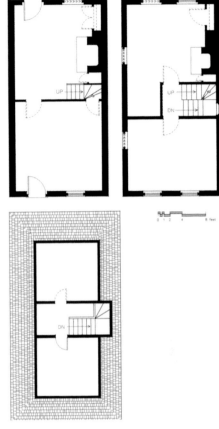

B First-, Second-,
and Attic-Floor Plans.
Drawn by Jeff Klee

FIGURE 3.17
Countinghouse and Shop,
Petersburg, Virginia
(early nineteenth century)

combining house and shop in a single structure—often with an unheated commercial room in the front (see Figure 3.17). In some instances, the back room served as a counting room, and the residential areas of the structure were placed entirely in the upper stories. In northern cities like Philadelphia smaller town houses with ground-floor premises followed the architectural textures of local practice but still incorporated the kinds of spaces seen in the Perronneau Tenement. Elizabeth Claxton kept a china store in the front room of her Crown Street dwelling. Her neighbors across the street apparently followed the same strategy, buffering the entry into their shop with a small lobby containing a glazed shop door. Similar buildings also occupied the streetscapes of English port cities. A two-story brick house in Cherry Street in Bristol, for example, offered a ground-floor shop with upstairs living apartments finished with paneled cupboards and other amenities. Similar town houses, in which parlors and best chambers occupy the stories above the ground-floor commercial rooms, still line High Street in the London suburb of Deptford. Erected in the 1720s, a house in High Street, Gravesend, offered entry directly into a shop heated by a small fireplace set in a paneled wall that contained two doorways—a narrow opening provided family access from the shop in front to a dining and sitting room in back, and a second doorway framed by an arched opening signaled the location of the stair that rose to the best apartments on the second floor (see Figure 3.18).[27]

The desire to create discrete commercial spaces within the house presented a common dilemma for shopkeepers and merchants throughout the Atlantic world. Plans for a wealthy Bristol merchant's town house in 1724 argued for an arrangement with a ground-floor office or "compter" separated from a drawing room by a vestibule and entry. The designer described the merchant's "compter" and its position in the house:

> On the left hand of the Vestibule is The Compter that People of Business may not have farr to go, and that the Master may see and hear of every thing that comes in at his doors: As this is the Support of the Family I have designed it large that there be sufficient Room to make such necessary conveniencys as shall be found wanting to keep every thing distinct: It has a private door by the Back stairs to retreat without being seen by people that are visiting, and the conveying away [of] anything that should not be exposed to view: And by it is the Back Stairs, to the Chambers that the young Men may at night go to their Beds and in the morning come to their business without disturbing or dirtying the best part of the House.

FIGURE 3.18

78 High Street, Gravesend, England,
Brick-Fronted House and Shop (circa 1726).

Copyright English Heritage © Crown Copyright NMR

A Elevation

B Ground-Floor Front Room Used as
   Commercial Space

C Stair

The Bristol merchant's house accordingly accommodated business rooms within the overall plan of the house, but commercial functions remained fully segregated from the spheres of domesticity and sociability. The key exception was the drawing room, a space that housed the combined functions of sociability and trade. The plan for the Bristol merchant's house is unique only in that the designer's written explanation offered a narrative for what was clearly common practice throughout mercantile society in the eighteenth-century Atlantic world.[28]

Architectural solutions that reconciled domestic and business uses within the house produced a variety of functionally allied buildings in American port cities. An early-nineteenth-century three-story brick town house in Thames Street in the Fells Point district of Baltimore offered a ground-floor shop with its own formal entry (see Figure 3.19). A second entry down a covered exterior passage opened into a plainly finished back room containing a winder stair leading to a second-floor drawing room that was finished with stylish neoclassical detailing and overlooked the harbor. The plan of the Leighton Mansion on Mechanic Street in Portsmouth, New Hampshire, incorporated a ground-floor corner office with its small fireplace turned at a slight angle into the room, echoing both the scale and finish of the house in High Street, Gravesend. Eighteenth-century Philadelphia town house designs offered a familiar solution that integrated business functions into the overall plan of the house and used the unheated entry and stair to achieve the separation of social, economic, and domestic personas.[29]

The desire to accommodate commercial and residential uses within the house linked urban dwellings in their late-eighteenth-century transatlantic context. The application of local practice in construction, choice of ornament, and details of the plan rendered the same houses local and distinctive. The architectural tension between local and Atlantic cultures reveals a deeper cultural tension between two mentalités. Town houses did not stand in isolation but constituted individual elements that communicated presence of place. Given the reality that the buildings that lined Charleston's Broad Street, Lancaster's King Street, and their respective side streets were the results of individual actions, how do we account for the many similarities in their organization and detailing? What were the mechanisms for consensus where statute and the building practices lacked architectural cohesion? Although some measure of agency can be assigned to the conventions associated with the building trades, it cannot adequately account for choices made about the actual interior organization of buildings. A different answer

FIGURE 3.19
Town House, Thames Street,
Fells Point, Baltimore
A Elevation

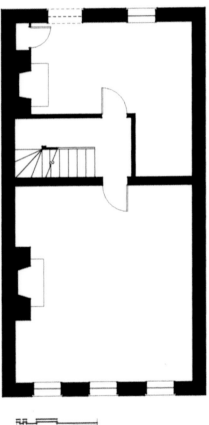

B Second-Floor Plans. *Drawn by Jeff Klee*

arises, however, when we take a closer look at the architectural textures of a very different early American city, Portsmouth, New Hampshire.

Following a series of fires that devastated the town center in the early nineteenth century, Portsmouth property owners and builders in the city recreated large sections of the urban landscape. Their efforts resulted in a town center composed of irregular rows of brick town houses, shops, and warehouses. The drive to build in brick, however, failed to take hold in the neighborhoods adjoining the city's core. In peripheral areas of the city like the South End, wood remained the preferred medium, even as builders experimented with new plans and decorative finishes. The relationship between the architecture of the urban core and the old and new frame buildings that dominated Portsmouth's periphery provides further insight into the larger cultural processes that shaped architectural choices in Lancaster and Charleston.[30]

No group of buildings illustrates this process and the expression of an architectural ideology better than the row of three-story town houses that speculators built on Sheafe Street in Portsmouth following a Christmas fire in 1813 (see Figure 3.20). Built of brick laid in plain Flemish bond and finished on the interior with stock mantels executed in a neoclassical style, the Sheafe Street houses presented elevations, plans, and details that eschewed local practice. The choice of building material rested to some extent on the provisions of the Brick Act of 1814, which legally stipulated that all new buildings in the city core use masonry construction. The roots of the Brick Act lay not only in the fear of conflagration but also in a desire for regularity and standardization in the urban landscape. In essence, calamity provided the circumstance to rethink and codify the visual identity of the urban core on a large scale. This new identity seemingly repudiated the architectural textures of a provincial place in favor of those that described the cultural ambitions of an emerging urban world where an architectural ideology of standardization blurred the visual distinctions between cities. The process that defined a transatlantic urban culture on the basis of private interests over public place was well established among Portsmouth's urban elite, as it was among the elites of other seaboard cities. What was new in early-nineteenth-century Portsmouth was the way in which town houses of the middling sort addressed issues of architectural identity in a manner comparable to the Reisinger House in Lancaster.[31]

The town houses on Portsmouth's periphery presented a different aspect. Brick construction outside the ordained "brick zone" was rare and generally

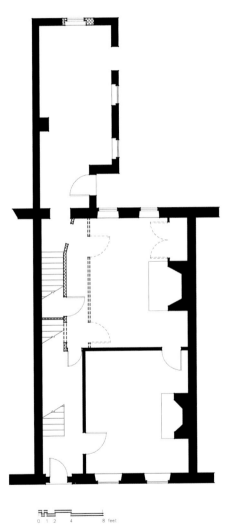

FIGURE 3.20

Sheafe Street, Portsmouth, New Hampshire

A Town House Row

B First-Floor Plan. *Drawn by Jeff Klee and Gabrielle M. Lanier*

0 1 2   4   8 feet

A Street Elevation

limited to the dwellings of the city's mercantile elite. Middling Portsmouth families with the means to build pursued design strategies that preserved multiple regional architectural precedents such as variations on center-chimney plan dwellings. The town house of Benjamin Holmes, Jr., on Pleasant Street in the South End illustrates the point (see Figure 3.21). Erected in the 1790s, presumably by Holmes, who advertised himself as a joiner and house carpenter, the two-story frame house followed a center-chimney plan with a lobby-entry front sitting room and dining room and back kitchen, scullery, chamber, and service stair. As a building type, the Holmes House represented a common feature in the landscapes of rural and village New England. Although New Englanders had built variations on this form since the early colonial period, dwellings like the Holmes town house did not emerge as a widespread and popular alternative until the mid-eighteenth century. By the close of the century, however, the center-chimney plan emerged as the regional house type evocative of the New England countryside. In Portsmouth, similar center-chimney houses appeared throughout the South End with the same frequency and general character of their counterparts in Newburyport and Salem, Massachusetts, and Providence, Rhode Island.[32]

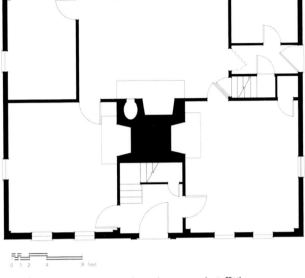

B First-Floor Plan. *Drawn by Jeff Klee*

The essential characteristic of the Holmes House and its cousins was a plan that incorporated a lobby entry and integrated service into the main body of the house but still held cooking and household work at bay in the back of the house. The builders of smaller center-chimney houses in Portsmouth and other northern New England seaport towns often realized these features through the simple expedient of siting the house with its gable to the street (see Figure 3.22). The orientation of the house in this way created a hierarchy of interior spaces that retreated from a formal front room or parlor, lobby entry, and back dining room and kitchen or "keeping room." Even the builders of center-chimney houses only one room deep and facing onto the street often took pains to announce the internal arrangement of spaces. In the Mary Rider house, built about 1800, the kitchen end of the house received only a single front window while the more formal parlor abutting the widow's shop received two (see Figure 3.23). By the close of the eighteenth century, however, the preference for center-chimney lobby entry plans was slipping in favor of town houses that made use of back wall chimneys. These plans synthesized provincial precedent and urban form in a new and distinctive manner that opened up the center of the house and created space for an unheated room behind the stair. In some instances, these new rooms provided an internal link between front parlor and back dining room. In other situations, the little room served just the back dining room as a pantry and staging area for meals. In either case, the new space facilitated service

FIGURE 3.23

Mary Rider House, Jefferson Street, Portsmouth (circa 1800, 1811). The Mary Rider House is interpreted in a museum setting as the residence of a nineteenth-century Portsmouth widow

A Elevation

B Reconstructed Kitchen Dresser

and communication by allowing the middling residents of smaller houses to enact more effectively the polite rituals of sociability. The formal logic perceived in these spatial arrangements clearly echoed the thinking behind the Reisingers' remodeled house.[33]

The rupture between the metropolitan face of the urban core and the backcountry traditions of Portsmouth's periphery resonated with Lancaster town houses and other urban environments. As elsewhere in New England, Newburyport suffered an early-nineteenth-century fire that ravaged its urban core. In the wake of the conflagration, builders erected two- and three-story brick buildings with commercial premises below and residences above. Away from the center of the city, however, local builders

FIGURE 3.24

Edward Langley House, by Nicholas King,
F Street, Washington, D.C. (circa 1796).
*Courtesy The Winterthur Library: Joseph Downs
Collection of Manuscripts and Printed Ephemera*

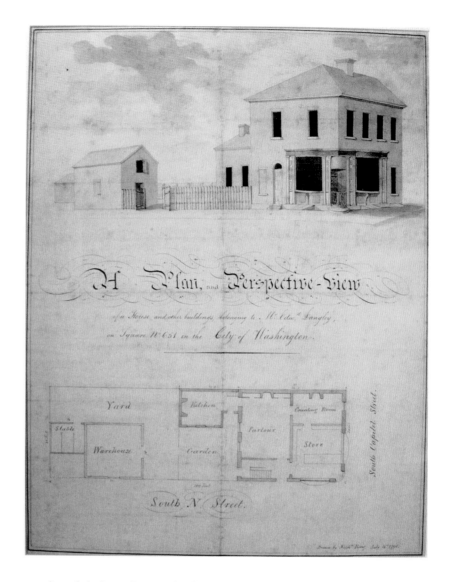

continued their preference for frame buildings based on plans that ranged
from center-chimney, lobby-entry forms to fully developed center-passage
plans with one- and two-room service wings. Similarly, the first generation
of town houses in Washington, D.C., exhibited an architectural tension best
described as one of "southern city, national ambition." In the nation's capital, some builders opted for the urban image of regular brick terraces inter-
changeable with that of other cities. Thus, Nicholas King's designs for the

F Street House and shop of Edward Langley reflected an architectural identity indebted to ideas of regularity and standardization closely associated with older and larger cities like Philadelphia (see Figure 3.24). Parallel developments in Virginia towns such as Alexandria and Fredericksburg show the same process of negotiation with urban cores putting forward the face of a broadly constructed image of urban identity familiar from coastal Virginia to northern New England to provincial British port and market towns.[34]

The negotiation of cultures is a familiar aspect of rural folk housing. The interpretation of the development of the Pennsylvania-German farmhouse in the eighteenth and nineteenth centuries, for example, recognizes the ways in which builders attempted to cram Old World interiors into New World skins, producing in the end a distinctive regional building type. The same process resonated in the concurrent rise of the Pennsylvania bank barn. Synthesized out of neighboring regional British and Continental agricultural traditions, these monumental two- and three-level barns symbolized changing technologies and ideologies in early-nineteenth-century farming. In the early American city, the cultural process of architectural design took on the additional baggage of a corporate identity. People saw their buildings as reflections of themselves, their worldviews, and the face of the city. But, even as the Reisingers, their Lancaster neighbors, the Charleston builders of Broad Street, and the Portsmouth planners of the Sheafe Street row each externalized one identity, they retained the comforts of another in the form of stove rooms and urban plantation compounds and keeping rooms. Their dilemma focused on making architectural sense in settings that blended local practice and cosmopolitan values. The resolutions to their deliberations are preserved in the fabric, plans, and finishes of their houses.[35]

THE SERVANTS' QUARTER

Billy Robinson claimed innocence. Standing before the justices trying the plotters in Denmark Vesey's thwarted insurrection by enslaved African-Americans in Charleston, South Carolina, Robinson listened attentively first to his accuser, then to the defense witnesses. Perault Strohecker, enslaved to a Cumberland Street blacksmith, implicated Robinson in the insurrection, averring that the defendant was intimate with other plotters already convicted and that in the wake of their arrests Robinson tried to organize a scheme to rescue Vesey and those condemned with him from hanging. Strohecker testified that at least two of the conversations he shared with the accused took place at Robinson's "own house." Robinson's counsel summoned Mrs. Miller, the white boardinghouse keeper who kept the premises where the defendant lived, to answer Strohecker's claims. Mrs. Miller stated:

> I live in a house in Elliot Street, there are two rooms on a floor—the first occupied by Mr. Howe [who worked as a grocer on nearby Tradd Street], the back by me. Billy occupies a room above my kitchen, and no one can go into his room without passing through my kitchen, I never saw Peirault go into Billy's room, or into my yard. Billy has lived in that room for 3 years.

Howe, along with two other witnesses apparently living in Miller's boarding-house, supported their landlady's contention that Robinson was innocent, because Strohecker could never have rendezvoused with Robinson in Robinson's quarters without their seeing him enter and leave. Because they did not witness such a meeting, it could not have happened. Moreover, they reported that Robinson, whose merchant master lived in nearby Tradd Street, was of good character and tractable disposition. On cross-examination, though, Strohecker described Billy's residence "exactly as Mrs. Miller had done" and effectively demolished Billy Robinson's architectural defense. The following day, the court sentenced Billy Robinson to death and then showed clemency, commuting hanging to "banishment beyond the limits of the United States."[1]

Billy Robinson's defense, largely forgotten in the greater gripping narrative of the Denmark Vesey Revolt, focused on the most basic of everyday actions and spaces, a private meeting between two enslaved African-Americans in their quarters, a place their masters claimed to control by surveillance. In his protestations of innocence, Robinson drew on white perceptions of town house space and the implicit assumptions whites held about their ability to regulate that space and the people in it. Robinson's defense depended upon a cultural blindness inculcated in white masters and mistresses. He might have attempted to exploit that blindness first to the ends of insurrection, but later he used it as a strategy to win his acquittal. The plot for the insurrection would never have advanced so far if black Charlestonians, enslaved and free, had not acquired a transparency engendered by white custom and racial arrogance. From this perspective Billy Robinson's defense reveals more than a desperate ploy to win acquittal; it is about urban settings where the authority and identity of the processional landscape of the plantation countryside and city merchants' mansions exist in a larger context of segmented yet interwoven social and cultural relationships.[2]

Seen from a slaveholder's vantage point, Robinson and his conspirators occupied the marginal spaces of the city: the street, work yards, and back lot domestic compounds. For enslaved and many free African-Americans those same spaces defined a locus of political and economic agency. But what were those spaces? What was the urban architecture of slavery in Charleston and other southern cities? And how did the slave spaces associated with Charleston town houses relate to the architecture of servants and service in northern and English cities? In the context of town house design, the answer resides in the organization of domestic work and lodging spaces in and behind the dwelling.

Miller's testimony in Robinson's defense offers a way into the architectural topography of urban slavery. Miller described a Charleston town house one room wide and two rooms deep where she lived with several other white lodgers occupying different rooms. Behind the house stood Miller's kitchen, and for three years Billy Robinson lived in its second-story apartment. Miller asserted that anyone going in or out of Billy Robinson's quarters necessarily came through her kitchen and to her notice.

A row of four town houses reflecting this arrangement remains standing on Elliott Street just above its intersection with the city's Cooper River waterfront (see Figure 4.1). Each of the dwellings occupies the full span of its street frontage and contains a ground-floor commercial area and upper-story living spaces. In 22 Elliott Street, the ground-floor arrangement included street access into a heated shop plainly finished as a commercial space with cypress boards. One outside entry provided direct access into this business room from the street; a second arched passage extended alongside the shop and provided separate access to the ground-floor back room, stair, and work yard behind the house. The stair leading to the upper stories rose from a position abutting the passage, turned over the passage, and ascended to a spacious landing that opened into a twenty-five-by-sixteen-foot front parlor and smaller back dining room. The two second-floor rooms were the best finished in the house. The front parlor possessed paneled wainscot with applied moldings and a relatively plain neoclassical mantelpiece distinguished by its reeded pilasters. The ground-floor passage also opened onto the yard that continued roughly fifty feet to the separate kitchen with its second-story servant rooms. The kitchen faced the rear of the house, which presented multiple possibilities for access. A covered passage led from the kitchen and work yard to the street, a door in the rear elevation of the main house opened into the heated back room of the main house, and a second, narrower door apparently opened under the stair. The yard was a work area presenting either a brick-paved surface or aggregate crush of shell, dirt, bone, and debris.

Robinson's lodgings occupied the single room most removed from the street. When Mrs. Miller testified that Perault Strohecker had to pass through "my kitchen" to get to Robinson's room, she recognized one element in a more complicated journey. Passing in and out of Billy Robinson's

lodgings required transit through and under the house. In the architectural settings of the surviving Elliott Street houses, householders like the Millers placed their living spaces above commerce and domestic labor and afforded themselves views of the work yard and street that were intrinsically proprietorial. Householders looked down into the open expanse of yard that separated the kitchen and its upper-story lodgings from the house. Householders occupying the second-story rooms of the main house stood above the world of work. Despite the advantages of elevation and passage, the householders' dwelling remained porous and vulnerable. The Millers, for example, asserted their control over Robinson's movements through the visual authority they presumed over adjoining spaces. The strength of the Millers' testimony, however, was weakened by their reliance on the presumed authority of their gaze—the power to exert control by looking. The Millers' claims in Robinson's defense center solely on what they saw from their residence. Nowhere in Robinson's trial transcript is there any indication that the Millers or any other white witness actually entered his room.

The Millers' narrative identifies several categories of town house space: their residence, their kitchen, Robinson's lodgings, and the urban lot that contained all of the buildings. The significance of the setting in the context of Robinson's trial centered on explicit distinctions drawn between those categories, in particular the architectural and social relationships represented by the location and placement of service and servant's quarter in relationship to the principal dwelling. The Millers' evidence identifies implicit relationships between rooms and buildings and the possibilities for movement, observed and unobserved, in and out of those spaces. Robinson's assertion of innocence based on the presumption of surveillance raises questions surrounding the transparency of servants and their ability to claim and transgress the household spaces of their masters. An understanding of the meaning of Robinson's defense depends on the ability to reconstruct those spaces, their settings, and their significance to the people who built and occupied them. The point of departure for the exploration of its meanings is a reading of Charleston's architectural history from the vantage point of Billy Robinson's quarter.

In Charleston the main dwelling represented only one element in an ensemble of buildings that included kitchen, washhouse, quarters, privies, stables, work yards, gardens, and a variety of other structures ranging from rickety garden sheds to two-story brick warehouses. Through the usage of everyday life and work, the urban lot with all its attendant buildings defined

FIGURE 4.1

Elliott Street, Charleston, South Carolina
opposite:
A Houses above East Bay Street

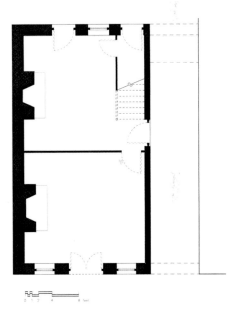

B 22 Elliott Street, First-Floor Plan.
Drawn by Jeff Klee

THE SERVANTS' QUARTER **123**

the Charleston town house. The organization and architectural content of individual lots varied according to shape and size of the property, the form of the main dwelling, the household economy, and the location of the property within the city. Regardless of size, the Charleston town house at a minimum was the product of two architectural elements: dwelling and kitchen.[3]

Billy Robinson's Elliott Street ran from the Cooper River waterfront to Church Street. One of the city's older and narrower streets, it comprised a neighborhood of modest houses and business establishments. In 1822, the year of the Denmark Vesey plot, the streetscape was composed largely of grocers' shops and boardinghouses. Of the twenty-two Elliott Street residents between East Bay Street and Gadsden's Alley, eight identified themselves as grocers and four as either boardinghouse operators or residents. The remaining population included a cooper, barber, hairdresser, mariner, and cigar maker. Lined with commercial premises and inhabited by individuals operating at the lower end of Charleston's economic spectrum, the streetfront architecture and occupational profile of Elliott Street possessed more in common with Philadelphia and Boston than with nearby streets in Charleston. The Elliott Street of Billy Robinson's day also represented a street in something of a social decline. Merchant houses, along with the shops of tailors, a printer, and watchmaker, had dominated the street a generation earlier. Unmentioned in street directories, however, were the enslaved African-Americans like Robinson who occupied quarters located behind the shops and boardinghouses.[4]

A mid-nineteenth-century plat for an Elliott Street property comparable to Miller's residence depicts the outline of one-half of a double tenement (see Figure 4.2). The brick two-story main house measured roughly twenty-six by fifty feet with a covered passage leading from the street to the back lot. The passage opened into a brick-walled *L*-shaped yard with a two-story brick kitchen pushed back into the far corner with its gable at right angles to the back of the house. In this arrangement, the cooking room occupied the front half of the kitchen building with a quarter similar to Robinson's placed in the second floor. In her own living accommodations, Miller presumed the power of surveillance. After all, the only way in and out of Robinson's quarter was through the kitchen, across the yard, and down the passage to the street—three spaces that Robinson's masters assumed they controlled.[5]

Kitchens with quarters for enslaved workers standing in the yards behind the town houses that lined Charleston's older streets generally assumed one of two forms. In the eighteenth century, the most popular configuration followed a plan with two rooms on a floor divided by a large centrally placed chimney with back-to-back fireplaces (see Figure 4.3). The room used as a kitchen faced a back entry into the ground-floor back dining room of the main dwelling across a small intervening yard. The second ground-floor room served as a washhouse. The stair to the living apartments in the upper stories of the kitchen-washhouse either opened into the kitchen or occupied a small lobby entry between the two rooms and was entered through a separate door. The upper stories were subdivided into numerous small rooms, each with its own door and window. Where the plans of upper-story quarters can be reconstructed, the typical arrangement centers on one heated room, which apparently served as a shared quarter when warmth was necessary.

Kitchens of this type include those behind the Heyward-Washington and Legare Houses in the older parts of Charleston. The Heyward-Washington and Legare kitchens presented four-bay elevations with the interior asymmetrically divided into a larger front kitchen closest to the back entry into the house and the smaller washhouse or laundry placed behind it. The Heyward-Washington kitchen also possessed a masonry bake oven abutting the larger hearth. The thirty-three-by-sixteen-foot Legare kitchen stood more than fifteen feet behind the ground-floor back dining room of the main house, a placement that was typical until the mid-nineteenth century, when Charlestonians began to fill in the yard between house and kitchen with intervening rooms. Less is known about the upper floors. The second story and garret of the eighteen-by-thirty-nine-foot Heyward-Washington kitchen were divided into multiple quarters. A winder stair built in the space between the ground-floor rooms and the front wall led upward to a narrow, unlit landing. A door on each side of the landing opened into one of the two front rooms, each measuring approximately eight by fourteen feet and illuminated by two windows. A second partition running parallel to the ridge of the roof created a back room of nearly equal dimensions but lit and ventilated by only a single window. Movement in and out of the second-floor back rooms appears to have required tramping through the front quarters, a practice that produced an environment of continual intrusion and little privacy beyond that afforded by everyday etiquette. The stair continued up to a pair of garret rooms, each provided with a dormer window and measuring just less than thirteen feet square.[6]

Toward the end of the eighteenth century a second type of kitchen-washhouse quarter gained popularity (see Figure 4.4). The new style of kitchen jettisoned the massive center chimney and placed the fireplaces

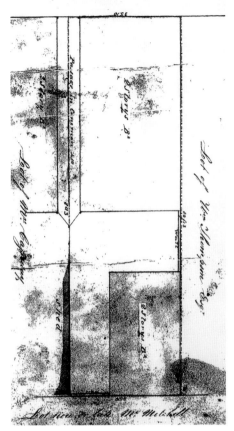

FIGURE 4.2
Estate of Robert Limehouse, Elliott Street, Charleston. *McCrady Plat Collection, #3385 (1851), Charleston County Register of Mesne and Conveyances (CCRMC)*

A Elevation

for kitchen and laundry in two separate stacks rising against the back wall of the building. In plan, the new kitchens kept the same sorts of work and living spaces found in the old center-chimney variety. A kitchen and washhouse occupied the ground floor; the second floor and loft contained enslaved servants' lodgings, some as small as seven feet square. The new plan also created space for a lobby entry and a larger stair in the middle of the building. By the 1820s this plan emerged as a favored, almost standardized form. At least two factors appear to have contributed to the ascendancy of the new kitchen plan. First, the removal of the fireplaces to the rear wall symbolically underscored the orientation of the building to the yard and thereby to the master's view from the main house. Second, the placement of a lobby entry with its own external access communicated the division of interior spaces. Doors opening onto the yard announced alternate paths into downstairs workrooms and upstairs lodging spaces and visually enhanced the architectural segregation of the quarter from the kitchen. The architectural segmentation and regulation of domestic spaces where servants often worked out of the sight and hearing of their masters was one intended objective of the new kitchen plan.

The back-wall-chimney arrangement achieved the same standardized quality as its center-chimney predecessor. The earliest examples of this form appear to date from the 1780s and include unfinished upstairs lodgings such as the servants' rooms above the Bocquet-Simons kitchen located behind 93 Broad Street. Here two roughly fifteen-foot-square lodging rooms housed an unknown number of resident servants (see Figure 4.5). In their original appearance the two rooms possessed whitewashed walls of raw brick, exposed but poorly finished ceiling joists, roughly-planed-board partitions, and unglazed windows. These rooms stood in contrast to the neatly executed brickwork and symmetrical, five-bay kitchen exterior. The juxtaposition of a public exterior and an interior seldom entered by masters and mistresses speaks to larger issues of architectural contiguity and social difference in a world where buildings were intended to signify and codify the nature of human relationships. For masters and mistresses, their gaze and the creation and maintenance of order in the seen world implied a similar control over what was hidden from the eye. Their authority rested in their presumption of the power of sight. For enslaved servants, the unseen interior world of the quarters enabled them to create spaces of their own, an ability that survives in decorative paint schemes featuring vivid colors, including bright greens and oranges. Their authority resided in their understanding and circumvention of the presumptive power of the gaze.[7]

As the back-wall-chimney kitchens gained popularity in the early nineteenth century, they also tended to incorporate multiple entries, more precisely defined work spaces, and slightly better finishes in the upper-story servant rooms. The Robinson kitchen on Juliet Street erected in the 1820s presented a symmetrical, five-bay front to the yard. Of the three doors, one opened into the kitchen, one provided access to the stair that led to the upper-story quarters, and the third led into the washhouse (see Figure 4.6). Unlike the center-chimney kitchens, where the front kitchen was typically

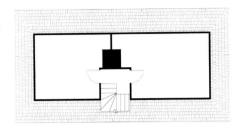

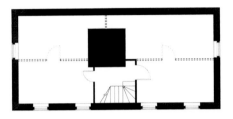

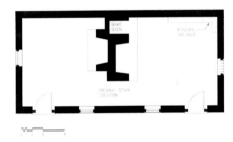

B First-, Second-, and Attic-Floor Plans. The dashed lines indicate the location of former partition walls. *Drawn by Jeff Klee*

FIGURE 4.4
Kitchen-Washhouse Quarter, 14 Legare Street,
Charleston (circa 1800)

FIGURE 4.5
Bocquet-Simons Kitchen-Washhouse Quarter,
93 Broad Street, Charleston (1780s). The
building also included a privy (now demolished)
at the end farthest from the main house

larger than the back room, the two main ground-floor spaces contained roughly the same amount of space. A suite of two small rooms on either side of the landing composed the second-floor plan. Each pair of rooms consisted of a heated, ten-by-fourteen-foot room that adjoined a smaller, seven-by-fourteen-foot, unheated chamber overlooking the dooryard below. All four rooms possessed individual entries opening onto the common passage that continued up to a finished loft containing a landing and two twelve-by-fourteen-foot rooms. Similar quarters erected on the Aiken-Rhett

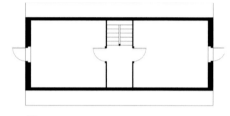

ATTIC

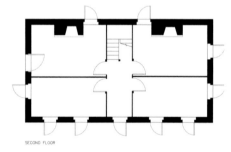

SECOND FLOOR

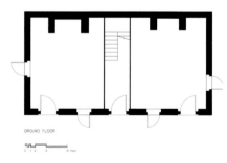

GROUND FLOOR

B First-, Second-, and Garret-Story Plans.

Drawn by Jeff Klee

House next door were remodeled in the mid-nineteenth century when the kitchen was doubled in length (see Figure 4.7). The new arrangement introduced a full-length passage running along the front of the rooms and terminating at either end in a large, heated room with multiple windows. Between these two rooms and off the passage the builders strung a range of smaller chambers along the wall backing onto the adjacent property. Without exterior windows of their own, these interior quarters required internal windows that borrowed light and air from the passage. Most Charleston kitchens with their attendant washhouse and quarter functions, however, adhered to the plan exemplified by the Robinson back building. Variation in size and level of finish distinguished individual buildings, such as the twelve-by-twenty-foot kitchen-washhouse erected as an ell behind 31 Hassell Street (see Figure 4.8). Each of the two ground-floor rooms contained less than one-half of the area of the Robinson kitchen, and the total

FIGURE 4.7
Aiken-Rhett House,
Kitchen-Washhouse Quarter,
Charleston (1820s, with mid-
nineteenth-century additions)
A Elevation

B Second-Floor Corridor, with Apartments
Using Borrowed Light and Air

area of the second-floor quarter just equaled that of the smallest Robinson kitchen chambers. Matters of scale aside, the Hassell Street kitchen and others like it displayed remarkable continuity in plan and the disposition of functions.[8]

Although back kitchens conforming to the types illustrated by the Heyward-Washington and Robinson back buildings document the most common choices, there were additional options, especially in the older, more congested parts of the city (see Figure 4.9). A survey of Edward Petrie's Queen Street property in 1797 recorded a single structure that contained

31 Hassell Street, Kitchen-Washhouse Quarter,
Charleston (circa 1840)

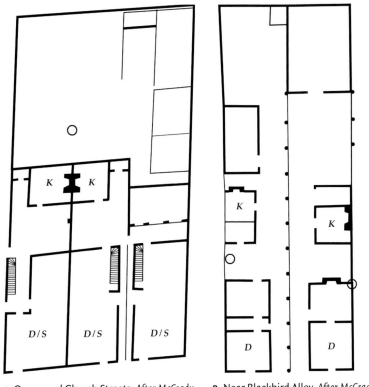

A Queen and Church Streets. *After McCrady Plat #464, CCRMC (1797)*

B Near Blackbird Alley. *After McCrady Plat #536, CCRMC (1799)*

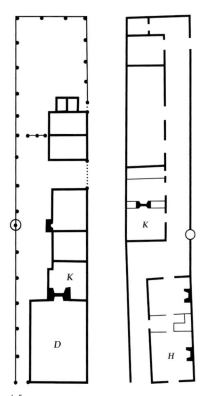

left:

c King and Hassel Streets. *After McCrady Plat #178, CCRMC (1798)*

right:

D Queen Street. *After McCrady Plat #3334, CCRMC (early nineteenth century). Illustration: Rebecca Y. Herman*

FIGURE 4.9

Four Lot Plans in Charleston. Showing the placement of houses on the street, with outbuildings placed behind them. Dwellings are identified as D, combination dwellings and stores as D/S, and kitchens as K. The remaining buildings represent varied functions, including storehouses, stables, sheds, and privies

two discrete kitchens with upstairs quarters for a pair of adjoining tenements. A plat drawn for two houses on Blackbird Alley in 1799 shows one with a one-room, two-story brick kitchen connected to a small carriage house, and the other with a two-room, gable-front kitchen quarter outfitted with only a single fireplace for the back room. Town houses erected in the rapidly developing reaches of upper King Street at the close of the eighteenth century employed other plans. A house and store sharing a lot on the corner of King and Liberty Streets, for example, were supported by a one-and-one-half-story wood kitchen with a small pantry built against its exterior-end chimney. In other settings kitchens were extended as part of a range of back building functions or acquired other uses specific to the property. The outbuildings behind a pair of Queen Street town houses begin with center-chimney, kitchen-washhouse combinations and then continue with storage rooms, stables, and privies. The operators of a bakery on Union

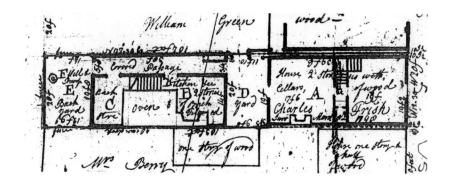

Street modified their center-chimney kitchen to include a commercial bake oven (see Figure 4.10). What unites these varied solutions is their near-universal concern with the explicit segregation of service from the main body of the house, their provision for quarters for the enslaved labor and for the servants, and their understanding of the total lot as a "house" of which the main dwelling was only one defining element.[9]

Lack of mention of quarters and servant rooms in the documentary record reinforces our perception of these spaces as defining the in-between spaces of the house and suggest a quality of transparency in masters' and mistresses' perceptions of domestic servants. Moving up and down back stairs, in and out of service passages and service buildings, and across work yards, servants were readily observed. The routine of their coming and going, however, generally failed to register their presence on the consciousness of masters and mistresses except when service went unexpectedly right or very, very wrong. Servants achieved transparency through the masters' blindness and servants' reading of their masters' and mistresses' assumptions. In essence, the habit of their masters' gazes was the servants' ally. While architectural, archaeological, and written evidence suggestively points to servants' occupying cellar rooms, pallets in kitchens, closets, and garrets, it remains far from conclusive. Servants lived in the margins of the house, in kitchen, yard, and passage and in the public world of the street, market, and shop. The advantage of quarters located over kitchens, like the one inhabited by Billy Robinson, is the degree to which the architecture of dominance makes the architecture of service visible. Thus, the view from the servants' quarter was intended by masters as a defining one. Standing in the door of the Miles Brewton kitchen, the enslaved servant's eye was drawn up to the house; standing behind the houses on Hassell Street, the servant's sight lines narrowed where the walled lot met the street. And yet these were places where servants could move unbidden and unseen.[10]

The organization of service and servant quarters around separate kitchens placed behind Charleston town houses was not without its parallels in other seaport cities and towns on both sides of the Atlantic. The extent to which these kitchens contained servants' quarters (rooms where servants slept, dressed, and stored their belongings), however, remains unknown. Throughout the North Atlantic rim, city dwellers confronted the twin problems of how to incorporate domestic servants into the household and how to integrate servant and service spaces into the house. Property surveys for eighteenth-century town houses lining Orchard and Prince Streets in Bristol, England, depict dwellings fronting the street with intervening courtyards, kitchens, and other work spaces extending behind the house to carriageways, shops, and stables opening onto back lanes (see Figure 4.11). A residence surviving in Broad Street continued to reflect this building strategy, with the house containing ground-floor reception room and commercial spaces, upper-story parlor and chambers, and back-lot kitchen and storehouse (see Figure 4.12). An open-front connecting porch or piazza hugged the property line and provided sheltered access between the detached two-story, one-room kitchen and the house. The organization of dwelling, kitchen, and yard found in Bristol town houses was reflected in the lot arrangements of other provincial English seaports such as Whitehaven, a tobacco port located in northwestern England.[11]

Across the Atlantic similar arrangements remained a common feature, especially in southern cities like Norfolk, Virginia. Insurance surveys made for Norfolk town houses from 1796 to 1802 routinely show small, one-story wood kitchens located behind houses. An eleven-by-fourteen-foot kitchen stood ten feet behind the Dyson family's two-story Church Street residence. William Plume's rented Main Street accommodations included a sixteen-by-twenty-foot wood kitchen along with a smokehouse and dairy. Wherever they appeared, though, a separate room in the house or freestanding building in the yard dedicated to food preparation and other forms of domestic service was the prerogative of the well-to-do.[12]

Separate kitchens represented only one of four primary architectural strategies for service. In addition to the construction of freestanding kitchens, town house designers and builders opted for kitchens located in cellars, ells, or within the main body of the house. Different options could signify different styles of life based on wealth and rank. Certainly the most

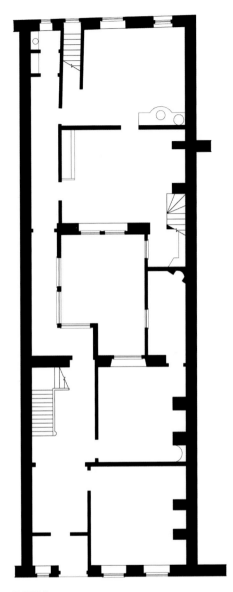

FIGURE 4.11

Town House Plan, Including Lot and Outbuildings, Orchard Street, Bristol, England. *Detail from a circa 1850 block plan in the archives of the Bristol Municipal Charities, courtesy of Roger Leech. Drawn by Jeff Klee*

FIGURE 4.12

41 Broad Street, Bristol
(mid-eighteenth century)

A Elevation

common approach in the vast majority of smaller houses inhabited by individuals of modest means throughout the North Atlantic community placed cooking and service functions in the house itself. At the close of the century, many residents in Whitehaven, for example, still prepared their meals in the main room of the house. These were also the houses that were most likely not to have resident servants nor to possess specialized spaces for entertaining. More elaborate arrangements appeared in town houses where space and money facilitated the luxury of many rooms. In larger houses and wealthier households, segregation of service and servants supported the genteel aspirations and activities of masters and mistresses. While the options for kitchens located in cellars, outbuildings, and ells were all exercised in the mid-eighteenth century, the preferred configuration by the 1830s narrowed to kitchen and service ells. Even as late-eighteenth-century householders and builders mulled over their choices for the location of kitchens and related work and storage spaces, they were broadly united in a common cause of creating functional and social divisions within the house. Accordingly, the lodgings for resident servants were tucked away in garrets and in the upper stories of working ells.[13]

The investigation of service in eighteenth-century English town houses typically locates kitchen functions but seldom the lodgings for the servants who supported the household. An early-eighteenth-century town house standing in Mawson's Row in the suburb of Chiswick, for example, incorporated a kitchen in the front room of the cellar in a space easily thought of as in the margins of the house (see Figure 4.13). Cellar kitchens with open areas equipped with stairs leading from the street down to a small paved yard and separate entry also contained limited lodgings. Sometimes a room was set aside as a servant chamber, but in other instances a bed stood in one corner of the kitchen. The often damp, twilit, poorly ventilated environment of the cellar kitchen and quarter elicited comments and recommendations from observers who believed that servant lodgings should be made more healthful. Similar arrangements of cellars with work spaces and occasionally servants' rooms appeared in other English cities. The Alfred House at 14 Alfred Street in Bath retains its cellar area complete with a hoisting mechanism for ease in provisioning the cellar kitchen and scullery (see Figure 4.14). Nearby town houses on the Circus possessed larger excavated areas that not only rendered the cellar kitchens airier and better lit than most but also provided an outside work area in front of the house (see Figure 4.15).[14]

Garrets provided the more common lodging spaces for servants in

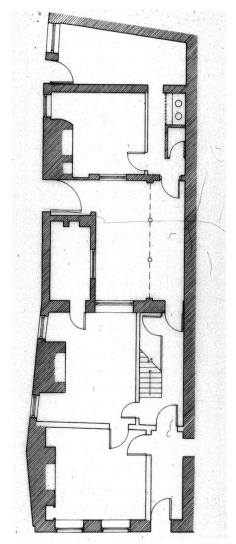

B First-Floor Plan, Including House and Outbuildings. Note the three entries: one from Broad Street into the house itself, one from John Street into the courtyard between house and kitchen, and one from John Street into the storehouse at the back of the property. *Based on an architectural survey circa 1920, courtesy of Roger Leech*

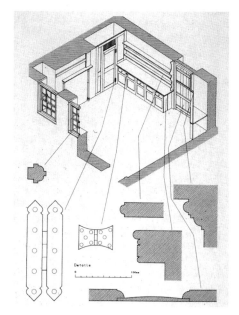

FIGURE 4.13

Mawson's Row, Chiswick, London,
Cellar Kitchen Plan (early eighteenth century).
Showing locations of built-in cupboards
and dressers and work areas. *Richard Lea
and Richard Bond, Copyright English Heritage,
© Crown Copyright, NMR*

FIGURE 4.14

14 Alfred Street, Bath,
England (circa 1773),
Wrought Iron Winch and
Hoist for Moving Loads into
and out of Cellar Area

English town houses throughout the eighteenth century. Often lacking fireplaces, garrets were divided into a number of rooms that varied in quality from unheated and low-ceilinged chambers to relatively spacious apartments usually reserved for the housekeeper. A particularly generous suite of garret rooms at the top of an eighteenth-century three-story town house at the corner of Clare and Marsh Streets in Bristol included a twelve-by-twenty-foot heated chamber equipped with shallow chimney closet (see Figure 4.16). A smaller, roughly twelve-foot-square, unheated room stood behind the principal chamber as did a nearly four-by-five-foot closet illuminated by light borrowed from the front room. Although the actual residents of these rooms remain unknown, the spaces they occupied are consistent with servant lodgings elsewhere in Bristol and other English towns and cities.[15]

Finally, servants occupied spaces between the principal rooms in many houses, lodging in chambers opening onto intermediate stair landings or sleeping in vacant rooms on one of the main floors. These spaces seem to represent makeshift solutions based on the convenience of less-utilized rooms and the need for attendance. Accordingly, the location of servant lodgings in the core of the house shifted in almost dunelike fashion. Pallet beds and other sleeping accommodations were introduced into household-

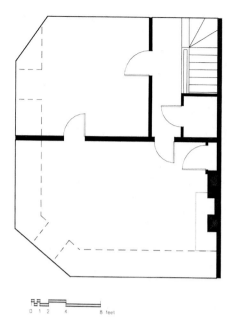

FIGURE 4.16

Clare and Marsh Streets, Bristol
(mid-eighteenth century), Garret Plan.
Note the single heated room and the
placement of windows in interior
partitions to capture borrowed light.
Drawn by Jeff Klee

ers' best chambers as circumstances required. The desire to have a nurse present during a serious illness, for example, surely directed some of this behavior, just as servants' lodging in their master's and mistress's bedrooms likely represented a practice associated with both the waxing and waning moments of life.[16]

The multiplicity of service rooms and servant lodgings in the English town house is well represented in the 1827 inventory of Penelope Iremonger, who lived an aristocratic life in her house at 12 Bolton Row in London's West End. Although Iremonger's house fails to survive, the listing of her possessions describes a three-story brick dwelling with the finest and most elaborately furnished spaces, including two drawing rooms and the best chamber, located on the second floor. Her inventory also indicates the location of service and servant spaces. The cellar contained the kitchen outfitted with an iron range, stove, and ovens set in brick. The half-dozen chairs, cradle, and worktable that furnished the room describe a space of domestic work and chat. The "servants hall," also in the cellar and placed between the kitchen, scullery, and laundry, held two cheap tables, one large and one small, along with a pair of stools, two chairs, and storage cupboards. Neither servants' hall nor kitchen contained bedding or other items associated with lodging, but the chairs scattered about the kitchen and the designation "servants hall" suggest two places for the congregation of the people who supported Iremonger's genteel life.[17]

Other rooms in the cellar and on the first floor were also associated with service and included the "Housekeepers Room" and "Butlers Pantry." Only the butler's pantry was furnished as a lodging room, with its fold-down "deal Press Bedstead with folding Doors and drawer," "old" chairs, and old-fashioned "Wainscot 2 flap Table." The four mahogany "Butlers Trays" suggest the chamber of an individual who was always on call. The housekeeper's room contained multiple cupboards with shelves and doors that could be secured. A mahogany drop leaf table, six "red stained" chairs, and chimney ornaments displayed above the iron heating stove set in the fireplace suggest a room located on the ground floor with ready access to the entry, kitchen below, and drawing rooms and best chamber above. Furniture and location strongly suggest that the housekeeper's room functioned as the office for household management.

In a house where the chatter of everyday work and domestic life occurred in rooms at the very bottom of the house, where did the housekeeper and the other servants sleep? Iremonger's inventory suggests that the attic story comprised those lodgings. The attic was divided into five chambers and a stair landing. The furnishings of those chambers suggest, in turn, other social divisions within the house. The front attic contained two chambers, one of which held a single low post bed and assorted furniture, including old and cheap tables and chairs. The adjacent chamber, however, was more crowded with three beds, old chairs, press, and dressing table. A middle chamber was similarly congested with two beds and an array of chamber furniture, much of which appears to have been old-fashioned hand-me-downs. Immediately adjacent, however, was the best chamber in the attic, heated by a grate set in brick and comfortably furnished with "a tent bedstead" and mahogany chest of drawers, dressing table, and bookshelf. Equally notable in this room were the artifacts of hygiene, a mahogany washstand, "night stool and pan," and japanned foot bath. Last, the room under the back attic mirrored the contents of the other garret chambers with multiple beds.

Although the attic rooms are not identified with individuals, the sense of their furnishings is clear. First, Iremonger created an attic proxy for her own authority. The best chamber with its one canopied bed and many amenities (including heat) claimed a central position of quality and location under the roof. As the housekeeper's chamber, this room possessed not only a modicum of comfort but also the rarer commodity of privacy. Iremonger accorded her housekeeper the privilege of privacy as visible recognition of her rank and an inducement to carry out the wishes of the head of the household even in the most removed precincts of the house. The surrounding chambers with two and three beds each suggest dormitory living conditions where servants slept and dressed themselves. The presence of tables and chairs in these rooms also raises the possibility of servants' socializing in their rooms after the family was asleep or during their limited free time. The one attic chamber with a single bed might have been so small that it admitted only the sparest furnishing possible, or it might suggest a room allocated on the basis of sex or age. The cradle in the cellar, for example, might just as well have been for a servant's infant and the single bed in a corner room in the attic for parent and child.

Iremonger's furnishings and their placement within her house emphasized the hierarchical organization of servants within the household. Attic lodgings and cellar work spaces divided servant life within the house just as they bracketed and centralized the authority of masters and mistresses. Operating on the physical margins of the house, however, also enabled ser-

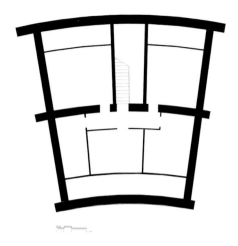

FIGURE 4.17
The Crescent, Buxton, Derbyshire, England
(circa 1780–1789), Lodging House Number 6,
Attic Floor Plan. *After Royal Commission for
the Historic Monuments of England / National
Monuments Record. Drawn by Jeff Klee*

vants to create spaces of their own. Although masters and mistresses might have presumed control over these spaces, the fact was that their authority was limited by their ability and inclination to enter servant rooms and work areas.

Although the Iremonger house does not survive, similar spaces for housekeepers' accommodations and their monitoring of service and servants remain in other town house contexts. The Crescent (circa 1780–1789) in the spa town of Buxton, Derbyshire, incorporated chambers for the service staff employed by both the hotel and its guests (see Figure 4.17). In the attics above the hotels that anchored each end of the Crescent, the builders introduced landings at the head of the skylit stairs. A collection of chambers of varying quality, each lit by a dormer window, was placed in orbit around the landings. Access in and out of these chambers could be regulated (at least theoretically) from the most centrally located rooms in the attic. Similarly, the attics over the range of lodging houses between the two hotels evinced the same characteristics. In the attic of lodging house Number 6 the main stair opened onto a common landing that linked five chambers, with each occupant's possessing a clear field of view of his or her neighbors' doorways.[18]

Throughout the eighteenth and nineteenth centuries, the desire to establish service and servant lodgings within the house was common currency among well-to-do urban householders around the North Atlantic rim. James Fennimore Cooper, for example, described "a species of second-rate, genteel houses, that abound in New York":

> They have, as usual, a story that is half sunk in the earth, receiving light from the area, and two floors above. The tenants of these are chiefly merchants, or professional men, in moderate circumstances, who pay rents of from $300 to $500 a year. . . . Each has his own roof and his own little yard. These buildings are finished, and exceedingly well finished, too, to the attics, containing on an average six rooms, besides offices and servants' apartments.[19]

The six rooms represented the first, second, and third stories of the house and were spaces generally reserved by the family for their own use; "offices and servants' apartments" in the cellar and garret made up the remainder of the house in the fashion of eighteenth-century British town houses. The placement of service and servant spaces in cellar and attic accomplished two things. It rendered the human infrastructure of the house invisible, or at least out of sight, and gave the emergent genteel, middle-class sensibilities of the householders center stage.

The range of options for the location of servant rooms and service spaces within the house is particularly apparent in the Norfolk, Virginia, town houses. Insurance surveys place the kitchens in one of four locations: in a separate building behind the house, in the cellar, in a rear ell, and in the main body of smaller houses. Moses and Elizabeth Myers, for example, built their Catherine Street house with a cellar kitchen located beneath the formal dining room above. The servants who worked in this dimly lit, often damp environment might have been lodged in an adjoining room or quartered in the garret. When the Myerses reinsured their house in the early nineteenth century, they had relocated the kitchen into a two-story brick outbuilding that stood behind the house. In addition to removing the heat and smell of cooking from the dwelling, the new building, designed with servant chambers in its upper story, both created and isolated a distinct residential domain for their enslaved servants, well away from the precincts of the family's chambers. The motives for this transformation are unclear, but architectural evidence indicates a sensibility driven by conflicting desires for control and segregation, privacy and surveillance.[20]

Servant rooms in Philadelphia town houses similarly occupied a range of architectural spaces. Lodging rooms for cooks, maids, and other domestic workers were situated in the uppermost stories of the house or in chambers over kitchens and other workrooms located in back buildings extending from the rear of the dwelling. Plaster walls and tiny fireplaces graced the best garret accommodations, but whitewash applied to the undersides of rafters and shingles and no provision for heat rendered these spaces uninviting habitations for the majority of attic residents.[21]

In Philadelphia town houses with back buildings or ells, the convention of the piazza played a crucial role in the division of the house. The piazza, occupying the space between the main block of the house and its service wing, contained the main and often only stair in the house. Both family and servants used the one stair in a strategic manner that clearly defined the front and rear of the house. Landings provided different paths of access to either the front of the house occupied by the family or the service rooms and servant chambers in the rear ells. Because the piazza and stair both divided and united the two halves of the town house, they enhanced the possibility for achieving both horizontal and vertical segregation within the house. Serving both family and servants, the piazza provided entries leading from the stair

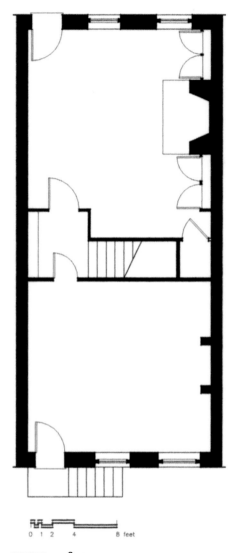

FIGURE 4.18

George Summers House, 612 Spruce Street, Philadelphia (circa 1805), Reconstructed Cellar Plan. *Drawn by Jeff Klee*

to the family's best rooms and chambers at the front of the house, kitchen and servant chambers at the back, and garret lodgings at the top. The result was a house that simultaneously centralized and segregated movement between the working and formal zones of the house.

The piazza proved particularly suitable to the sociology of well-to-do Philadelphia households in the late eighteenth and early nineteenth centuries. In several recorded instances, piazzas replaced older arrangements (see Figure 4.18). As built about 1805, the Summers House at 612 Spruce Street followed a plan that included an entry passage that led to a stair sandwiched between the front and back rooms in the style of London town houses popularized by the second half of the eighteenth century. The house was vertically divided from cellar to attic by a stair rising between the front and back rooms. From the cellar up, the front rooms of the house included a storage room, entry and parlor, best chamber, chamber, and garret. The back of the house ascended from kitchen to dining room to chamber to chamber to garret. The rooms of the house clearly worked en suite by floor. The cellar kitchen and adjacent storeroom consolidated service; the first-floor parlor and dining room unified the rituals of polite sociability. In the early nineteenth century, however, the owners of 612 Spruce Street decided to better integrate the flow of activities between rooms on each floor and to lift service out of the cellar and place it in a new rear wing. To do this, they removed the old stair that rose through the core of the house and replaced it with a piazza and stair at the back of the entry. The new piazza and service ell did not simply enlarge the house; they transformed the sociology of the house in decisive ways. The internal hierarchy of rooms within was now dispersed more horizontally, with the result that the new order of architectural importance ran from the front of the house back to the workrooms in the attached wing: entry, front parlor, back parlor (dining room), piazza, kitchen, and service. The new arrangement of the Summers House mirrored a process that was well established in elite town houses erected in the last quarter of the eighteenth century. The Pancoast-Lewis-Wharton House at 336 Spruce Street, for example, was erected in the 1780s as a house where ells or back buildings were preferred over cellar service spaces. A generation earlier in the 1760s, the builders of the Powel House, the home of an elite Philadelphia merchant family, pursued a similar strategy.[22]

The choices reflected in the remodeling of the Summers House and the original plans of the Powel and Pancoast-Lewis-Wharton Houses shared a preoccupation with town houses in Charleston about the most effective means to segment and regulate the domestic environment—a difficult task given the long-standing history of skirmishes between masters, mistresses, and free or enslaved servants, who asserted their own authority within the house's service spaces. The essence of servant autonomy and voice is captured in the narrative of the last days of a Philadelphia cook employed in the wealthy household of the Drinker family:

> Other individuals thrived despite the limits of service. Sally Dawson lived, first as an apprentice and then as a paid cook, with the Drinkers for ten years. During that time she repeatedly incurred her mistress' displeasure with her stubborn independence. In 1803, Dawson contracted yellow fever. After a few days, the Drinkers' physcian conceded defeat and ordered Dawson to remove to the public hospital. Both the Drinkers and Dawson recognized that she could not expect to survive the disease. Undaunted, the maid "shifted herself and was dressed rather smartly—[as she] stood at the kitchen door while her bed and bedcloaths was put into the Carriage. . . ." To the end (she died two days later) Sally Dawson regarded herself, not as a drudge, but as a spirited young woman. Her identity was self-made and her servitude was but a small part of it.[23]

Standing in the doorway of her kitchen with her bedding brought down from the chamber above, Sally Dawson asserted her own proprietorial interest in her employers' house. The back of the Drinker family's house was her domain, and she relinquished it only with reluctance and grace.

The idea of lodging servants (both individuals and families) is particularly problematic. Like the lodgings Iremonger provided for her servants, the rooms assigned eighteenth-century Paris servants segmented everyday lives. It was uncommon for servants to share their allotted accommodations in their employers' house with their spouses and children. The resulting social landscape of servants acquired a decidedly fractured quality. The lodging strategies for eighteenth-century Paris servants shed some light on this aspect of life in the servants' quarter. Some Paris servant families rented a separate apartment where the family united after working hours, thus dividing their lodgings between their assigned chambers located in the master's and mistress's house and rented rooms taken in another location. The effect was a dwelling defined by two or more rooms located at different addresses and connected by occupants' ability to shuttle between employers. The evidence for Paris servant spaces underscores the divided nature of the servants' quarter—its most significant characteristic. In English town houses like Iremonger's, servant domains were divided by the householder's rooms—and each of those nominal servant spaces was situated in a way that theoretically provided constant oversight. The same arrangement held true for Billy Robinson, who depended on the presumption of constant surveillance for his defense.[24]

As revealed in Billy Robinson's defense, servants also discovered the blind spots in these domestic landscapes and readily found ways to transgress the spatial authority of their master's house. Seventeenth-century Dutch genre painting and eighteenth-century French and English literature are rife with allusions to the many ways in which servants comported themselves in the world of market, street, and tavern—and imported that worldliness into the household. The depiction in text and image of the obedient and virtuous servant was a rarity in the eighteenth-century urban world; instead, servants were repeatedly represented as saboteurs of civil discourse. The comedic depiction of servants in art and fiction relied on the representation of their place in their master's house, not in their own spaces. Similarly, the transgressive acts of servants depicted in popular culture from the seventeenth through the early nineteenth centuries stand as symbolic reversals where the authority and propriety of the masters' world was turned on its figurative head. Significantly, these representations were elite productions and constituted an appropriation of the servants' world to the ends of satire. Thus, the actions of servants were a two-sided mirror held up by elites reflecting their own foibles while affirming their power—an authority that, no matter how buffeted and abused, inevitably seems to bounce back into some semblance of its ordained shape. When the perceived actions of servants shifted from embarrassing antic to mortal threat, as in the Denmark Vesey revolt, the response to the transgressive character of the servants' world sharply and brutally shifted from amused tolerance to fearful, angry repression.[25]

The possibilities for transgression were literally built into town houses where servants worked and lived. Cellar kitchens under English town houses, quarters over kitchens in Charleston domestic compounds, and piazzas and external passages of Philadelphia dwellings all offered direct access between the working world of servants and the street. Bypassing formal entry into the house, servants literally turned their masters' and mistresses' residences inside out, exposing the private affairs of the family to the street through gossip and direct observation. The routes in and out of Charleston's town house compounds, in particular, underscored both the assertion of domestic authority and its very vulnerability. The 1774 Pringle House on

Tradd Street illustrates the larger pattern of access in and out of the city's urban plantation landscape (see Figure 4.19). The main house abutted but did not front the street. Access from the street into the single house therefore followed one of two routes: from the sidewalk onto the piazza, or from the sidewalk or street and down the carriageway. The piazza route, in turn, offered three options. It led to the main and most formal entry into the stair passage, to a secondary entry into the dining room, or to a set of steps at the far end of the piazza, which led down to the dooryards of the work buildings in the yard and the gardens beyond. The carriageway provided access into the single house compound at street level. Servants entering by the carriageway literally passed beneath the occupants of the main house as they went about their business at the rear of the house or among the back buildings. Their path physically reminded them of their subordinate status and exposed them to their masters' and mistresses' elevated gazes. The inattention of masters, however, undercut the practical authority of their architectural setting. Carriages or horses carrying social equals entered nearly at eye level with the piazza. Passengers and riders stopped at the rear steps, stepped down into the yard, then up onto the piazza, and back toward the main entry. This mode of entry was only slightly less formal than entry from the sidewalk. In all instances the organization of the single house unit ran from street to backyard in a pattern of decreasing formality, declining architectural detail and finish, and increasing dirtiness.[26]

In an environment where architecture codified stature, the enslaved servant's view of the "big" house from the quarter and the work yard spoke to very different relationships and forms of movement than those defined by the master's and mistress's guests and business associates (see Figure 4.20). Billy Robinson, Perault Strohecker, and other African-American city residents relied on custom, inattention, and familiarity. They moved through Charleston's domestic landscape with an autonomy that at first surprised and ultimately terrified their disbelieving masters. The ability to exploit urban domestic space to their own advantage relied on a culture of dependent architectural and social relations. The kitchen and its occupants served the house, and the house and its occupants depended on the kitchen. Household servants asserted their voice in the operations of a hierarchical urban landscape that constantly cast them as dependent on white authority but was also one where white masters inescapably depended on black domestic labor. From the master's perspective, the status of servants and enslaved domestic workers objectified the inmates of the kitchen, washhouse,

FIGURE 4.19

Pringle House, 70 Tradd Street, Charleston
(1774). *After a lot survey drawn 1789. McCrady
Plat Collection, #569, CCRMC*

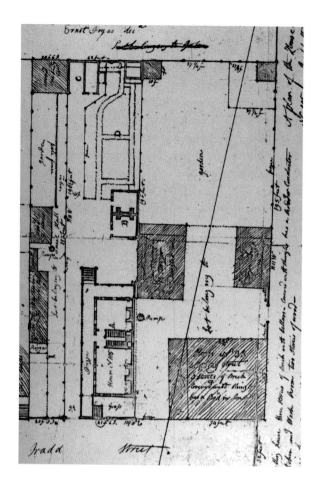

and quarter. Like household furnishings that functioned as backdrops and props in the world of sociability, servants found a degree of autonomy in the transparency that Billy Robinson sought to exploit first for insurrection and then in legal defense.

Diarist Timothy Ford, a successful Charleston lawyer and public figure, captured the quality and the implicit critique of authority of dependent relationships upon his arrival in the city from his native New Jersey in the mid-1780s:

> It would readily be supposed that the people require a great deal of attendance; or that there must be a vast superfluity of Servants. Both are true though not in equal degree. From the highest to the lowest class they

must have more or less attendance—I have seen tradesmen go through the city followed by a negro carrying their tools—Barbers who are supported in idleness and ease by their negroes who do the business; and in fact many of the mechanicks bear nothing more of their trade than the name.

The presence of servants as fixtures was of particular importance in the genteel households of the "higher classes" where "one or more servants (in many places) plant themselves in the corners of the room where they stand and upon the slightest occasion they are called." Servants were not without the ability to protest the whims of their masters and found opportunity to in the execution of their duties:

> At dinner it wd. seem as if the appetite were to be whetted and the victuals receive it's relish in proportion to the number of attendance. They surround the table like a cohort of black guards and here it appears there is a superfluity; for no sooner is a call made than there is a considerable delay either from all rushing at once; or all waiting for one another to do the business.

In situations like the one Ford describes, servants exposed the social failings of their masters.[27]

Actions and situations that revealed the dependency of mistresses and masters were not limited to tableaux played out in Charleston dining rooms. Not only were free and enslaved servants in a position to penetrate the most intimate recesses of their masters' houses, mock them through contrived displays of ineptitude, slander them through gossip exchanged in kitchens and market stalls, and subvert the authority that bound them, but they were also able to exploit the false confidence engendered in their perceived personas as animated furnishings. In Richmond, Virginia, for example, Sally, an enslaved woman, stole into the shop of James Boyce and purloined an impressive array of shawls, cloaks, and cloth from the master's stock-in-trade. Sally, carrying her plunder, exited through "the Dining Room of Mr Boyce where his Lady and Mrs. Booth were." Sally's actions suggest that she knew that her mistress and her guest would not see her even though they sensed her presence in the room. Sally exploited their blindness accordingly. The transparency engendered by habit and custom shielded Sally's actions in much the same manner that it rendered Billy Robinson's movements in his master's house invisible.[28]

FIGURE 4.20

View of the Miles Brewton House, Charleston, from the Kitchen-Washhouse Quarter Dooryard (circa 1769)

The indifference and inattention of masters echoed in the coarse textures of the servant and service spaces. The spatial divisions of the servant's world inadequately describe the daily experience of service spaces like the kitchen and quarter occupied by Robinson. Kitchens were often floored with slate or brick pavers, a practice that enhanced maintenance but further darkened an already dim interior and exhausted the legs of those who stood and crouched on those hard surfaces. Windows in the upper-story quarters were shuttered but often left unglazed, leaving the occupants in summer prey to mosquitoes, flies, and other insects or sweating in close, poorly ventilated rooms. In winter the same loose-fitting shutters offered little protection from the cold and damp. The smell of meals and laundry filtered year-round into the servants' quarter along with the earthy stench of cesspits and stables. In the kitchen dooryard bits of shattered pottery, intermixed with chicken bones and fish scales, crunched underfoot. The kitchen yard of the Brewton House (one of Charleston's most refined colonial mansions) remained unpaved for more than fifty years. The mashed layers of crushed household waste were finally capped with paving bricks in the 1820s. Still, the yard remained the site for odious domestic tasks, including gutting and cleaning fish and slaughtering and dressing fowl—activities revealed in the fish scales and bones that clogged the brick drains installed with the paving. Wooden fences and brick walls constrained sight lines in a city where back lot gates and service alleys were a rarity. The view from the quarter outward focused on the work yard, the back of the house, and the narrow passage or carriageway that led past the house and beneath the implied gaze of white masters (see Figure 4.21). Voices in conversation, some whispered, some shouted, penetrated the crevices between board walls, melding together in an unremarkable white noise where the plotters engaged in the thwarted Denmark Vesey revolt calculated their moves seen but unseen, heard but unheard.[29]

Quarters over kitchens were not the only lodgings for enslaved blacks in Charleston. Additional quarters were placed above storehouses, shops, and carriage houses. The desire to have enslaved domestic workers available around the clock produced accommodations where servants slept on pallets in their masters' rooms or occupied attic chambers. Still, the architectural expression of the servants' quarter had its closest association with the kitchen in the domestic yard behind the house. The yards in which kitchens and quarters stood varied considerably in the numbers, types, and organization of buildings they contained. Early-nineteenth-century newspaper ad-

FIGURE 4.21

View from the Work Yard of 30 Hassell Street, Charleston (circa 1840). Looking past the piazza and across the street to the back wall of the kitchen-washhouse quarter behind house fronting East Bay Street

vertisements offer a glimpse into the types and importance of the buildings behind the house. Mentioned most often were kitchens, followed by stables and carriage houses, wells and cisterns, gardens, and storehouses. The notice for "An elegant and healthy Family Residence" at 3 Meeting Street and the corner of Smith's Lane epitomizes the extent of the most elaborate of these urban plantation compounds. Behind the three-story, brick, slate-roof town house was arranged "every necessary appertenance for the residence of a genteel family." "The outbuildings," touted the ad, "are also of brick, 60 feet long, and consist of a two story brick kitchen, washhouse, double coach house and coach man's room, with stabling for three horses; also, a cistern of excellent water, and a boiler on the outside, and necessary pipes to permit water at pleasure; also, a large wooden store house, and a brick office or study 19 feet square, with fireplace, together with a good garden." Absent from real estate advertisements, though, is specific mention of servants' quarters. Kitchens, stables, carriage houses, storehouses, and counting-houses explicitly supported the genteel family, but the upper-story rooms that lodged domestic servants above the kitchen and in the margins of the house were, at best, assumed.[30]

Room-by-room inventories for furnishings of the spaces where Charleston servants lived and labored are similarly scarce and invariably emphasize the working environment. Inventories list predictable arrays of objects related to cooking, washing, stabling, and craftwork. The appraisers found in Martha Godin's kitchen, for example, a pair of firedogs, large and small iron pots, skillets, stew and dripping pans, a spit, and pewter basins. Beds and bedding, chairs, and tables for the four adult enslaved blacks and their four children escaped note. The functional division between kitchen and washhouse is reflected in bricklayer and builder Matthew William Cross's inventory that lists fifty dozen hearth tiles in addition to a full assemblage of cooking utensils described as a "Lot of Pots, Kettles, dutch-Ovens, fry-ingpans, grid Irons, pot-Covers, pails, piggins, etc." The washhouse half of the building held large iron pots for heating water, washtubs for launder-ing, smoothing irons, ironing table, and clotheshorses. The location and furnishings for the quarters of the thirteen enslaved workers employed in Cross's building enterprise went unrecorded, as did those for the fourteen servants (and their children) employed in the house.[31]

Although few clues exist for the lodgings of Charleston house servants outside of the quarters above kitchens and washhouses, tantalizing refer-ences to the furnishings in the house, particularly garret rooms, suggest an additional location for quarters. George Ingliss's 1775 inventory itemizes the contents of both the front and back garret rooms. The front room, with its mahogany clothes chest, writing desk, bed outfitted with pavilion and curtains, and framed prints hanging on the walls, belonged to a member of Ingliss's family, but the back garret room with its poorer quality bed-ding, mahogany chest of drawers, and "Hair Trunk containing Remnants of Negro cloth, callico, etc." might well have quartered one or more house servants. Other inventories more typically mention only the front garret chamber, leaving the contents of the rear garret, like those of the kitchen quarter, unrecorded.[32]

The indeterminate qualities of servant lodgings speak to the greater problem of servant identity and urban material life. The cumulative absence of direct evidence documenting the presence and contents of Charleston servant quarters suggests three interpretive possibilities. First, enslaved household servants could and did possess personal property independent of their master's authority. Second, from a mistress's or a master's perspec-tive, enslaved workers' personal possessions were by default the property of those who owned the servants. Third, despite the brutal constraints of slavery, Charleston's chattel servants were able to claim some measure of privacy and independence in spaces located at the very heart of the urban plantation.

No objects provide a stronger sense of the way these three strands came together than the artifacts recovered by archaeologists from kitchen and quarter dooryards. Often shaped in the form of a common, footed, English creamware bowl, small African-American colonoware vessels speak directly to the ways in which enslaved potters appropriated and transformed European form through African technology (see Figure 4.22). The mass-manufactured creamware bowls that inspired the form of the colonoware example were cheap and easily available, suggesting a practice that blended African and European traditions but not their aesthetic value systems. Scraps of eighteenth-century sweetgrass baskets recovered from the muck of cisterns and privies testify to the presence of African-American objects in everyday use, objects that likely held little monetary worth but vast associative power. Cowrie shells, pierced coins, and beads that adorned the body possessed deeper cultural and often symbolic associations for their African-American owners. The ornament of body and dress also asserted an autonomy of self that could never be fully regulated through servitude. Often ephemeral servant possessions in Charleston households exerted an additional proprietorial claim to the spaces in the margins of the house and the city. Thus, caches of crystals archaeologically recovered from Annapolis cellars and the ornamented coffin lids and waist beads recovered from New York City's African Burial Ground describe urban environments where a rich African presence flourished. Nowhere was this more apparent than in the foods prepared for white and black consumption in southern cities like Charleston and Norfolk. Ingredients like rice and okra and dishes such as gumbolike stews attested to the impact of African cuisine on elite white diets. Still, the divided worlds of the house extended to the very cooking hearth where masters and mistresses often purchased separate provisions for their servants and where the boundaries between those worlds were compromised every day in the very acts of cooking, tasting, and sampling.[33]

In the town house environments of service and servants' quarters and the paucity of evidence describing how those spaces were used, what are we to make of Billy Robinson's architectural defense? The most striking element in the court case is the white witnesses' belief that, by virtue of location and custom, Robinson (and by implication other servants, enslaved and free) was perpetually visible. Perault Strohecker's testimony exposed the fallacy of this assumption. The autonomy of the spaces inhabited by enslaved blacks within the quarter and the interstices of the house, house lot, and city is revealed again and again in other trials associated with Vesey's revolt. Cross-examined in the trial of John Vincent, Charles Drayton stated, "I think it was in his own room in an Alley on Church Street, viz. Elliott Street, that he told me about his master." Other witnesses and defendants narrated encounters behind the house: "Edwin brought the first news of the rising into our yard," and "Peirault, when hauling cotton from my master's store, told me in the yard, secretly." Laid bare in these terse accounts is the vulnerability of elite power at its most intimate point—the house. Servants throughout the North Atlantic rim at the turn of the nineteenth century laid claim to spaces within their masters' houses—and made those spaces their own.[34]

THE WIDOW'S DOWER

We can recreate the occasion when Hannah Rand, widowed at age thirty-six, invited the three-man committee appointed by the Rockingham County probate court into the house she had shared with her deceased husband. Samuel Rand, a shoemaker and small-scale housing speculator, lived, worked, and died in debt in early-nineteenth-century Portsmouth, New Hampshire (see Figure 5.1). Town clerk Thomas Drown led the delegation. Saddler and property developer Nathaniel B. March accompanied Drown on the walk from his State Street office located near Rand's shoemaker's shop. Carpenter Benjamin Holmes, Jr., the Rands' next-door neighbor, completed the party. The task assigned to Drown, March, and Holmes required the division of the Rand family house and yard into two portions—one-third for the widow's dower and the residue for the benefit and support of the remaining heirs, all orphans in the eyes of the court. Observing the proceedings with Hannah were her twelve-year-old stepson Aaron and three of her five own children by Samuel: Albert, Ruth, and Joshua, who ranged in age from nine to six. The significance that the surveyors' deliberations held for the family was beyond the comprehension of the two youngest, Samuel, nearly three, and Martha, nine months.[1]

Walking through the house, peering around previously inventoried furniture and personal possessions, inspecting the yard, sharing observations,

FIGURE 5.1
View of the South End, Portsmouth,
New Hampshire. Looking from Puddle Dock
Neighborhood toward Mechanic Street.
Photo Collection of Strawbery Banke Museum

and making notes, the court surveyors deliberated over the division of the two-story frame house fronting Pleasant Street just above its intersection with Cottars Lane (see Figure 5.2). The final division submitted to the court began by listing the widow's rooms, continued by specifying spaces held in common with the other owners, and concluded by affirming Hannah Rand's privilege of passing in and out of the second household's apartments in the prosecution of her daily chores (see Figure 5.3). The dower allotted to Rand:

> The front lower room, front chamber and garret over the same of the House on Pleasant Street . . . a part of the wood house, beginning at the Northerly end of the necessary and running Northerly ten feet, a part of the garden, extending from said Pleasant Street on the easterly side of the

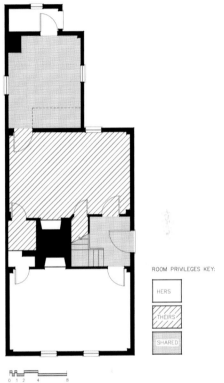

FIGURE 5.2

Hannah and Samuel Rand House,
Pleasant Street and Cottars Lane,
Portsmouth (circa 1795)

ROOM PRIVILEGES KEY:

HERS

THEIRS

SHARED

0 1 2   4   8

FIGURE 5.3

Hannah and Samuel Rand House,
First-Floor Plan. *Drawn by Jeff Klee*

House and adjoining a passage way . . . back as far as the Northerly end
of the scullery to a line intersecting said garden parallel to said Pleasant
Street; and the privilege in common with the owner of the other part of
said premises of the front door, front entry and front stairs to the garret,
cellar stairs and the outside cellar door, the scullery, the necessary and
the gate opening to Meeting House Square, also the privilege of passing
and repassing through the kitchen to and from the cellar and to and from
the scullery, and also the privilege of passing and repassing through that

part of the cellar not set off as a dower . . . [and] a passage way six feet wide running from said Pleasant Street by the Easterly side of the house and wood house and adjoining the same back to Meeting House Square.[2]

Rand's dower offers a striking description of a house. The delegates of the county court painstakingly designated the widow's rooms, spaces in common, and the division of the yard. A court's preoccupation with what constituted the widow's "third" reached beyond a monetary proportion of the estate and assigned the heirs specific parts of the house, each space freighted with its own social significances.

As legal documents, dowers provided for the maintenance of the estate for the heirs and the financial security of the widow by awarding her a life right in a third of the estate. For women whose husbands died without wills, dower rights ensured their material well-being at a prescribed level commensurate with the value of the estate; for those whose husbands sought to dispossess their wives in death, dower rights secured a widow's property without prejudice. In New England cities, the division of seemingly indivisible property like a house and lot resulted in "'special' assignments of dower." In a legal culture where "indivisible" was poorly defined, if at all, common practice and local knowledge shaped the specific terms of individual dowers. Custom and opinion in Portsmouth dower divisions centered on the issue of the social standing of women and informed architectural decisions. Dowers recorded in other early American cities, like Philadelphia and Charleston, lacked the kind of architectural detail expressed in Hannah Rand's division. In most locales the allocation of house and property was simply noted as a dower, portion, or right intended to support the widow in her lifetime and preserve the estate for the future.[3]

The dower ideally provided a competency—a term denoting the financial and material resources providing the basis for the economic maintenance of the individual. The concept of a competency, an imprecise and variable ideal, carried associations with a person's economic independence and material comfort that were rooted in the possession and responsible stewardship of property. Lack of a competency conveyed a sense of moral inadequacy and social instability. Although the dower supposedly endowed a lifetime competency for the widow at an economic and material level appropriate to her station, it defined a culture of dependency surrounding the perception of women and property. Should the widow remarry and enter a new state of marital dependency, she commonly forfeited her claim to the estate. Should she die, the estate reverted to the surviving heirs. In a narrow economic sense the widow's dower anticipated a lifetime annuity and little more; in a broader cultural context the dower defined expectations about the appropriate station and future of widows—wives without husbands—until choice or fate carried them across a different threshold.[4]

Rand's dower and others like it from Portsmouth and other northern New England port towns argue for the idea of a widow's competency informed by more than economic considerations. The precise division of a house by dower communicated a sense of material expectation on the part of both the widow and her community. In the eyes of the community, the allocation of specific rooms to the widow spoke to a symbolic sense of station negotiated by the widow and the court. The fact that different household spaces (for example, parlors and kitchens) expressed different social identities was not lost on the widow or the court appointees who rendered the division.

The question of what architecturally symbolized a widow's social competency stands at the heart of Hannah Rand's dower. The rooms a widow received expressed a sense of rank and status determined by the viewers, who were at once men, neighbors, and instruments of the court. But widows surely took a hand in negotiating their own architectural situations and the material communication of their circumstances to the world through the spaces they received—constituting a sense of self that was mediated by the delegation. There was also the knowledge that the division of a house by dower was temporary. Rarely did a dower result in major physical changes to the house. In the isolated cases where some remodeling was required, modifications focused on improving access for the widow through relatively minor alterations. Finally, the dower divisions really did intend to divide the house only for the life of the widow. While a widow could formally protest the division of her house, few widows were inclined to. Lack of formal protest, however, neither equaled resignation nor translated into passivity.[5]

The architectural circumstances for individual widows varied greatly, and within the range of experience dower committees discovered a range of housing possibilities. Hannah Rand's dower provided for a widow of the middling sort. She received a share in the house, but the compact scale of her dwelling reduced her portion to an architectural fragment—a widow's apartment. The dower committee did not discuss the contents of rooms Hannah Rand or other widows received but concerned themselves solely with the particular allocation of space within the circumstances of a specific house. Whereas furnishings communicated social value and identity, unfurnished rooms in a divided house exhibited architectural ambiguity. The division of the house disrupted the ways in which architectural finishes articulated the relative importance of rooms. Features such as built-in cupboards and bake ovens remained in place, but their presence was often refashioned into a new architectural identity that conflated household functions, producing combinations such as chamber-parlor, dining room–kitchen, or parlor–dining room. In essence, the dower committee found a house within the house. Acting within her architectural portion the widow could craft a new domesticity suitable to her situation, her resources, and her ambitions. A widow without real property received no dower, because the estate had none to offer. Her lot left few alternatives other than lodging with friends or relatives, finding rooms of her own, or seeking the austere comforts of the almshouse. Wealthy widows, especially those entitled to thirds in estates comprising several properties, often received a house in its entirety. The reality of their thirds did not intrude into the intimacy of their houses.

Understanding the architectural competency of Rand's dower begins with the artifact. Hannah and Samuel Rand's house represented one house type built in Portsmouth's South End in the late eighteenth and early nineteenth centuries. The Rands' house was a middling affair. Built with its gable to the street, it measured eighteen by thirty feet with a two-story, twelve-by-thirteen-foot scullery extending from the rear of the house. The house followed a plan based on a lobby entry and centrally placed chimney. The dwelling faced onto a six-foot-wide walkway, or "passage," and adjoining garden and was entered through a door opening into a roughly seven-by-eight-foot lobby containing the main stair to the upper stories and doorways on either side leading into the adjacent rooms. To the left of the entry stood the parlor with its molded window cornices and neatly worked mantel. The kitchen–dining room was to the right and contained not only the cooking fireplace but also the bake oven, the inside stairs to the cellar, and access to the scullery. The scullery occupied an unheated ell fitted with a second, smaller stairway and extended from the back wall of the house proper. Upstairs, the Rand House was finished with simply styled mantels decorating small chamber fireplaces. With its center chimney and timber skeleton using heavy framing posts to define the rooms inside, the Rand House drew on long-established local construction practices found in Portsmouth's South End as well as in the rural, village, and urban settings of northern New England.[6]

The Rands' house stood in an urban landscape characterized by wooden

FIGURE 5.4

Langdon Mansion, Pleasant Street, Portsmouth.

Courtesy of Strawbery Banke Museum

houses varying considerably in size and elegance. These houses also repre-sent the spectrum of dwellings that were periodically divided by bequest and dower. The Wentworth-Gardner House, with its rusticated wood front overlooking its owners' Piscataqua River wharves, and the Langdon Man-sion, complete with its brick dependencies, defined the best houses of Portsmouth's elite merchant families (see Figure 5.4). Slightly more modest urban mansions, such as the Margaret and Thomas Manning House on Man-ning Street, drew on similar plans and finishes and were scattered through-out the neighborhood. Interspersed with these larger houses were smaller

dwellings, many drawing on plans that incorporated a central chimney and lobby entry similar to the Rands' house. The largest of these center-chimney houses extended a full two rooms in depth, as did the two-story frame house of Mary and James Holmes nearby (see Figure 5.5). New to the South End in the early 1800s were more compact houses that made use of unheated stair passages. When Samuel Rand, for example, invested in the development of Cottars Lane, he and his partners commissioned a pair of houses following a side-passage plan of the type more familiar in cities like Philadelphia and Baltimore (see Figure 5.6). Still other builders embraced a new generation

FIGURE 5.6

Samuel and Joshua Rand Houses, Cottars Lane
(now Franklin Street), Portsmouth (circa 1805).
Speculative houses erected by Samuel Rand

of center-passage plans a single room in depth, with cooking and service functions relegated to an ell extending from the rear of the dwelling into the house lot. The resulting landscape of the South End presented the jumbled rooflines and irregular silhouettes of houses that defined diverse living accommodations.

Street directories listing residents' occupations (and often designating the status of women as widows) and tax assessments enumerating real property (including the estates in which widows held dowers) complete the picture of Hannah Rand's community. The 1821 street directory and 1822 tax rolls identified four of every five women listed as widows, a proportion that was one-quarter greater than Charleston in 1822 and one-third greater than places like the Southwark district of Philadelphia or the port of Norfolk, Virginia, at the turn of the nineteenth century. The reasons for Portmouth's seemingly high population of widows might have been due to the hazards that men in this largely maritime community routinely encountered at sea.[7]

Widows' "houses" rated in the tax assessments represented all types of dwellings in Portsmouth's architectural landscape. The most highly valued residences were urban mansions, personal monuments commemorating social and economic attainment. Wooden dwellings one or two rooms in plan and roughly finished defined the opposite end of the spectrum. In the middle were dwellings like the Rands'. Built of wood and standing two stories tall, these houses often contained neatly executed woodwork, including decorative cornices and mantelpieces. Modest in scale and finish, these middling houses were not without their pretensions.[8]

Composing 11 percent of all the individuals listed in 1821–1823, widows occupied houses and apartments throughout the city. Of the 218 widows enumerated citywide, slightly more than one-fifth were assessed for houses. In the South End where Rand resided, widows constituted an even higher proportion of householders. An additional fifty properties were listed in estates, many of which incorporated provisions for the widow's lodgings. Similarly, other widows continued living in houses where dower rights had been sold but not relinquished. Thus, Betsy Floyd living on Cottars Lane around the corner from the Rands' house found her husband's creditors nibbling away at her dwelling, selling in 1816 the west front room and the privilege of the entry, and the remainder in 1823 to Phineas Tyler, a carpenter who already rented rooms in the house (see Figure 5.7). As with many Portsmouth widows, Betsy Floyd's dower left her vulnerable to being dispossessed of housing. The widow's third was an ephemeral asset that provided for her well-being only for the duration of her widowhood or her natural life. The division of the house also exerted an emotional and psychological effect. The contraction of widows' houses into suites of rooms compressed and diminished the symbolic social and domestic competencies signified by the undivided dwelling. Although reduced architectural circumstances could contain all the old functions of parlor and kitchen, the loss of widows' spatial separation signified a parallel erosion in social standing. Like Betsy Floyd, Hannah Rand found herself living in a divided dwelling. Within the

FIGURE 5.7

Betsy Floyd House, Cottars Lane,
Portsmouth (circa 1813)

worldview of her community both Rand's widowhood and her divided house
were liminal circumstances. Death or remarriage would resolve Hannah
Rand's status and, in effect, unify and heal the house.[9]

   When Rand's dower is plotted on a plan of her house and lot, the significance of the location and textures of the spaces she received become apparent. Rand's dower assigned her the best rooms at the front of the house.
Composed of the parlor and parlor chamber, Rand's new accommodations
overlooked Pleasant Street and were the most elaborately finished spaces
in the house. Illuminated by four windows, the parlor presented a stylish

appearance, complete with a chimneypiece employing an ogee silhouette, dentil cornice, and pronounced mantelshelf. Upstairs, a molded cornice ran across the top of the chimney wall that incorporated a recessed fireplace with beaded trim and a mantel consisting of a simply molded surround, plain frieze, and pronounced mantelshelf.

The architectural hierarchy of Hannah and Samuel Rand's house resonated in its furnishings. The dower division was only one of a series of court-ordered actions assessing the value, debts, and disposition of Samuel Rand's insolvent estate. Twelve months earlier the court instructed the estate administrator, John Lock, to admit traders Benjamin Carter and Thomas Treadwell along with baker Nathaniel Souther, the Rand's neighbor from across the street, into the house for the purpose of inventorying Samuel Rand's personal property. The inventory takers recorded one dozen chairs, a birch table, and a looking glass in the front parlor overlooking Pleasant Street. The adjacent entry contained fire buckets and little more; the kitchen, which doubled as a dining room and was located at the back of the house, held seven "old" chairs (one for each family member except then-unborn Martha), two pine tables, cupboard, and tin and ironware for cooking. A desk completed the contents of the back kitchen–dining room, a space that served as the family's "keeping," or common, room where the theater of everyday life played out. The scullery stood behind the kitchen–dining room and likely contained the family's provisions. Carter, Treadwell, and Souther found the hides, unfinished boots, and shoemaker's tools Rand employed in his trade located in his shop in nearby State Street.[10]

The best table and chairs in the front parlor and the family dining table and cookware in the back kitchen reinforce the distinctions between the architectural competencies of sociability and domesticity expressed in the building's decorative finishes. Personal property, including two-thirds of the contents of the Rands' house, however, was subject to creditors' demands, and the court ordered the public sale of Rand's furniture and other possessions. Out of her husband's modest estate the widow could retain only the essentials for the maintenance of her reduced household.[11]

The records of the Rand estate remain silent on who occupied the other parts of the dwelling. Other estate proceedings, however, suggest that there were two alternatives. The portion of the house not claimed by the dower could be rented out or remain in the occupation of children, a solution that in effect kept the dwelling intact. In the circumstances of the Rands' residence, the dower committee decreed the entry and scullery as spaces that the two households would share along with parts of the yard, the woodhouse, and privy behind the house. For Hannah Rand to reach these "shared" areas required provisions for her passage through the spaces occupied by the second household. Finally, there are the spaces Hannah Rand did not receive, most strikingly the kitchen with its cooking fireplace and bake oven. Denied the use of the working spaces in the house, Hannah Rand found herself with the appearance of the parlor but lacking a kitchen. The dower compressed the household of Hannah Rand and her six children into two heated rooms, where their new circumstances compelled them to import cooking, dining, and the other functions of everyday life into the former parlor.

The paradox of Rand's architectural competency is clear. The dower assigned her the parlor, but it gave away the kitchen. Given the letter of the law and the size of the house, the dower committee discerned no alternative to dividing the house through the central chimney stack and creating front and rear tenements. What remains unexplained, though, is why Rand received the spaces she did. The architectural competency of the parlor meshed with particular forms of social life associated with images of gentility and sociability. The competency of the kitchen is one of domestic work. When the house was divided, the dower privileged one set of associations over the other—in the case of Rand's allocation, the architectural sphere of gentility (the parlor) was favored over that of domestic work (the kitchen).[12]

Hannah Rand's dower was not unique in Portsmouth. Mary Hill, who occupied the house on the opposite corner of Pleasant Street and Cottars Lane, endured the same process and received

> all the Ell part of the House . . . also the Priveledge in Common to Pass and repass at all times a Certain piece of Land adjoining the southeast side of said Ell of the House . . . also the priveledge to pass and repass thro the Entrys of said Mansion House which are to be in Common, also the priveledge of a suitable passage way to pass and repass to the Cellar under the said Ell of the said House.[13]

Hill, the widow of mariner James Hill, occupied a three-story frame mansion markedly different in appearance and plan from the Rands' dwelling (see Figure 5.8). The Hills' house fronted Pleasant Street with a balanced, five-bay elevation and a plan incorporating a broad center passage containing the stair to the upper stories and opening onto a room on either side. A two-story frame ell extended from the rear of the house and overlooked Cottars Lane and a back garden. The interior arrangement of rooms followed

A Elevation

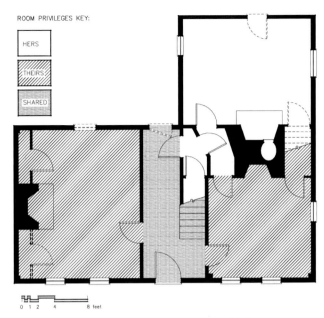

ROOM PRIVILEGES KEY:

HERS

THEIRS

SHARED

0 1 2 4 8 feet

B First-Floor Plan, Indicating Widow Mary Hill's Third.

Drawn by Jeff Klee

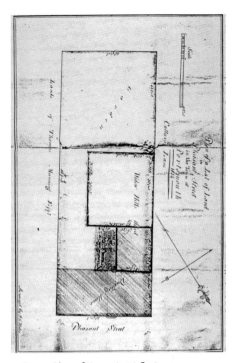

C Dower Plan of House Lot (1814).

Redrawn from original in the Rockingham
County Probate Office, Exeter

a functional and decorative progression from the first-floor parlor, across the entry, through the dining room, and into the kitchen. Although the 1814 inventory for James Hill notes that the building stood unfinished, the Hills were clearly in residence, and the house was furnished on the lower floors. A predictable array of plain and fancy chairs, ceramics, and tables, ranging from a maple table in the kitchen to a birch card table in the parlor, graced the rooms. The inventory also recorded "Articles said to be given to the Widow by her Parents": a feather bed, birch bureau, a pair of mahogany card tables, and twelve yards of English carpet.

Hill's dower, "impartially made," bestowed on her a life right in the service wing and a portion of the garden on Cottars Lane. The more formal rooms of the house, the parlor and dining room, constituted the spaces set aside for the other households, most likely renters. Because the entry separated the parlor and dining room, the building could be divided into three tenements, each one room in plan and either two or three stories in height. Like Rand, Hill also received rights of access. The stair passage opening onto Pleasant Street gave her a fashionable front door on a principal street that belied the interior arrangement. Hill's actual "front" door, added as a result of the division, stood at the very back of the passage underneath the stair and opened into an unlit lobby fronting on the side of the chimney stack. Her dower apartment consisted of two rooms, a first-floor, all-purpose space that included the kitchen fireplace, bake oven, and service stair that led up to Hill's second-floor chamber. Hill's dower differed from Hannah Rand's in significant ways. First, despite her larger and grander house, Hill received an architectural competency that emphasized the domestic sphere of the kitchen. Second, Hill's dower placed her behind the house facing on Cottars Lane rather than in rooms on Pleasant Street. Where the dower committee carved Hannah Rand's apartments from the genteel world of the parlor, they partitioned Mary Hill's from the workaday world of the kitchen.

Relocated into the two rooms most closely associated with domestic service, Hill retained the accoutrements to furnish these workaday spaces with the genteel belongings she brought to her marriage. Her parents provided her with four objects constituting a recipe for married life and, paradoxically, for widowhood. The feather bed and bureau symbolized the household space associated with the most elemental site of reproductive married life: the chamber. The mahogany card tables and carpet reflected the social capital of sociability. Just as her parents equipped her with material trappings to enter married life, the dower committee, very likely through discussions with Hill, determined the rooms appropriate to her new circumstances as a widow. Hill's possessions enabled her to redefine the old working spaces of the house as a middling widow's apartment. The card tables and English carpet softened the utilitarian kitchen precincts through their signification of polite games of cards and evocations of the parlor. With the sale of her house to another mariner, Hill's brief dower tenure ended in 1817 as a likely casualty of the economic dislocations of the second and third decades of the nineteenth century and a rising culture of litigiousness.[14]

The assignment of specific rooms to widows like Hill did not always follow the same progression even when houses were similar in plan. The lack of architectural consistency between dowers appears in the division of the Cabot Street house owned and occupied by Abigail and Samuel Beck. Similar in plan to the Hills' house, the three-story, L-shaped Beck dwelling included a parlor, entry, and dining room fronting Cabot Street and a service wing and stables extending back into the lot (see Figure 5.9). When Abigail Beck was widowed in 1819, the dower committee awarded her the rooms in the best end of the house. These included the parlor, the small room behind the entry, and a portion of the garden. Like other Portsmouth widows, Beck

A Elevation

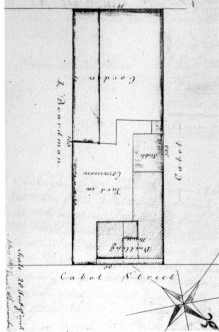

B Dower Plan. *Rockingham County
Probate Office, Exeter*

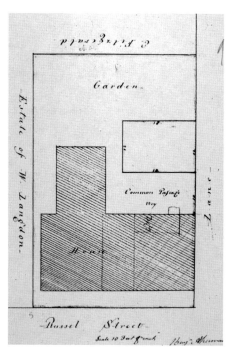

FIGURE 5.10

Lovey Hill's Third, Russell Street, Portsmouth
(1821). *Rockingham County Probate Office, Exeter*

also received a right of access that allowed her to reach other individual or shared spaces: the front entry and stairs, the back stairs to the third story, and "also the Yard in common with the other owners, as it is now fenced, also a privilege of passing from the yard into the scullery for the purpose of getting water." Beck's dower, like Hill's, placed the widow in a suite of rooms at one end of the house. But, where Hill set up housekeeping in the kitchen ell, Beck found herself with the task of converting the parlor into a more generalized space. Lovey Hill encountered the same dilemma in the 1820 division of her house on Russell Street. The dower for the *L*-shaped, center-passage-plan house awarded her the lower room, chamber, and garret in the parlor end of the house, along with a portion of the garden and unrestricted passage both from the street into the entry and through the garden from an adjacent lane (see Figure 5.10). The remaining heirs received the dining room, service ell, and associated chambers in the upper stories.[15]

The discrepancy between the rooms awarded Mary Hill and those given to Abigail Beck and Lovey Hill highlights conflicted notions of widows' architectural competencies. For Mary Hill the dower focused on the architectural sphere of domesticity; for Beck and Lovey Hill (like Hannah Rand) the emphasis fell on interior spaces associated with the culture of gentility. A notation in Lovey Hill's dower offers some insight into the logic identifying the spaces she received in her divided house. "Her late husband's estate," the committee wrote, would be divided in a "manner having respect to quality as well as quantity." Quantity, the widow's thirds, presented little problem to most dower delegations, but quality and the intrinsically "indivisible" nature of houses demanded social judgments about both the rooms within the house and the person receiving them. Dower committees apparently entered their deliberations with a free hand in matters of quality and chose for the widow the rooms that they viewed as both befitting and sustaining her station. Guided by custom, convention, and perception, the rationale for their choices remains clouded because there was little public discussion about the proper appearance of widows' houses.[16]

The rooms bestowed on widows in the course of dower divisions enable us to infer social status on the basis of the quality of architectural spaces. But who were these widows who occupied divided houses, and did the rooms allotted to them truly communicate a sense of rank in Portsmouth's urban society? They hailed from Portsmouth's middling sort and were the widows of mariners, artisans, shopkeepers, and minor merchants. They were women who, with their husbands, had enjoyed a degree of economic and material success that yielded sufficient resources to purchase a house and acquire debt. They were also the mothers of children who would eventually inherit their fathers' estates once they came of age and their parents' creditors had been satisfied.

Some widows received a dower that included shops and other work spaces. Nathaniel Souther, the baker who participated in designating Rand's dower, died in 1824. Like Rand, the newly widowed Mehitable Souther, who lived across Pleasant Street from the Rand household, greeted the court-appointed delegation that arrived at her house charged with the responsibility of dividing it into two properties. Again, the dower committee recorded their deliberations with care:

> The corner room on Pleasant Street and Cottars lane, with the chamber and garret over and cellar under the same and also the chamber adjoining the one before mentioned over the bake-house, also a piece of land beginning at the corner of said bake-house adjoining the land of Phineas Tyler . . . with the privilege of passing and repassing through the front door and the front stairs from the lower floor to the garret, also the privilege of passing and repassing through the bake-house door to the yard and through the front gate and the yard to the back part of the house, and, also, the privilege of the well and pump and of the necessary, with the privilege in common with the other part of the said house of the cellar under the front entry. . . . Preserving to the owner of the other part of said house the privilege of making a cellar door in the front entry and of passing down and up the cellar stairs.[17]

The familiar dower provisions awarded the widow her rooms, her portion of the garden, and the right to move between those spaces. But Souther's dower describes a different kind of house. Occupying the corner opposite Mary Hill's former home, the Souther house conformed to an *L*-shaped plan with the bakehouse located in a wing along Cottars Lane. The Souther house followed a first-floor progression from bakehouse to shop to entry to best room (a combination dining room and parlor). As the hub of economic activity, the bakery and shop represented the most important working spaces in the Southers' house.

The Souther dwelling with its bakehouse and shop represented the typical conflation of home and work in a single building. Houses with retail spaces, barrooms, workshops, and other economically productive spaces were typical of urban landscapes on both sides of the Atlantic. Widow Eberth living on Vine Street in Philadelphia's Northern Liberties occupied a town house with shop in front, kitchen in back, and parlor and sleeping chambers upstairs (see Figure 5.11). Similarly, eighteenth-century Paris bakers occupied houses where work spaces spilled into domestic areas and the bakehouse easily doubled as the family kitchen. Such was the case in the Souther house, where the "Baker's tools" apparently included all the family cookware. Still, the Souther house contained two clearly articulated sets of rooms: the parlor and dining room with mahogany and birch tables, windsor chairs, tea tray, and looking glass occupied the room on one side of the first floor entry; the shop with its display tables, desk, and chairs stood opposite. The distinction between commercial and domestic spaces did not rise to the upper chambers.[18]

Souther's dower created a set of tenements, displaying a much more fragmented sense of the house than did the decisions that divided her neighbors' dwellings. Read in combination with Nathaniel Souther's inventory, the dower reveals a remarkable reworking of the house through expedience. First, the dower committee assigned the shop room to the widow along with the chamber overhead and the chamber over the bakehouse. Second, the dower limited her right in the bakehouse (a room that also served as the family kitchen) to one of passing back and forth to the garden, well, and privy. Like Hannah Rand and Lovey Hill, Souther ceded possession of the kitchen hearth. Third, the dower committee devised the best room and chamber at the end of the dwelling farthest from the bakehouse to the other heirs. Like Mary Hill, Souther lost her parlor. Although she lacked a right in both bakehouse and parlor, she retained the shop room. This commercial space offered her two possibilities. She could claim the old bake shop as her own parlor overlooking Pleasant Street, or she could continue to employ the room as a shop, either for rent or as her own, and dedicate the chamber upstairs as her parlor. Souther continued to occupy her rooms through the 1820s, but she left no record describing how she actually used them.

The ambiguity of Souther's dower did not extend to all Portsmouth houses where families pursued domestic and business life under the same roof. Lydia Amazeen, widow of trader Joseph Amazeen, occupied a frame house at the corner of Jefferson and Atkinson Streets. A local tax assessment compiled just before Joseph Amazeen's death placed the couple among the city's middling sort. A dower delegation visited the newly widowed Amazeen in 1824:

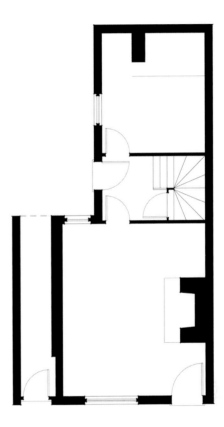

FIGURE 5.11

Eberth House, Vine Street,
Philadelphia (circa 1785)

A Elevation

B First-Floor Plan (reconstructed).
Note the front shop with its street entry, the
side passage under the party wall, and the
back entry into the service wing and family
quarters. *Drawn by Jeff Klee*

FIGURE 5.12

Joseph and Lydia Amazeen House,
Jefferson and Atkinson Streets, Portsmouth
(circa 1795)
A Elevation

We have sett off to the said Lydia Amazeen, the western part of the House
in said Portsmouth . . . consisting of the following rooms and privileges.
Namely, a small Shop in the front part of said House and Northwest corner of the same: A Setting Room, small Bed Room, and two chambers
over the said Rooms, likewise, a small Bed chamber on the back part
of said House next adjoining the chamber on the South west corner of
said House, with the privilege of passing and repassing through the back

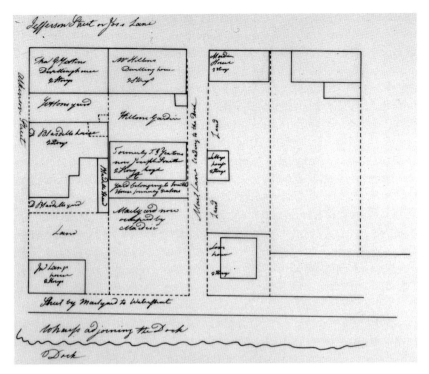

B Block Plan (circa 1800; reconstructed),
Showing Location of the Amazeen House.
By Gabrielle M. Lanier

ROOM PRIVILEGES KEY:

HER'S
THEIRS
SHARED

SECOND FLOOR PLAN

FIRST FLOOR PLAN

0 1 2   4   8 FEET

C First- and Second-Floor Plans,
Showing Widow's Third and Shared Areas.
By Gabrielle M. Lanier and Jeff Klee

chamber entry, over the back stairs—from the said Chambers—forth and back into the back yard.[19]

The dower also awarded her use of the kitchen in common with the other households within the dwelling, the right to use the "front Door entrance in the front entry, over the front stairs, in common with those who may occupy part of said House," and a share in the cellar, including the well and cistern (see Figure 5.12). Along with the right to these spaces, Amazeen acquired unimpeded access into and out of the cellar, to the backyard, and to the necessary.

Because Amazeen's house contained more rooms than Rand's dwelling, her dower seems comparatively generous. The division of Amazeen's house identified her rooms, areas in common, and the right to "pass and repass" through other apartments. Unlike Souther's dower, Amazeen's new accommodations incorporated a full functional range of spaces. In addition to a "setting room" and upper- and lower-floor sleeping chambers, the dower committee assigned her the shop at the front of the house and a "privilege in the kitchen to wash, bake, and do other necessary work." Although held in common with the other household occupying the building, the dower emphasized Amazeen's free use of the kitchen, an arrangement found in the division of similar houses. The court reserved the shop for Amazeen, but whether she occupied or rented out this room remains unknown. Although the parlor went to the other heirs, Lydia Amazeen kept the "setting room"—a space that served as a dining room and communicated polite associations with a rising middle-class culture. The size and complexity of the Amazeen house also yielded more readily to division than did the more compact dwellings occupied by Rand and Souther. Thus, Amazeen's house and others like it represent an architectural threshold: a dwelling large enough to divide and still retain the symbolic competencies of sitting room, kitchen, and shop—spaces embracing sociability, domesticity, and commerce.

Like Mary Hill, Amazeen brought her own possessions to her marriage. Enumerated at the end of her husband's inventory, the "personal property that belonged to Lydia Amazeen before marriage" signified the twin competencies of sociability and domesticity. Dining and card tables, along with appropriate accessories such as crockery and cutlery, pictures for the walls, and copper implements for the hearth, described the polite social settings of middling gentility. A "Post Bedstead" with its pillows and bolsters, sheets, blankets, quilts, and bed curtains furnished the chamber, the most intimate site of domestic relations; cooking implements equipped the hearth in the kitchen, the most utilitarian and casual dwelling space. The presence and enumeration of these possessions in a separate and discrete list reveals a relationship between the material culture of dowry (objects generally provided by a bride's family and brought to the marriage) and dower (objects provided by the husband's estate and brought to a wife's widowhood). Although the two entitlements were not the same, they both relied on objects to signify the status and expectations held for individual women entering and leaving marriage. As cultural markers, the objects of dower and dowry were instrumental in the maintenance and control of social identity.[20]

Portsmouth widows who held life rights in larger estates consisting of multiple properties rarely encountered the necessity of a divided house. When wealthy sea captain Thomas Manning died in 1819, his estate contained four separate properties, including house lots on Washington Street, South Road, and Manning Street and the adjacent Dock Lane waterfront. Margaret Manning received the two-story house and lot on Manning Street where she had lived with her husband. Among her property were an extensive garden, wood house, carriage house and barn, store, and wharf. An inventory for the house specified rooms by function. The first floor included socially prominent rooms (dining room, front entry, and parlor), commercial areas (shop room), and domestic work and storage spaces (kitchen, pantry, scullery, garret, and cellar). Although the second-floor rooms were all designated chambers, their relative importance was expressed through their relationship to the rooms below; these second-floor rooms ranged from parlor chamber to kitchen chamber. Together with her waterside wharves and stores, Manning's dower offered the widow full access to the architectural competencies of sociability, domesticity, and trade.[21]

Manning's dower ensured an architectural competency commensurate with her standing in Portsmouth's elite mercantile society. The concern for the architectural and material display extended to wealthy widows in other cities. Elizabeth Petrie of Charleston, South Carolina, for example, received from her husband Alexander the bequest of an annual allowance of seven hundred pounds and "the use and service of the Negroes Named Pegg, Jean, Moll, Judith and Pompey." Petrie's slaves represented the most common form of property Charleston men willed to their wives, daughters, and sisters. Petrie also specified his wishes for his wife's house and its furnishings. First, the widow received "the use and Occupation of a House that I have directed my Attorneys to Build." Second, an itemized list of household goods gave her the means to furnish her house. While the cash allowance provided a degree of financial independence, the house and furnishings affirmed her husband's expectations regarding her life after his death. Elizabeth Petrie's "trust," her estate bequest, also reflected expectation born of mutuality and the consanguineous culture of mercantilism.[22]

Petrie's town house followed the form and style of Charleston's favored and distinctive "single house" (see Figure 5.13). Two stories in elevation and built on a raised foundation, the frame house sat gable end to the street with access into a narrow carriage yard or onto a piazza. One room wide, the house extended three rooms in depth, including a front parlor, stair passage, and back dining room, before it opened onto a work yard containing the kitchen quarter and other outbuildings. Erected on the site of the old Orange Garden away from the commercial core of the city, Petrie's house, with its well-finished interiors featuring neatly carved fireplace elements and open stair, conformed to a range of houses with solely residential functions.

Alexander Petrie's bequest addressed an architectural and material competency focused almost exclusively on the material culture of polite society. Elizabeth Petrie's allotted furniture emphasized the social rituals of tea and dining. She received two large dining room tables and a complement of eighteen mahogany chairs, along with silver salts, a pepper box, all the table china, and a case containing a dozen silver-handled knives and forks and a dozen silver spoons. Petrie's material competency extended to a round tea table, "all the Tea China ware," and a silver coffeepot and stand. In addition to the objects that defined the setting for sociability, Elizabeth Petrie received her choice of her husband's library and all his liquors—two provisions guaranteed to facilitate the content and flow of polite conversation. Through the bequest of a house and furnishings appropriate to its most formal social precincts, Alexander Petrie sought to establish the material conditions for his wife's widowhood. His concern for material display extended into two other areas of the widow's house. First, Alexander Petrie specified the furnishings of the widow's chamber: the "best" bedstead, a chest of drawers, and a dressing table and glass. Second, he assigned his wife the use of a horse and carriage. These two bequests focused simultaneously on the more removed and intimate precincts within the house and the public world of the street. The material provisions for Petrie's widowhood are steeped in a sense of comportment extending from the innermost reaches of the house through its most public rooms and out into the city. While Petrie's annual allowance gave her liberty, her house and its key furnishings reinforced her husband's assumptions concerning the style and manner in which his widow would act.[23]

Elizabeth Petrie's enslaved servants speak most eloquently to the architectural competency of the widow's dower. The interplay of sociability, domesticity, and trade that informed the division of northern New England town houses resonated in the skills of the chattel workers inherited by Charleston widows. The five African-American servants named in Alexander Petrie's will were part of a larger complement that included a total of sixteen people at the time of the widow's own death. Possessed of her own servants and those provided by her husband, Petrie held ample resources in human capital, which included ten women (five designated "old") and six men (who received the highest dollar valuation). In an urban context where enslaved labor occupied multiple spheres, cooks, seamstresses, and washerwomen symbolized a domestic competency, and house servants, especially maids and coachmen, stood as human emblems of sociability. Enslaved workers with skills in trades such as carpentry or smithing could be rented out as a source of income, signifying a competency in trade.

Elite white Charleston widows were measured by their management rather than their execution of the affairs of the hearth, the salon, and shop. The managerial nature of their households paralleled that of elite women in other cities where slavery was not a general practice. Northern widows typically hired workers; southern women tended to own them. Latitia Lavergne of Philadelphia invested considerable care in providing for her unnamed "girl" following her death. Lavergne resided in a substantial Philadelphia town house consisting of a front parlor furnished with the best dining table, two card tables, and tea table, a back parlor established as a considerably plainer dining room, and a back kitchen furnished with only a pine table and two old windsor chairs. The plan and hierarchy of front and back rooms repeated itself upstairs. The second-floor front room with its mahogany and walnut furniture, bed hangings, and carpets contrasted with the back chamber, which seems to have been used largely for storage and bathing. The garret at the very top of the house contained the stuff of a servant's apartment: a small pine table, "field" bedstead, and a "toilet table" of slight value. When Lavergne died in 1803, her final bequests assigned the bulk of her estate to her friend Rebecca Braverd and a small portion of "Goods allotted for the use of the girl."[24]

The "girl," apparently a servant, received an ensemble of objects that enabled her to recapture the textures of her mistress's house on a greatly reduced scale. She received a small walnut table and four chairs, a looking glass, two brass candlesticks, and five pictures for the walls. A cattail bed with bedstead, bolster, pillows, sheets, blankets, bedspread, and curtains defined a chamber. A kitchen table and array of tubs, buckets, pots, and "Lott of Kitchen Ware" were associated with domestic space. Whether these objects were ultimately packed into a single room or spread through a small town house is unimportant; they defined a set of expectations constructed around broadly held ideas of respectable women's households—regardless of wealth or station. Lavergne's "girl" gained the material capital of a respectable servant with which she could establish herself in another household just as Elizabeth Petrie preserved her own architectural competency through the possession of slaves.

One twist remains in understanding Elizabeth Petrie's architectural competency in Charleston. Just before his death, Alexander Petrie invested in the old Orange Garden property running between Tradd and Broad Streets on the south side of King Street. Laying out a string of uniform lots along newly formed Orange Street, he set aside the first parcel in from Tradd Street for his wife. The house built on this lot, along with the provisions for the widow's cash allowance, slaves, and household furnishings, stood as a material directive for the development of the remaining lots. The widow

Petrie's single house and its stylish furnishings emphasizing the society of the dining table and salon advertised the fruition of her husband's intent. As a speculative venture, Orange Street was designed to attract affluent Charlestonians with a desire to live in the city but not in its older and more congested neighborhoods. Petrie's house in this circumstance acquired the quality of a model home in an urban environment where the everyday life of urban elites defined much of the public sphere. The widow's house, indeed the widow herself, assumed a persona that marketed respectability and lured like-minded builders into the new street. Petrie's dower established her as a fixture in a larger architectural competency centered on the outward show of genteel sensibilities and urban land speculation.[25]

Elizabeth Petrie's inheritance, Latitia Lavergne's bequest, and Margaret Manning's dower asserted material circumstances far removed from the concerns that plagued Hannah Rand as her husband's creditors clamored for their due. Two of Elizabeth Petrie's less fortunate Orange Street neighbors, for example, found their architectural competencies successively compromised by financial exigencies. Like many Charleston husbands, Tobias Cambridge willed his wife Elizabeth a life right in his house at 12 Orange Street, described as a wood dwelling measuring roughly sixteen by twenty-six feet and including a brick kitchen, countinghouse, stable, and carriage house. A suit leveled against the estate forced the widow Cambridge to sell the property at public auction, where she purchased it back. In her own will, Cambridge, sensitive to the near loss of house and lot, stipulated that "Should Either of my said Daughters wish to dispose of her Share of the house in which I live that She Shall not be at Liberty to do so to any Stranger until She has made an offer of the Same to my Other Daughters." The daughters united and sold the house and lot in 1823. When the new owner died the following year, his widow converted part of the house into a "Seminary to teach young Ladies and Gentlemen." The widows who occupied 12 Orange Street as dowers never faced the legal prospect of Rand's divided dwelling, but they did confront the threat of claims against their houses. Cambridge responded by using her assets to purchase the house in her own right; her successor preserved the house by dedicating part of the dwelling to the instruction of "young Ladies and Gentlemen."[26]

Widows of more limited means living in houses divided by dower or renting rooms were typical in early American seaports in the eighteenth and early nineteenth centuries. In Boston, for example, Elizabeth Greenleaf owned and occupied on Salutation Alley "one end of a house one room on a floor three stories high" in a divided dwelling reminiscent of Rand's dower. Sarah Doubt, living on Middle Street in Boston and working as a milliner, resided in a similar set of rooms composed of a parlor, kitchen, and chamber. Doubt's parlor held a looking glass, three tables (two mahogany and one marble), bureau, and seven chairs; her kitchen contained only cooking and ironing utensils and three chairs. The absence in Doubt's possessions of hats, bonnets, ribbons, and the stuff of a milliner's stock-in-trade suggest that her parlor doubled as fitting room and salon for custom work that she marketed through another milliner's shop. Widow Johanna Conner and her two parrots shared a similar set of rooms in her rented Fish Street residence. The 576-square-foot house fronted Fish Street and likely followed a plan with two rooms on a floor, with the widow occupying one in each story. Although Conner held no legal stake in a divided house, her rented portion still contained the sorts of rooms associated with Rand's dower. There is no evidence in the two-story frame house for the "slop shop" where Conner sold ready-made clothing. The constellation of rooms and the furnishings found in her parlor, kitchen, and chamber, however, speak to the same culture of domestic competency seen in Portsmouth's dower-divided houses. The absence of clearly identified commercial spaces, such as Amazeen's shop room, suggests that, even as these poorer Boston widows occupied and furnished their architectural competencies, they did so in ways that tended to compress the worlds of domesticity, gentility, and business.[27]

The same holds true for widows' households in Philadelphia, where the contents of houses and the material competencies they reflect are revealed in the inventories and wills associated with their estates. Mary Harper owned and occupied a house on North Front Street above Elfreth's Alley and near the Northern Liberties. Her house conformed to a standard Philadelphia type consisting of two rooms on a floor and a kitchen ell. Harper occupied a suite of three rooms, most likely on the second floor, and rented the more valuable ground-floor rooms to cutler and surgical implement maker William Pintard for use as shop and residence. Within the confines of the front room, Harper established her sphere of sociability. A mahogany dining table with six leather-bottomed chairs and a round tea table provided the focal points for a room that doubled as dining room and parlor. Ten small pictures on the walls, japanned waiters, clock, copper coffeepot, fireplace tools, and array of crockery and glass provided props in a display that announced possession of social knowledge and the material means to act on it. A windsor armchair, the least-valued article of furniture in the room and the most comfortable, completed the setting and provided the vantage point from which widow Harper surveyed her salon.

If the front of Harper's house projected the material culture of sociability, the back chamber and kitchen embodied domesticity. An old kitchen table and bench provided working surfaces for cooking and washing, and a second "small" table with two chairs defined the site of everyday meals. A corner cupboard contained cheap English earthenware dishes for ordinary use, side by side with the widow's pewter plates and dishes. Kettles, pots, pans, a colander, ladle, fleshfork, gridiron, flatirons, and teakettle furnished the fireplace. Water for washing clothes and scrubbing floors sloshed in wooden tubs and buckets; a bellows coughed life into the kitchen fire, and a hearth brush, shovel, and tongs carried away its ashy remains. A woodpile stood at the door. A bureau and a broken looking glass in the kitchen were convenient fixtures where Harper could inspect and adjust her appearance before going out or receiving guests. Upstairs, the chamber held the widow's feather bed, a case of drawers, trunk, chairs, and linens. Harper's chamber also gave her a private place to secret her valuables, including a sizable sum of cash and her silver teaspoons, sugar tongs, and cream jug.[28]

Phebe Duncan, widow of an African-American mariner, shared a smaller, three-story house on nearby Mulberry Street with her brother, cooper John Broomwick. Unlike Harper, who listed herself in the street directories as a "gentlewoman" and occupied her house solely as a residence, Duncan seems to have combined sociability, domesticity, and trade in a dwelling that contained two households in the late 1790s. Furnishings established the best room on the second floor of the three-story, eleven-by-twenty-three-foot brick house. Here, Duncan placed objects of sociability (her card table, windsor settee, china, and glassware) alongside the beds and bureau that defined the same room as the chamber she shared with her two children. Cooking and cleaning utensils, tables, and chairs filled "the Room down stairs or Kitchen" located in a two-story ell measuring seven by nine feet. The third-story room served as the storage space for Duncan's sundry possessions, which included her cache of pewter plates.

The three rooms associated with widowed Phebe Duncan constituted roughly one-half of the rooms in the house. The ground-floor front room, the chamber over the kitchen, and the garret were spaces most likely held by Broomwick and six other residents. Together, the two households carved out individual apartments and common spaces within the compact confines of a dwelling divided like the court's prescription for widow Rand. The primary distinction between the ways that Harper and Duncan furnished and occupied their houses and the ways that they illuminate the situation of Rand's dower lies in a sense of scale. Harper and Duncan utilized the architectural competencies of their widow's apartments in different ways. Harper pursued a presentation of neatly divided and clearly presented competencies of sociability and domesticity of parlor, kitchen, and chamber. Duncan possessed exactly the same types of rooms but combined the domestic lives of two households and collapsed the functions of the widow's parlor and chamber into a single second-story room. The ambiguity of the first floor, identified as a kitchen and likely given over to other income-generating activities, spoke to the relative luxury and accessibility of material respectability that Harper enjoyed.[29]

Just as the dowers assigned to Portsmouth widows describe a range of individual circumstances, the estates of Philadelphia widows address visible differences based on wealth and status. Elizabeth Lawrence represents one extreme. Her town house in a fashionable block of Chestnut Street included a parlor, small back parlor, and entry on the ground floor and a second-floor "drawing room." Each of these rooms held the familiar icons of elite sociability. Predictably, the material culture of domesticity was relegated to the back of the house, where Lawrence's roles, like Manning's, Lavergne's, and Petrie's, assumed the genteel air of a household manager. Isabella Caldwell's two-story frame house standing near the waterfront in the southern reaches of the city presented a markedly different aspect. Containing one room on a floor furnished only as chamber and kitchen, widow Caldwell's house was devoid of the objects and spaces that affected gentility. Still, Caldwell enjoyed a situation superior to that encountered by impoverished and homeless women who sought the refuge of Philadelphia's "Bettering House."[30]

Many urban widows seized an active role in the disposition of their affairs and worked within the dower system to reclaim economic and social status. Such was the case with Alice Hill's dower in Wilmington, Delaware, where the symbolic power of objects crystallized around competing competencies and prescribed expectations. Alice and Scotland Hill owned and occupied a "small frame house" sited on a rented corner lot. Although "small" is not specified, the most compact town houses in the nearby cities of Philadelphia and Baltimore ran between ten and fourteen feet square. The Hills' house contained at least six tables, ten chairs, two beds, three spinning wheels, five chests, an iron stove, and several other pieces of furniture in addition to the occupants' clothing, personal effects, dishes, cutlery, cooking utensils, and remaining household flotsam. Domestic furnishings spilled out into the yard along with shovels, rakes, grindstones, and various casks and kegs. In sum, the Hills' yard held the standard broken-down scatter of domestic and working debris associated with urban and rural households throughout the mid-Atlantic region. The contents of the house also describe a level of domestic, potentially knee-shattering congestion. One-half dozen tables, a supply of hams and pork jowls, and a debt to a neighborhood brewer suggest that the Hills kept a tavern in their house and yard. The open expanse of the yard cluttered with Scotland Hill's many tools and his listed occupation as a laborer suggest that he actually equipped and supervised a work crew. The types of tools subsequently sold at his estate auction indicate that Hill and his workforce labored variously as gardeners, excavators, and firewood cutters.

Under the administration of executor Samuel Hillis, Alice Hill received household furnishings, objects related to foodways, and some personal items, chiefly her husband's apparel. The household furnishings describe the basic stuff of a small apartment: an old mahogany table with six chairs to go around it, a "desk table," two bundles of bedding with some bed clothes, a "small square looking glass," and a pair of andirons for the fireplace completed the furnishings. Hill also received their "small frame house," a teakettle, ten silver teaspoons, a skillet, flatirons, and the family pork supply—three hams, two shoulders, two jowls, and a pig. These items, plus her own clothing and a "lot of books," completed the assemblage of objects with which she was expected to begin her new life as a widow.[31]

More than simple furnishings for a bereaved woman's solitary household, the items she inherited symbolized expectations about Hill's new social and economic standing as a widow of modest means. Her widow's allotment of bedding and other household goods conforms to court-mandated distributions of property throughout the eastern United States, where the primary goals were the maintenance of the widow in an appropriate situation and the preservation of the estate for future distribution. The expectation for widowhood from the perspective of probate law and the executor's responsibilities can be read in two ways. First, the widow's allotted property guaranteed a minimal independence by endowing Hill with sufficient property to continue running the tavern, albeit under significantly reduced circumstances. Second, the actions of the court defined the widow as a ward of state and estate, an enforced circumstance of dependency and passivity.

In Hill's case, the distribution of personal property intended the removal of Hill from her working role as her husband's business partner to that of the widowed ward of his estate. In this context, the material world of Alice Hill accords with the worlds of Phebe Duncan, Hannah Rand, Sarah Doubt, and other middling widows in early American cities.

Hill refused to be content with the meager contents of a single-room widow's apartment or with the limited vision of her future advanced by court and custom. At her husband's estate auction, apparently using cash advanced by Samuel Hillis against the value of the estate, she purchased three tables and two sets of bedsteads for her feather beds. She added to her stock of cooking and dining ware one-half dozen knives and forks, mortar, small pot, and two bottles. More than one-half of her purchases, however, fell into a different category—tools. David C. Wilson, the auctioneer, sold hoes, rakes, digging forks, pick, spade, maul, wedges, grindstones, and other laborer's tools to Hill. Although she could not reassemble the whole of the working capital she had built up with her husband, Hill acquired for herself as much of their productive property as she could. With additional tables and cooking and dining utensils, she recovered at least the basic equipment to run a tavern in her house. Her acquisition of tools enabled her to equip laborers for excavating, gardening, and firewood cutting.

Hill's actions are two tiered in character. Her purchase of tools represents the acquisition of capital. Her shovels, digging forks, hoes, and other tools enabled her to carry on the practice of contracting work crews for various projects and to serve as an important source for jobs in the local community. Her possession of capital in the form of tools bound her workers to her and her to them; her ability to use those tools to recruit and equip a labor gang allowed her to contract with clients who needed manual work performed. Whether she contracted directly with clients or used a crew foreman to negotiate terms is unknown. More than a measure of economic self-sufficiency, these working relationships and the sociology of labor they describe represent a level of functional symbolism found in genuinely ordinary objects. For Hill, tools signified not just income but also, for all its limitations, a kind of liberty.

While questions of architectural competency and dependent relations lie at the heart of Hill's actions and Rand's dower, there is finally the ephemeral quality of the dower. The dower nominally divided the house, but rarely did the division extend into remodeling work more extensive than modifying an existing passage for the widow to gain her apartments. Regardless of the widow's life expectancy, the court saw the dower as a short-lived arrangement. When John Knapp of Newburyport, Massachusetts, died in 1814, the county court sent a committee of three men with instructions to view and divide the house and allot widow Mary Knapp her thirds. The remainder of the house was set aside for the economic benefit of the Knapps' four children. The three-man committee performed its charge with the same assiduity of their Portsmouth counterparts. Like the houses of Amazeen and Holmes in Portsmouth, the Knapp dwelling, built early in the eighteenth century, followed a plan incorporating a lobby entry fronting on a large central-chimney pile and flanked by a room on either side. A range of rooms, including the kitchen, stretched along the rear of the two-story frame house. Following a practice based as much on custom as law, the court assigned Knapp a front room and chamber in the southwest corner with rights in the kitchen, cellar, and yard. Both Knapp and the other occupants of the divided house held privileges of passing in and out of one another's lodgings on their way to these common spaces. As an architectural and social competency, Knapp's dower approximated the dowers granted Holmes and Amazeen.[32]

Knapp's tenure was short. When she died a year later in 1815, her dower reverted to the estate, her children were assigned to the guardianship of a local tanner, and the family's house and lot were sold to satisfy her husband's old debts. The new owners of the Knapps' house set about the task of literally dividing the house into two dwellings (see Figure 5.14). They pulled down the old center chimney and in its place inserted a new entry containing both an open stair to the second story and a passage to the rear of the house. In place of the old chimney, the new owners inserted two new stacks, each fitted with back-to-back fireplaces. A small fireplace heated a formal front room, and a larger fireplace with bake oven provided a cooking hearth in the back kitchen. Neatly divided in half, each of the old dwelling's two new residences also possessed its own gable entry and separate back stair. Along with the transformation of the building's plan, the new owners outfitted each half of the two new tenements with up-to-date decorative trim. The few bits of woodwork that survived the renovations found fresh use recycled in the upper stories of the building.[33]

The remodeling of Knapp's old house calls attention to a particular feature of houses divided by dower. While occasional provisions were made to create a second entry for the widow (as in Portsmouth widow Mary Hill's new front door) or a partition in the cellar, the separation of households necessarily relied more on social conventions than walls. Physical barriers,

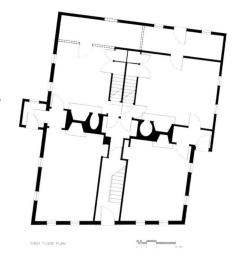

FIRST FLOOR PLAN

FIGURE 5.14

Mary Knapp House, Federal Street, Newburyport, Massachusetts (remodeled early nineteenth century). Plan of the first floor with alterations and additions following the conversion of the house into two tenements. *Drawn by Jeff Klee*

after all, complicated a subsequent owner's ability to make the house whole again. Every dower that divided a house contained numerous provisos detailing the widow's right to move in and out of the other household's allotted spaces, but none of them instructed widows on how they should behave in their new lodgings. Dowers also seldom offered any directive for the construction of the walls and doorways necessary to achieve real architectural divisions. The court viewed the dower, no matter how long the widow's tenure, as a temporary condition, and it assumed that she would occupy her dower in a respectable fashion. Comportment, it seems, erected invisible partitions until remarriage or death concluded a widow's dower rights and the house reverted to its idealized, single-family character.[34]

Knapp's and Rand's dowers lay bare the perception of widows from the perspective of the masculine world of property. First, each dower division addresses symbolic architectural competencies revolving around sociability, domesticity, and commerce. While dowers drawn up for wealthier widows accommodated all three competencies, those for poorer women in smaller houses forced choices that reflected customary expectations held by both men and women about the status and maintenance of widows' households. Second, dower divisions represented a liminal point between marriage and an uncertain future that death, remarriage, or debt resolved. The lack of material investment in physically dividing the house into two households suggests that the widow's dower was a passing condition. Third, the dower division of the house created awkward domestic environments. Crowded houses filled with unrelated lodgers and multiple families were a common feature in the early American city, but they also represented a condition associated with the households of the lower sort or with households organized around extended dependent relationships. The widow's dower represented both diminished and dependent circumstances that seemingly could be restored only through remarriage or death.

Finally, the dower divisions of houses like Rand's underscore the symbolic power of objects in everyday life. Rand's position in Portsmouth society (like other women's in similar straits in other cities) had been labeled as ambivalent, ambiguous, and liminal—terms that buttress the economic authority of men. In a strongly patriarchal society widows were trapped between the realities of their everyday lives and the social expectation of their dependency. Widows in American cities encountered a similar ambivalence at the turn of the nineteenth century when male perceptions of political virtue further compromised their position. In post-Revolutionary America personal independence was strongly associated with economic independence. Although economic dependence held strong negatives for men, it carried more positive associations for women cast in the role of helpmates whose labors were theoretically owned by husbands and who were seen as bearers of moral authority. Widowhood complicated the equation. Whatever the provisions of dowers and wills, widows possessed a measure of economic independence steeped in a thoroughly male culture of property. Dowers in Portsmouth and wills in Philadelphia and Charleston engaged both the material and symbolic dimensions of circumstance and comportment. They constituted actions that textured rhetoric and anchored ideology in the practice of everyday experience. To what extent did widows negotiate the terms that represented their status and station in the material world? Constrained by law, widows were not without voice. We cannot know the words that passed between Rand and the dower committee, but we can be certain that she assumed an active stance as she asserted her preferences for herself and her children. Given the variation in the rooms assigned in Portsmouth dowers, we can also be assured that the delegation took her words into account. Rand negotiated the cultural associations embedded in household space; in doing so, she affirmed who she was in the eyes of her neighbors and her own.[35]

And what of Hannah Rand and her dower? Rand moved out of her house. As she settled her husband's debts and looked to her children's futures, she petitioned the court for and received the reversion of her dower right in May 1823. At the court-mandated public sale of Samuel Rand's property in June, painter Ebeneezer Pike purchased the heirs' two thirds for just less than four hundred dollars. Two weeks later, Rand sold her third to Pike for an additional three hundred dollars; Rand then concluded a mortgage with Pike in which he agreed to pay her one hundred dollars annually over a four-year period. Nine months later, Rand invested her money in a lot on Partridge Street, purchased from her brother James Locke, Jr., a painter who would teach two of his sister's sons his trade. The deed registered between brother and sister stipulated that Hannah Rand's sister-in-law release and "surrender up and forever" her own right of dower and her power of thirds.[36]

THE SHIPWRIGHT'S LODGINGS

In early June 1800 David Watson and James Harris made their way through the streets of Baltimore to the Fells Point residence of Angus and Jane Grant. The Grants' one-story frame house containing a single room stood on Wolf Street in a setting of similar town houses and larger and taller brick and wood dwellings. Watson and Harris's task was to compile an inventory of the dwelling's contents as part of the probate court proceedings occasioned by Angus's recent death. A predictable array of furniture cluttered the twelve-by-sixteen-foot residence: three tables (two described as "small"), three chairs, and a bed and bedstead composed the major movable contents in the house. Smaller objects, a pair of brass candlesticks, flatirons, tub and bucket, a shovel, tongs, and andirons for the fireplace, and "furniture" for table and kitchen, nearly completed the list of Grant's worldly assets. His silver watch (his most valuable possession), his joiner's tools, a tea caddy, and tea tray rounded out the inventory.[1]

Two houses very much like the Grants' dwelling survive on Wolf Street (see Figure 6.1). The remnants of a row of approximately seven identical units of which the Grants' was surely one, the Wolf Street houses as originally built each enclosed 192 square feet of living space, supplemented with a finished loft. Framed with sawed and hewed studs, some with the bark left on, the houses were clad with beaded-edge weatherboard. Front and back

FIGURE 6.1

Wolf Street Town Houses, Fells Point, Baltimore. Extremely rare, these two residences stand as the last remnants of a longer row of one-story frame urban dwellings

A Elevation

windows admitted light and air. On the interior, a fireplace provided heat and a cooking hearth. Hand-split lath and plaster covered the walls. As the dwellings of urban artisans, houses like those on Wolf Street were familiar fixtures on the streets of Fells Point. Erected at the very end of the eighteenth century during Baltimore's rapid post-Revolutionary growth, these houses

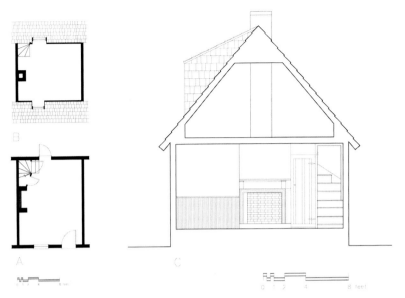

were notable chiefly for their ordinariness. Although regionally distinctive with their single-story elevations and construction details, the town houses of Fells Point shipwrights were similar in quality to artisan residences in other seaport towns.[2]

Of 626 Fells Point houses recorded by tax assessors in 1798, two-thirds were wood, of which nearly one-fifth stood only one story tall. Only one in ten of all the houses assessed was as small as the Grants' dwelling. In assigned value, the Grants' town house clung to the bottom rung of Fells Point dwellings, with only two others worth less. The Grants, as property owners, were better off than many of their neighbors who occupied rented houses and defrayed their rent by taking in additional lodgers. Still, the Grants' house was their own, and its ownership placed them in a propertied minority. Their possessions, chiefly their tea tray and tea caddy, were not without some pretension to polite forms of sociability. Thus, the poverty of the poor shipwright's house is relative.

Many urban artisans lived in tenement quarters that they shared with others in similar economic circumstances. Rooms taken in houses owned and occupied by women heads of households, such as widows, represented one common rental option. Widow Elizabeth Claxton of Philadelphia, for example, boarded plane maker James W. Massey in the upper rooms of her

A Elizabeth Claxton's House

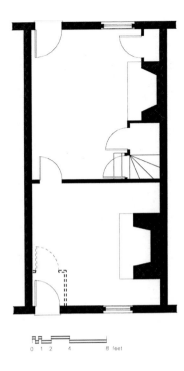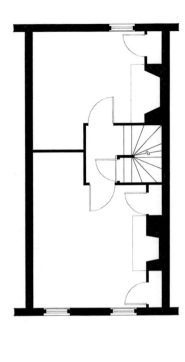

0 1 2   4   8 feet

house on Crown Street, where her daughter Mary Claxton kept a small china
shop in the ground-floor front room (see Figure 6.2). The Claxton house was
one of a row of late-eighteenth-century terrace houses designed with two
rooms on a floor and a cellar kitchen. Spaces like the Claxtons' common
room were home to artisans who possessed little capital greater than their
tools, clothes, and a few personal items packed in a trunk. They were individuals who ranged from older tradesmen eking out a precarious existence
under the supervision of multiple employers to younger, more ambitious
workers beginning their careers.[3]

Other self-styled artisans enjoyed life at the opposite end of the spectrum,
and their situations hold significant caution for constructing generalized
patterns about material life and social status on the basis of occupational
classifications. Langley Boardman, who identified himself as a cabinetmaker, commissioned and occupied a well-finished mansion at the head of
State Street in Portsmouth, New Hampshire; his contemporary, blockmaker
John Leighton, acquired and remodeled an eighteenth-century merchant's
house on Mechanic Street (see Figure 6.3). Their assets exceeded the nominal scope of their craft. Boardman was involved with both international

FIGURE 6.3

Boardman and Leighton Houses, Portsmouth, New Hampshire

A Langley Boardman House (right) (circa 1803–1806), 152 Middle Street

shipping interests and speculative real estate developments throughout the early-nineteenth-century city. Leighton profited as one of the chief rigging suppliers for the shipyards of the fledgling United States Navy. The fine finishes found in their respective houses amplify the paradox between the expression of mercantile aesthetics and the claim of republican virtue based on artisanal identity in the post-Revolutionary United States.[4]

Boardman's and Leighton's less successful peers pursued similar economic, social, and architectural goals—only on a much more limited basis. Thus, two of the houses erected on Portsmouth's Cottars Lane in the first decade of the nineteenth century were speculative efforts undertaken by shoemakers Samuel and Joshua Rand. These houses, built on plans incorporating stair passages, parlors, kitchens, and multiple upstairs chambers, were a far cry from the Grants' Baltimore dwelling. The 1820 street directory for Portsmouth, however, reveals that, while the Cottars Lane houses archi-

B John Leighton House, Corner,
Mechanic and Gardner Streets (right)
(early eighteenth century; remodeled
early nineteenth century)

tecturally projected the image of respectable single-family town houses, they all sheltered additional artisan lodgers in rented rooms. When individuals listed in directories and tax lists for 1820 and 1822 are linked to Cottars Lane, the disproportionate ratio of people to houses becomes evident, as does the interpretive problem of presumptive associations based on looking at architecture without people.[5]

A great many artisans occupied town houses between the extremes of the struggling itinerant lodger and the successful entrepreneur. Their houses and furnishings reflected the situation of individuals who achieved modest levels of material attainment but whose grander economic and occupational ambitions often failed to materialize. What distinguishes this middle ground of artisans' houses is how their residences in plan and finish illuminate an often tenuous grasp on the culture of property and what town houses and their furnishings signified in the early American city.

The study of urban material life through tax lists, inventories, architecture, and objects typically focuses on issues related to standards of living and their reflection of status and class. But the material world is as much about context and appearance as it is about property and possessions. The way things look (appearance) and the ways in which objects stand in relationship to one another in specific settings (circumstance) describe the ways that individuals imagine and represent themselves (comportment) in the complex web of everyday social interaction. The possession of a single artifact may compensate for the presence or absence of the full sets of objects associated with particular forms of behavior: such single objects can signify the associated social sensibilities and behaviors of the larger set. In the absence of a tea set, a tea tray will do; in the absence of a dining service, a dining table will do. Through this lens, the Grants' tea tray and tea caddy ideally exist in a larger imagined assemblage of tea table, tea service, and tea—which they do not own. The presence of genteel possessions in the Grants' house offers no surprise. After all, consumer culture in the early modern world relied on the broadest possible market for luxury goods and people's attachments to their possessions. Our task is to explain how people viewed, used, and valued those objects in everyday life. The web of relationships found in the Grants' Wolf Street town house and its furnishings provides an opportunity to ask questions about what architecture and household furnishings signified rather than what they were worth. The role of objects, specifically buildings, is instrumental in our understanding of how artisans perceived and negotiated their circumstances in status and opportunity. How buildings and objects convey social meaning enables us to recreate a much more dynamic understanding of the past.[6]

The Grants' tea tray and caddy asserted the possession of the social knowledge necessary for their proper use. Still, in a context of genteel prescribed behaviors, the Grants' tea assemblage is incomplete, revealing the tension between knowledge of the forms and rituals of genteel comportment and insufficient resources to fulfill its associated behaviors. Thus, the tea tray works as an emblem for a particular category of social knowledge:

the taking of tea and its attendant rituals. The lone tea tray in the one-story frame house cannot meet the task of acting out the sociability of the tea table as performed in the cosmopolitan parlors of the city's economic and social elite. In the Grants' possessions a gulf lay between the forms and iconography of social knowledge (the world of appearance) and the resources necessary to act on that knowledge (the limits of circumstance). The degree to which the Grants' gentility could be displayed and enacted through the material representation of social knowledge varied according to the situation and the presence of other actors. Accordingly, we could read the Grants' tea tray in a different context that critiques social hierarchies. Through the selective possession and display of symbolically charged artifacts, the Grants and their contemporaries engaged a process of appropriating, recontextualizing, and reinterpreting the material language of gentility into their own cultural system. From both perspectives, the signifying power of the Grants' incomplete tea service was not fixed but depended on occasion and audience. The households of the Grants and many other artisans operated in a fluid urban society where an individual's ability to imagine, recognize, and articulate the materiality of economic and social advancement is significant, particularly when related to the range of material experience within specific crafts.

Artisans' possessions, especially tools, yielded a material competency. As a part of the means of production they were economic capital. But household possessions, in addition to economic capital, signified social capital, an investment in the assertion, acquisition, and display of reputation. In this context, the Grants' tea tray assumes a role comparable to that of the contents of traveling merchants' trunks and the furnishings of captains' shipboard cabins, where key objects, like a traveler's silver service, are brought forth as a visible assertion of rank and status. They demonstrate the requisite knowledge for the successful social use of objects that tested and reflected status. Mere possession, though, did not communicate social rank. Ownership simply represented sufficient means to acquire a constellation of objects that demanded specific forms of social knowledge for their effective use.[7]

Domestic furnishings as a form of social capital in the preindustrial city, then, could serve as social signifiers only through the enacted reality of face-to-face interaction. To own the tea tray assumes social knowledge; to display it presumes an owner and an audience able to access that knowledge; to use the tea tray demonstrates the means to act on that knowledge. The interaction between possessor and audience sets objects in motion, but partial constellations of objects may signify imperfect action or a symbolic reversal where high-status behaviors are ridiculed and critiqued by people routinely excluded because of caste or rank.[8]

Objects represent categories of behavior: what is ideal, what is sufficient, and what is possible. The realization of the ideal through a material sufficiency produces a variety of possible outcomes, not the least of which is the caricaturing and satirizing of the world of manners. Here the demonstration of imperfect knowledge set in play produces an effect opposite to the one desired; the artifacts of gentility reinforce categories of social difference. Nowhere is this more apparent than in the early-eighteenth-century engravings of William Hogarth. Two prints from *A Harlot's Progress* of 1732 make the point (see Figure 6.4). In plate 3, the Harlot takes tea served on a four-legged stool in her chambers just as she is about to be arrested; plate 2 illustrates the bumptious Harlot upending a tea table, sending its accoutrements smashing to the floor. Hogarth's representation of the artifacts of tea compromised and violated signifies an elite view of genteel virtue and its inaccessibility.[9]

In contrast, Hogarth's early contemporary, the poet John Gay, used the moment of tea taking and the setting of the tea table to ridicule elite gossip:

> And now through all the room
> From flow'ry Tea exhales a fragrant fume.
> Cup after cup they sipt, and talk'd by fits,
> For *Doris* here and there *Melanthe* sits.
>
> ·
>
> *Melanthe*'s tongue could well a tale advance,
> And sooner gave than sunk a circumstance.

The symbolic moralizing and satirizing themes announced by Hogarth and Gay in the early 1700s continued with topical variations into the early decades of the nineteenth century. The symbolic possibilities of objects found in the fine arts were very much a part of the everyday. In use, the Grants' tea things provided the opportunity for them to emulate or parody elite manners, but, most of all, they provided the tangible means to make those behaviors part of their own world.[10]

The question emerges just how well the Grants, their house, and the possessions within represent the artisan's world in Baltimore and beyond. The 1799 street directory for Baltimore lists forty-eight shipwrights, shipbuilders, ship joiners, and ship carpenters living in Fells Point—including Angus Grant. Of the thirty-four ship carpenters, one-half are represented in the 1798 tax on buildings and property, and one-half occupied rented dwellings. Architecturally, their circumstance ranged from two comparatively wealthy shipyard owners who occupied two-story houses containing in excess of 2,400 square feet, to fourteen individuals who lived in dwellings that measured between 192 and 600 square feet and stood one to two stories high. Angus Grant and John Sable were at the very bottom of a list where the average house size was 394 square feet. The Grants' dwelling also reflected a local preference (likely based on cost) for wooden houses in a landscape where frame residences outnumbered brick ones by a margin of two to one.[11]

In Philadelphia, poor and middling artisans and mariners composed much of the population recorded in tax lists and directories for the alleys and lanes of Southwark, a neighborhood demographically and occupationally similar to Fells Point. Eleven Becks Alley houses assessed in 1798 ranged from a commodious high of 17 by 25 feet to a low of 12 by 10. Four of the eleven incorporated additional space in the form of attached kitchens, and three more were being enlarged with back buildings that contained provision for cooking and additional upstairs chambers. At least seven of the houses were frame, and all were two stories tall. All but one were owner-occupied, although it is likely that several householders took in renters. In 1813, thirteen individuals listed their address in Becks Alley; ten of these were artisans, including five shipwrights, two carpenters, and a mastmaker, boatbuilder, and blacksmith. Parhams Alley presented a similar aspect with twenty-one properties ranging in size from an 18-by-40-foot building that likely incorporated a pair of town houses to two 14-by-16-foot dwellings. Somewhat larger at an average 308 square feet per floor, the Parhams Alley houses were home, in 1813, to a mix of artisans, mariners, and widows. While the housing for artisans living in places like Parhams Alley suggests a standard for households of modest means, other artisan dwellings represented significantly higher levels of amenity.[12]

The buildings and occupational profiles for larger streets provide an important contrast to the architectural and occupational composition of Southwark's alleys. Forty-two houses were recorded in 1798 on Almond Street, a broad cross street that ran from Second down to Front and the city waterfront (see Figure 6.5). One-half of the Almond Street town houses were brick, and one-half of those were a full three stories tall. The average house contained 369 square feet, but seventeen of the forty-two were significantly

A Plate 2, *The Quarrel with Her Jew Protector* (detail)

FIGURE 6.4
William Hogarth, *A Harlot's Progress* (1732).
Courtesy Colonial Williamsburg Foundation

enlarged through the presence of kitchen ells. Unlike alley lots, the spaces behind the Almond Street town houses enclosed sufficient area for additional buildings like shops and stables. However, the space and elevation of the Almond Street houses were somewhat deceptive when we consider that the 1798 street directory listed twice as many surnames as houses. The occupational profile of Almond Street was distinctively maritime, with one-half of the residents listing themselves as mariners, pilots, and captains. The remaining residents included artisans, merchants, widows, shopkeepers, and laborers. To make determinations of social rank based on the outward appearance and interior appointments of artisan houses is problematic.

Unquestionably, the houses of Parhams Alley and Almond Street were visibly different. When we repopulate those dwellings, however, social distinctions between houses asserted on the basis of appearance erode in the face of the practice of urban living.[13]

By the early 1800s multistory, one-room town houses were a standard option for Southwark's laboring sort. Built in the style of single-family dwellings, these residences typically contained multiple households. The six three-story town houses proposed for Jackson Court in 1829 each contained

a 14-by-15-foot room per floor. The ground-floor room, like the Grants' Wolf Street residence, contained fireplace, stair, and cupboard. Only a single window in the front brought air and light into each room. In 1832 similar off-street tenements were constructed behind a pair of Becks Alley houses. Three stories high, each of these houses possessed cellar kitchens equipped with "mantel shelf and closet under the stairs." The main floor aspired to greater elegance, with the two 14-foot-square town houses invested with "side closet and neat wood mantel, grecian ovolo mouldings and wash-boards." While the presence of cellar kitchens and multiple stories placed these Philadelphia brick houses well above the Grants' single-story frame dwelling, the use of a one-room plan spoke to a common sensibility that conflated domestic life into 196 square feet in increasingly congested urban settings.[14]

The contents of these one-room houses associated with Southwark artisans are reflected in the estates of individuals like Matthew Johns, a hatter, who occupied a 16-by-20-foot "old frame" house on Front Street with his wife, Mary, and six children. In addition to the eight residents, the 320-square-foot dwelling held on the ground floor a dining table, breakfast table, three pine tables, and one-half dozen chairs. The upstairs chamber contained two beds (but only one bedstead) and a bureau. Given the lack of outbuildings or ells in the description of the house, cooking likely occurred in the cellar, as was common throughout eighteenth-century Philadelphia and contemporary English towns and cities. Missing from the Johnses' estate are references to the tools and supplies of the hatter's trade. Like Grant, Johns appears to have worked elsewhere in the city. Also absent from Johnses' estate are knives, forks, spoons, and chairs in sufficient numbers that would have allowed the eight-person household the luxury of individual places and place settings at the table. In the Johns family, as with other poorer households throughout the city, dining occurred in shifts, or with people sharing utensils, or in settings where some folks stood and others perched on window sills or leaned against walls or tables. Like the Grants, though, the Johnses claimed a fragment of material gentility with the possession of dining and breakfast tables, which suggests at the very least a basic knowledge of the trappings of polite sociability, and, with limited seating and cutlery, a reduced means for enacting the associated behaviors.[15]

Directories and tax lists for the Southwark district note the presence of at least thirteen other men employed in the hatter's trade. Scattered through the district, ten of the hatters found their lodgings in other people's houses.

opposite:

FIGURE 6.5

Houses in Almond Street, Southwark, Philadelphia (left, early to middle nineteenth century; right, middle eighteenth century)

A Elevation. *Photo: Historic American Buildings Survey, Library of Congress*

FIGURE 6.6

Thomas Davis Kitchen in Christian Street, Southwark, Philadelphia

Two of the remaining three lived in two-story houses of sixteen by fourteen feet each. The assessors noted one of these houses as a double house, indicating the existence of a second dwelling unit of comparable size and construction. Stephen Pesse owned the largest town house among the hatters—a three-story, eighteen-by-twenty-two-foot dwelling standing on Front Street. Similar in area and elevation, Johns's "old frame" house was inferior in material and condition to the brick residences of his fellow tradesmen. But Johns's house was also different in its lack of additional spaces. Two of the three hatters owning houses carried on their trade in separate shops behind the dwelling, where they practiced the noxious, poisonous arts of the hatter's trade. All three houses included kitchen ells that extended from the back of the house, averaged about eight by fourteen feet, and were two stories in height with shed roofs sloping down to the kitchen dooryard.[16]

The small houses of Southwark's hatters were common fixtures in the community, where the dominant trades were associated with shipbuilding, and the dwellings owned and occupied by shipwrights and caulkers follow a similar pattern of a single room on each floor. The average area of the twenty-six recorded shipwrights' dwellings was 236 square feet, reflecting a range of two-story dwellings from a maximum of 17 by 19 feet to a minimum of 10 by 12. The eleven caulkers fared little better, with the area of the typical house still falling below 300 square feet within a size range of 22 by 20 feet to 13 by 14. The town houses of both groups split about evenly wood versus brick and the presence versus absence of kitchen ells extending from the rear of the house.[17]

The houses that survive tend overwhelmingly to be of brick construction. Their frame counterparts largely disappeared from the late nineteenth through the mid-twentieth centuries, when they were pulled down and replaced with larger, less combustible brick residences. Still, the surviving dwellings suggest a number of problems in drawing conclusions about housing quality based on size alone. As small as these houses might have been, they were often reasonably well finished. Wharfbuilder Thomas Davis, for example, owned a pair of thirteen-by-twenty-foot kitchens built for an unrealized eighteenth-century speculative venture (see Figure 6.6). The 1798 tax assessments record Davis as living in one of the kitchens while renting the other to a shipwright. These kitchen dwellings, however, were far from rough temporary accommodations. Both were finished with plaster, moldings, mantel and overmantel, and paneled doors. Similarly, the two Drinkers Court houses that fronted Delancey Street exhibited fully paneled fireplace walls in the compass of a single-room and kitchen plan (see Figure 6.7). The back buildings in the courtyard, home to a currier, tailor, seamstress, shoemaker, shopkeeper, washerwoman, cook, two mariners, and an accountant, were smaller and not nearly as elaborately finished. Still, they possessed what insurance surveyors would have designated "neat" chimney pieces, a description conveying a sense of modest quality.[18]

The level of interior finish within Philadelphia's smaller houses, many situated in alley developments and home to artisan families similar in wealth and status to the Grants, remained reasonably high into the early nineteenth century. Summers Court, developed at the close of the eighteenth century, consisted of a row of two-story brick dwellings measuring roughly twelve by fourteen feet on the ground floor (see Figure 6.8). The single ground-floor room, which originally served as kitchen, dining, and sitting area, was finished with plaster walls and enclosed stair that led to a second-story chamber, outfitted with a simply constructed mantelpiece with a beaded surround and molded cornice. The same quality of ornament appeared in the three-story, fourteen-foot-square Fitzwater Street houses erected by the Pritchard brothers in the early nineteenth century. Each of the Pritchard tenements received a built-in cupboard, enclosed stair with raised-panel door, and mantelpiece composed of a beaded surround and neoclassical moldings. Both the Summers Court and Fitzwater Street dwellings were home to mariners, clerks, and skilled artisans—including blacksmiths, shoemakers, and engravers. This mix of professions supports the contention that people tended to define their identities, not through their occupations, but through a complex weave of associations and behaviors that engaged all aspects of their everyday lives. Both the quality of the dwellings and the array of trades pursued by their inhabitants describe an urban landscape characterized more by a blurring of social identities than discrete social categories.[19]

Like the Grants' Wolf Street dwelling in Fells Point, the town houses of Southwark artisans most often consisted of a single room on a floor. But, unlike the Grants, Southwark artisan houses had the amenity of a full second story, most often set aside as a best chamber, and often a full cellar, which in many cases contained a kitchen. Small, well-finished houses occupied by artisan households were not limited to Philadelphia and Baltimore. In Whitby, England, eighteenth-century back lot court and alley housing was similar both in size and quality of finish to dwellings like those in Summers Court and on Fitzwater Street. In Linskill Square, two-story brick town

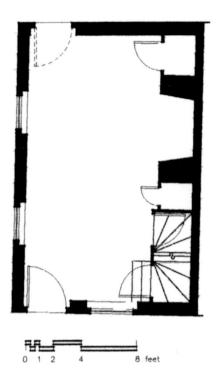

0 1 2   4   8 feet

B Plan. Erected as a service ell in advance of an intended main house that was never built, this building remained a residence for its entire history. *After Historic American Buildings Survey, Library of Congress. Drawn by Jeff Klee*

FIGURE 6.7
Drinkers Court, Delancey (formerly Union)
Street, Philadelphia. *Photos: Philadelphia Historic
Commission*
A Drinkers Court Entry

houses faced each other across a cobbled and guttered court and contained a total ground-floor area of 256 square feet—divided into a large front room and two or three smaller rooms each 6 feet deep and ranged across the rear of the house (see Figure 6.9). A roughly 3-foot-square lobby entry screened access into the 10-by-16-foot main room, and one of the smaller back rooms comprised a small landing and winder stair. Most notable, though, were the molded mantel cornices and paneled partition walls gracing these compact spaces. The even smaller, roughly 14-foot-square dwellings in neighboring Loggerhead Yard display an equally advanced notion of finish with their paneled upper stories (see Figure 6.10). Certainly, architectural details like molded mantel cornices and plain paneling were standardized by the mid-1700s; consequently, as decorative details gained greater circulation, their ability to communicate social difference diminished.[20]

Smaller houses, often built by and for artisan families, emerged as common building forms in towns throughout seventeenth- and eighteenth-century England. In the Trinity area of Frome, a cloth manufacturing town in Somerset that grew dramatically through the eighteenth century, builders erected modestly scaled but well-finished town houses (see Figure 6.11). Anchored by the dwelling of cardmaker Samuel Whitchurch, a row of four three-story stone houses originally consisting of a single roughly ten-by-twelve-foot room continued up Naish's Street. Similar town houses completed the streetscape. The interiors of the Naish's Street houses and others throughout the Trinity area were furnished with large open fireplaces, winder stairs, and paneled cupboards. Similar housing appeared in eighteenth-century Leeds as building clubs strove to maximize profits derived from properties purchased on speculation, in Hull as property owners filled in their back lots, and in Lancaster as builders subdivided older houses.[21]

Artisan dwellings standing two and three stories tall and ranging one or two rooms in depth were a standard element in late-eighteenth-century American port towns like Boston. Furnishing strategies reflected a broadly understood sense of social space. Boston shipwright Joseph Hambury, for example, lived in "a small tenement" in a lane opening into Lynn Street. Three stories tall, Hambury's wooden house contained 266 square feet of living space on each of its floors. Two beds, trunks, a chest of drawers, and a "chamber table" crowded the roughly 14-by-19-foot chamber on the uppermost floor. The principal parlor occupied the second story and was furnished with a desk, tables, chairs, and a seaman's chest. The ground floor, containing worktable, kitchen utensils, tinware, and a straw bed, defined

B First-Floor Interior

C Second-Floor Interior

the everyday nature of the room as kitchen, ordinary dining room, and family sitting room. Joseph Hambury's mahogany desk stands out as the most valuable object in his house. Like the Grants' tea tray, Hambury's desk enshrined a particular category of social capital—in this instance literacy and the means to conduct business within the house in a proper fashion that embraced the exchange relations associated with the trade and social interaction of a shipwright who found employment both in the city's shipyards and on board ships at sea.[22]

Desks appear repeatedly in the inventories of early-nineteenth-century Boston artisans and often represent one of the most expensive pieces of furniture in the house. Housewright William Moore owned and occupied a two-story wooden dwelling in Hawkins Street that included a ground-floor parlor and back kitchen within its eighteen-by-thirty-foot compass. The parlor, which served as a combination sitting and dining room, contained Moore's best table, leather-bottom chairs, silver plate, and china. Moore also furnished the parlor with a desk, globe, and bookcase, a constellation of objects that conveyed cosmopolitan values within the discourse of business that was held in domestic settings.[23]

The presence of desks and related objects in Boston artisan households recurs in estate inventories in other parts of the city. Samuel Aves, a cooper occupying a two-story brick town house located in the North End and abutting his shop on the corner of Salem and Bennett Streets, kept a front room furnished with a desk, his best tables, chairs, china, glassware, and a dozen pictures on the walls. Aves's kitchen, like Moore's, stood behind the front parlor and contained little more than worktables and cooking utensils. Boatbuilder Jeremiah Smallage's house, located in Battery March Street across town from Aves's dwelling, adhered to much the same formula. His wooden two-story house stood in front of two brick-and-frame tenements he owned on Smallage Court and contained a parlor and kitchen on the ground floor and chambers in the second story and garret. The parlor, with its dining table, leather-bottom chairs, and pictures on the walls, presented a familiar material setting for sociability. Smallage also owned a desk. Unlike Aves and Moore, though, Smallage regarded his desk with seeming ambivalence: it represented one of his least valuable pieces of furniture, and it appears to have occupied a spatially ambiguous position between the parlor and kitchen. The desk and its social connotations were clearly visible within the house, but Smallage, more than his peers, struggled with the placement of those objects associated with trade.[24]

FIGURE 6.8

Summers Court (now Beck Street), Philadelphia, Single-Room Houses (late eighteenth century)

opposite:

A Elevation, 207 Beck Street

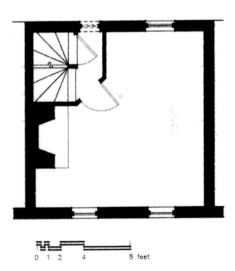

0 1 2 4 8 feet

B Second-Floor Plan. *Drawn by Jeff Klee*

FIGURE 6.9
Linskill Square, Whitby, Yorkshire, England

A Courtyard Elevations

The presence of desks was not limited to Boston's middling artisan households. Merchants, shopkeepers, widows, and clerks were all equally likely to own similar objects. Desks identified particular sets of social relationships centered on intersecting spheres of domesticity, sociability, and commerce within the house. The material culture of business existed in juxtaposition with the objects of dining, vividly revealing a system of linked values like those seen in the fixtures and society of the merchant family's dining room or the respectable widow's dower-divided house. The furnishings of the artisan's parlor, even in one-room houses like Angus Grant's, asserted social knowledge. For the Grants the signification of that knowledge focused on the trappings of tea as a form of social exchange; for Aves, Moore, and Smallage the material equipage for sociability was more extensive and emphasized different categories of exchange-based relationships. While the culture and rituals of sociability were broadly understood in the North Atlantic world, they nevertheless assumed local characteristics and class distinctions.

The investment by householders in the material culture of urban sociability varied according to local preference and practice. In Washington, D.C., brickmaker Samuel Baker occupied a two-story town house with kitchen next to his brickyard—a workplace made up of sheds, kilns, stacks of bricks, and piles of oyster shells for making lime. The precincts of Baker's house ranged from dusty to muddy to smoky, depending on weather and work. Within his modest house, Baker pursued a furnishing strategy comparable to the Grants' in Fells Point. Two prints and a looking glass hung on the walls. Major furniture included two tables, a bureau, cupboard, and settee. A tea tray and two caddies rounded out the assemblage that defined the character of the most public and formal room in the Baker household. Like the Grants, the Bakers invested selectively in display, but with limited means to act on the social possibilities associated with these objects. The pattern holds true for other Washington artisans like builder Jeremiah Hemsworth, whose frame house contained a dozen chairs, desk, two tables, and cooking utensils in its main room. The presence of his teapot and one-half dozen cups, saucers, and silver teaspoons suggests an assemblage sufficient for taking tea in a manner that met the standards of genteel behavior. The household topography where the functions of parlor, salon, kitchen, and dining room converged in a single room, however, inevitably compromised the prescribed propriety of the event.[25]

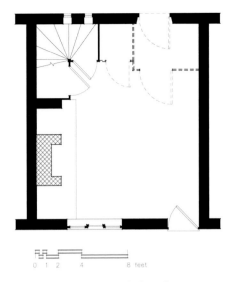

B 3 Linskill Square, Ground-Floor Plan.
Drawn by Jeff Klee

FIGURE 6.10
Loggerhead Yard, Whitby, Yorkshire

A Elevation

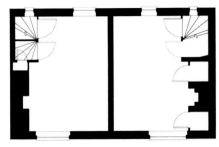

SECOND FLOOR PLAN

0 1 2   4   8 feet

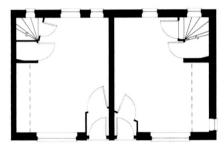

FIRST FLOOR PLAN

0 1 2   4   8 feet

left:

B Second-Floor Fireplace Wall

right:

C First- and Second-Floor Plans.
   Drawn by Jeff Klee

FIGURE 6.11

House of Samuel Whitchurch, Cardmaker,
Naish's and Baker Streets, Frome, Somerset,
England, with Attached Tenements in Baker
Street

In southern seaport cities, like Charleston and Norfolk, the textures of artisan houses and furnishings were complicated further by the presence of a large enslaved and skilled African-American labor force. Although poor white and free black artisans resided in the city, they were a distinct minority. The result was a distorted social and economic landscape with little room for middling artisan families like the Grants. Even the most modest town houses associated with free Charleston artisans tended to reflect a higher standard than those built in other cities. Cooper David Saylor, for example, erected a new house on Elliott Street in 1778 following a fire that devastated the neighborhood (see Figure 6.12). Located just off the city's busy Cooper River waterfront, Saylor's seventeen-by-thirty-five-foot brick house stood a full three stories tall. The first floor of the house was divided into two principal rooms divided by a centrally placed entry and stair to the upper stories. The front room possessed a door providing direct street access and likely functioned as a small shop or counting room for Saylor's business; the smaller back room with its plain beaded mantelpiece appears to have served as a family dining room that possibly incorporated cooking functions. The second floor followed a similar plan with the exception of the addition of a small unheated closet located in the space over the entry and entered from the second-floor front room, which, with its more elaborate interior finishes, served as the "best" room. The second-floor back room and both rooms on the third floor were uniformly finished with plain board mantels and used as family chambers.[26]

The internal arrangement of rooms in urban dwellings like the Saylor House has its parallels in other cities. The kinds of spaces they contain and their functional juxtaposition are redolent of late-eighteenth- and early-nineteenth-century town houses in Philadelphia's Northern Liberties. An early-nineteenth-century residence on Lawrence Street offered a plan where the first-floor front room included a "balk" or box entry—a small, board-enclosed vestibule with glazed shop door—and the back room served as kitchen and dining room (see Figure 6.13). A Philadelphia-style piazza that could be entered either from the outside or from the front room effectively divided the house in the same manner seen in the central entry of the Saylor residence.

The Saylor House also reflects choices less frequently observed in Charleston's surviving artisan houses. More common were dwellings following a pattern of commercial usage that relegated the entire ground floor to business purposes and placed the shopkeeper's parlor, dining room, and

FIGURE 6.12
Saylor House, Elliott Street, Charleston,
South Carolina

A Street Elevation

chambers in the upper stories. Typical examples of this arrangement stand in the nearby Queen Street neighborhood, just up Elliott Street from the Saylor House. Built as a rental property, the Johnson-Poinsett House at 22 and 24 State Street is a late example (circa 1841) that placed a heated shop at the front of the house and a counting room at the back. The stairs to the upper stories occupied one corner of the back rooms and were entered from an unfinished brick passage that divided the two tenements and ran straight back to the yard. In town houses of this type, the placement of service spaces and servant quarters followed Charleston practice and shared the back lot with work yards, shops, and storehouses.[27]

Dwellings where craft and domestic life were combined under a single roof made for snug quarters. John Douglas, a cabinetmaker living and working on Meeting Street with his three slaves, Frank, Abraham, and Sandy, devoted the ground-floor rooms to a showroom, where, at the time of his death, on display were five chests of drawers, two secretaries, a combination secretary and bookcase, three wardrobes, five sideboards, five bedsteads, two sofas, a dozen chairs, a set of dining tables, and a pair of card tables. His shop, equipped with workbenches, tools, and unfinished work, might have occupied either the back room of the house or the building in the yard where he stored his stacks of mahogany, cedar, and pine. Douglas's upstairs rooms reflected a more modest standard of living than that of the clientele suggested by his stock-in-trade. His household furniture included a bedstead and bedding, chest and chamber table, looking glass, and "old" chairs. Eight "pictures" enlivened the plaster walls of Douglas's lodgings.[28]

Blacksmith Aaron Fairchild furnished his house with objects that exceeded the standard in quality, quantity, and value set in the Grants' Fells Point town house but fell below the material threshold of Charleston's well-to-do artisans. The house contained desks, tables, chairs, a settee, and an unspecified assortment of crockery and glass. Like Douglas, the Fairchild family decorated their house with a "lot of Pictures" valued in sum at only $1.50. In a house without tea or card tables, the presence of the settee and art (no matter how slightly valued) on the walls defined a material setting for sociable conversation just as the Grants' tea caddy and tray evoked the setting and site for similar social rituals. Carpenter John Eddy, living on St. Phillips Street located on Charleston's expanding northern edge, invested more extensively in the material culture of gentility but apparently at the expense of a larger array of possessions. Eddy's house was distinguished by the presence of a tea table, a set of dining tables, and little more beyond

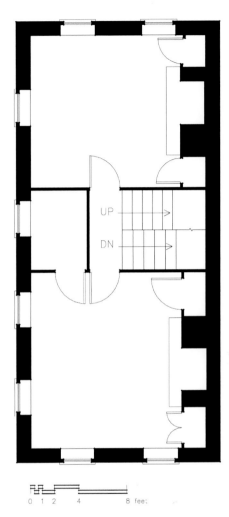

0 1 2 4 8 feet

B Second-Floor Plan. *Drawn by Jeff Klee*

A Street Elevation

FIGURE 6.13

North Lawrence (formerly Crown) Street, Philadelphia

beds, chairs, and chests for storage. While the tea and dining tables identified sites for sociable exchange in the Eddy house, the paucity of smaller objects shaped the context of those exchanges. Absent from Eddy's inventory were valuations for the tea wares or dining service that would have graced the tables of Charleston's more affluent households. Instead, eight wine glasses and a decanter were the objects that set the social rituals of the house in motion.[29]

Like Fairchild and Douglas, Eddy owned a portion of the larger constellation of objects associated with polite social behavior. Like the Grants' tea tray, the importance of those objects resided as much in how they signified particular forms of social knowledge as in how they directed its application in polite society dominated by the art of conversation and the display of manners. Charleston artisans occupying small, modestly furnished houses like the one-room dwelling of Angus and Jane Grant were an anomaly. Even craftsmen of moderate means, like Fairchild and Douglas, owned skilled slaves who completed much of the artisan's work. In these settings, slave-owning artisans aspired to a degree of material gentility that placed them at the threshold of elite sociability and removed them from the workaday world of their craft.

By the turn of the nineteenth century, artisan households defined by the old identity of the master craftsman were giving way to a new one of the businessman. Changes in the organization of craft work and self-perception led these families to acquire and display the material culture of sociability more aggressively. Thomas Baas, a pump-, mast-, and blockmaker on Gillion Street, oversaw a slave workforce that included a carpenter and three pump-makers who conducted the business of fashioning water pumps and ship rigging in a work yard behind his dwelling and in the shipyards on the waterfront. Jean Desbeaux, a cooper residing on Cumberland Street between Meeting and Church Streets, similarly conducted his trade through the "Five Negro Coopers" listed in his estate. But the absence of cooper's tools, stockpiles of materials such as hoops and staves, and completed wares suggests that Desbeaux conducted his craft through the common Charleston strategy of contracting out his skilled slaves, a practice that would ensure his widow Anne Desbeaux a continuing income from the cooper's trade even after the "cooper" was dead. Both Baas and Desbeaux occupied houses where the material culture of sociability predominated. Baas's house displayed the same array of objects associated with merchant family dwellings in Charleston and other cities. Tea, card, and dining tables were prominent fixtures in the Baas household, as was the supporting cast of objects, including silver, glass, and china. The Desbeaux's slightly more modest accommodations strove for the same standard with the same kinds of tables and their associated behaviors reflected in possessions like silver tea and dining service, a "filtering fountain" for the table, and one dozen pictures in frames.[30]

The town houses occupied by Norfolk artisans reflected domestic arrangements in a southern seaport city where enslaved African-American servants performed much of the actual labor. Closest to the furnishings of households like Jane and Angus Grant's were those of poorer artisans like boatbuilder Richard Lewelling, who lived in Catherine Fields on the edge of Norfolk. Lewelling's inventory describes the furnishings of a house composed of two or three rooms that provided spaces for a sleeping chamber, kitchen, and the social and business functions of dining room and parlor. The focus of Lewelling's rooms was the mahogany desk and pair of mahogany tables. Mahogany, an exotic wood closely associated with wealth, linked the furniture to the cosmopolitan tastes and merchant culture of the Atlantic world. The desk, tables, and the family's incomplete tea service (including a canister and sugar box) signified social capital. John Mitchell, a gravestone cutter living in the two-story brick Water Street dwelling he shared with boardinghouse keeper John Stutson, inhabited a similar array of rooms with elements of the familiar assemblage of desk, dining table, pictures on the walls, and tea service.[31]

Accommodations like those of plasterer Finlay Ferguson defined the upper range of Norfolk artisan dwellings and the transition from craftsman to entrepreneur. Ferguson occupied a two-story house consisting in plan of an entry passage containing the stair to the upper story and opening onto two rooms on the ground floor. The family kitchen was located in the back cellar under the dining room, and the lodgings for the family's four slaves appear to have been in the attic and other spaces that defined the margins and interstices of the house. Within his town house, Ferguson furnished the ground floor with the material culture of sociability, including objects related to dining, tea, gaming, and conversation. On the second floor, the best chamber, which occupied the front of the house, served both as Ferguson's chamber (furnished with his bed, bureau, and japanned dressing case) and as his study (equipped with his desk, scientific instruments, and library, including "1 book of plans of Architecture"). Within sight and sound of these polite spaces, Ferguson superintended his plaster shop and work yard behind the house. Here he operated his plaster mill, stored raw materials,

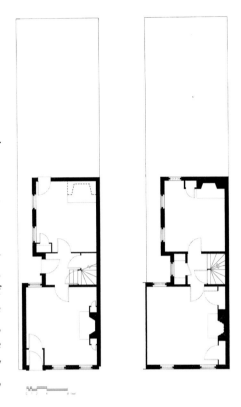

B First- and Second-Floor Plans.
Drawn by Jeff Klee

and stacked scaffolding and architectural fragments. Like Jean Desbeaux in Charleston, Finlay Ferguson nominally preserved his artisan identity even as he and his family acquired the material culture and engaged in the social rituals associated with genteel society.[32]

The houses and furnishings of more affluent Charleston and Norfolk artisans were not unique to slaveholding cities. Philadelphia house carpenter William Palmer shared a three-story town house with his wife, Ann, on Tenth Street near Chestnut Street. Apprenticed to carpenter Joseph Govett in 1787, Palmer made his first appearance in the city's street directories in 1805 when he listed his address in Filbert Street. Six years later the Palmers had moved to Tenth Street, where they occupied a three-story brick town house just four doors below Chestnut and on the edge of the rapidly growing city. After Palmer died in 1815, his wife remained in the neighborhood, moving first to Eleventh Street and subsequently back to Tenth. The Palmers' Tenth Street town house consisted of a ground floor defined by an entry with stair and a pair of back-to-back rooms with the front room serving as the family parlor and the back room as a formal dining area. As in many Philadelphia houses, the kitchen occupied one of the cellar rooms, most likely the rear one under the dining room, and opened into the work yard behind the house. The upper stories of the Palmers' house served as chambers that declined in quality even as they rose in elevation. The best chamber occupied the room above the parlor, and the poorest was located in the garret.[33]

The Palmers perceived the functions of parlor and dining room as flowing together. Their parlor contained a sofa, side table, table glass and decanters, sideboard, and a set of eight windsor chairs; the adjoining dining room was outfitted with a settee, dining and side tables, serving trays, and a portable mahogany desk. Following early-nineteenth-century practice, the two rooms probably could be transformed into one by opening a pair of doors in the partition, and the mantels and trim in the rooms were most likely visually nearly identical. The presence of pier glasses, or mirrors, in each room reinforced the effect of a single, unified space but also signaled the relative qualitative differences between the two rooms. The parlor pier glass set in its gilt mount exceeded by threefold the value of its mahogany-framed dining room counterpart. While the parlor and dining room explicitly displayed the material culture of polite dining and conversation, they only hinted at other forms of genteel behavior such as cards and tea. Still, the Palmers' town house with specific rooms dedicated to the forms of polite behavior described a very different set of living circumstances than Angus and Jane Grant's smaller, more poorly furnished residence. The Palmers and other better-off artisan families clearly demonstrate the problems inherent in defining social groups on the basis of occupation, particularly where factors of mentalité and ambition come into play as in the instance of Philadelphia shoemaker Thomas Rimer.[34]

Rimer, an English immigrant and widower, established himself in the 1790s as a shoemaker working first out of his house and shop on South Second Street near Philadelphia's principal public market and later on Front Street, a block closer to the waterfront but well south of the city center. From 1797 until 1810 Rimer listed himself in city directories as a shoemaker. But, in 1811, Rimer changed his occupational persona to that of "gentleman," a designation that lasted only a year until in 1812 he recast himself as "late shoemaker" or "late cordwainer," an identity he preserved through subsequent listings well into the 1820s, when he ceased to identify himself by his former trade. Meanwhile, in 1816 Rimer set up residence in a two-story brick town house in Carters Alley, located between Second and Third Streets just below Chestnut Street—conveniently situated between the city's thriving commercial thoroughfare to the north and its more fashionable residential areas to the immediate south. Rimer's self-wrought transformation from artisan to gentleman to retired artisan confronts us with the problem implicit in the households of more affluent artisan families like those of the Palmers, the Desbeaux in Charleston, or the Moores in Boston. Rimer wrestled with the means to convey symbolically the substance of his changing and rising status within urban society. For Rimer, as for the Grants, one avenue for the assertion of self lay in the material world.

Rimer's dwelling in Carters Alley followed a standard Philadelphia town house type composed of an entry passage extending past two ground-floor rooms and the stair leading to the upper story before terminating in a two-story kitchen ell. In a street where more than one-half of the eighteen residents registered in the 1825 directory pursued artisan occupations, including carpenter, printer, chairmaker, and shoemaker, Rimer's house asserted his status as an individual of means who had made the leap from tradesman to investor and entrepreneur owning rental property, bank certificates, and insurance company stocks. His house reflected his sense of status. The first-floor front room was set out as an office or study dominated by Rimer's most expensive piece of furniture, his secretary. With its writing surface, bookshelves, and filing slots and drawers, Rimer's secretary made visible the business acumen that informed his success and stood as a model for his less affluent artisan neighbors. In the same spatial gesture Rimer isolated and presented the material culture of business in the most public room in his house and compressed the material culture of gentility (in the form of dining, tea, and other objects of sociability) in the first-floor back room, which came to serve as parlor and dining room in the manner of more middling artisan houses elsewhere in Philadelphia and other cities on both sides of the Atlantic.

What allies Thomas Rimer with Angus Grant is the frame of reference for the presentation of self (or selves) through objects. Despite one fleeting directory listing, Thomas Rimer continually asserted his position within an artisan community. The aspirations to gentility reflected in his self-reference (gentleman) signified both a moment of transformation and its subsequent redefinition within an occupational reference. To be an artisan "gentleman" was an open-ended process defined in larger measure by the skill with which an individual comported himself in the highly competitive world of civility. Bounding the context of genteel behavior by reasserting his occupational identity enabled Rimer to situate his social identity in a context that both was familiar and enhanced his position. Despite his business successes, Rimer remained outside the elite circles of Philadelphia's merchant community. As a retired gentleman shoemaker turned capitalist residing in a street dominated by middling artisan households, Rimer grounded his status in his origins. In this sense, he and other modestly successful artisans established a context for the material culture of sociability that achieved its measure of success in their visible engagement with the material culture of sociability, gentility, and taste. Rimer and his contemporaries were not trying to be urban elites, but they were quick to seize upon the conventions and objects associated with elite culture and use them to position themselves in the rapidly changing world of artisan society.

The same range of artisan houses and furnishings appears in northern New England port towns like Portsmouth. Individuals engaged in shipbuilding and its related trades evince a range of domestic settings, running from modestly furnished one- and two-room dwellings to more elaborately equipped mansion houses. Within that span we discern two expressive trajectories in the artisan house: one defining a broadly constituted material identity at the juncture of middling society and occupational associations, the second revolving around elite claims to artisan identity as a gesture of republican ideology. No single individual more clearly illustrates this duality than Langley Boardman. In 1823, Boardman, who steadfastly identified himself as a cabinetmaker, ranked as one of the ten wealthiest individuals in Portsmouth, with an assessed wealth almost seventeen times the city average. Between 1803 and 1806 Boardman commissioned a three-story frame house on Middle Street at the point where it intersected with State Street, which led inland from the town's commercial center (Figure 6.3A). Assessed at three thousand dollars in 1823, the Middle Street residence stood as one of the thirty-five most valuable privately owned structures in town. With its center-passage plan, elliptical stair, neoclassical detailing, and fine decorative carving (including a parlor mantel elaborated with "sheaves of wheat, central fruit basket, and vine-entwined Ionic columns"), the Boardman mansion represented a category of experience far removed from the material realities of middling artisan households (see Figure 6.14).[35]

Boardman, for all his claims to artisan identity, stood on the economic heights of early-nineteenth-century Portsmouth society. His successes as an enterprising land speculator, builder, shareholder in ships and shipping, and a member of the town elite clearly were manifest through his house in scale, plan, finish, and siting. Boardman selectively asserted his artisanal identity in a manner reminiscent of John Singleton Copley's pre-Revolutionary portrait of Paul Revere in his shirtsleeves, where Revere, politically connected and financially well-off, constructed an image of himself as an artisan in a medium generally associated with elite self-representations. Similarly, the silver teapot Revere cradles in his hand connects him to both the world of craft as maker and to the world of gentility as possessor. Revere, like the Grants in Baltimore's post-Revolutionary decades, does not represent himself engaged in the ritual of taking tea, but simply in the position of claiming possession of its artifacts and customs. Boardman, like Rimer and William Palmer, worked from a similar position, where artifact and knowledge intersected at issues of comportment and identity. In urban settings artisanal culture and identity carried political and economic associations often viewed in counterpoint to mercantile society.[36]

The symbolic associations that charged objects like teapots, dining tables, and desks with meanings far beyond their utilitarian nature were present in the houses of Portsmouth artisans of more modest means, just as they were in other early American cities. Joseph Walker, a caulker who

FIGURE 6.14
Langley Boardman House, Middle Street, Portsmouth, First-Floor Parlor Mantel Detail

owned and occupied "one Half of a Dwelling House" in Congress Street until his death in the 1820s, and Robert Harold, a joiner living in Gates Street in the city's South End at the close of the eighteenth century, illustrate this point. Walker's one-half of a house contained kitchen and chamber spaces and a room that doubled as parlor and dining room. The furnishings arrayed in Walker's best room included a pair of mirrors, serving trays, and three tables—respectively labeled as "common," "dining," and "Pembrock." The tables, albeit slightly valued, still articulate a perceived hierarchy encompassing the utilitarian, the social, and the fashionable in a manner consistent with the furnishings seen in the houses of other artisans such as the residence of Philadelphia hatter Matthew Johns. Robert Harold, like Charleston cabinetmaker John Douglas, occupied a building that contained both residential and commercial functions. His shop containing tools, stock, and unfinished projects such as "16 new Chair frames" and a clock case abutted the lodgings he and his wife, Lilly Harold, shared and furnished. In a street characterized by older wooden dwellings, many following variations on regionally familiar center-chimney New England house types, the interior of the Harolds' residence held the expected range of useful objects, including tables, kitchenware, and seating furniture. Like the Grants in Fells Point, though, the Harolds also possessed fragments of a tea setting, including a "Stand and tea Chest."[37]

The existence of "respectable" artisan houses should not obscure the living conditions of the urban laboring sort. Although their true numbers will never be known, truly wretched accommodations for artisan-laborers existed in every American seaport city at the turn of the nineteenth century. The worst of these houses included tumbledown wooden hovels on back lots, cellar and garret lodgings in divided houses, and cobbled-together dwellings on the city's edge (see Figure 6.15). Some dwellings, like William Butler's Washington "Small frame house" inventoried in 1822 (containing his "lot of old tools and rubbish," "wheel barrow with some old tubs," an old table and two chairs, "with some old boards" and "two old doors out in the weather"), were outside the symbolic threshold of genteel material expression.[38]

And so we return to the Fells Point town house of Angus and Jane Grant. Houses like those of the Grants and their peers, where expressive possibility collides with material actuality, signal the need to look at the contexts of architecture and artifacts for evidence of how people negotiated their lives in multiple, often conflicted, always complex circumstances. In the Grants' dwelling and other artisan town houses like it, public and private bumped against each other in quarters where the material culture of sociability and social ambition were enacted. In an urban world where popular ideologies penetrated into the most intimate precincts of the household, the Grants appropriated elements of prescribed middle-class behavior and made them their own.

THE TRAVELER'S PORTMANTEAU

Far from home, Richard Brush, "late of the Island of Madeira but last residing in Boston, merchant," died. Following the directive of the Suffolk County, Massachusetts, probate court, the assessors of Brush's estate sifted through the contents of his rented room. Like travelers in every port city, the bulk of Brush's portable personal wealth resided in his dressing case, clothing, and gold watch; his business assets included the floating capital of 150 gallons of wine (presumably Madeira) intended for sale and two blank books in which he planned to record his transactions. He also carried his own mattress, a prudent safeguard against the ravenous vermin lurking in lodging bedding. But the deceased wine merchant's baggage also contained other objects that tease the imagination. A case of knives and forks, a pair of candlesticks, two pairs of cups, a set of china, and a fiddle rounded out the contents of Richard Brush's portmanteau. These objects lent the alien room a touch of familiarity and gave at least a faint hint of Brush's social deportment when visitors came calling.[1]

When the Rockingham County, New Hampshire, court probated the estate of Portsmouth merchant Joshua Martin in 1794, it conducted what amounted to a room-by-room inventory of his luggage, which included trunk after trunk of books constituting a personal library composed of scores of volumes dealing with topics ranging from navigation, geography, and shipbuilding to poetry, drama, history, and fiction. His "house" included a large desk, hair trunk, and writing desk furnished with the tools of his trade (blank books, seals, sextant, quadrant, and nautical charts) as well as the badges of status (gold and silver sleeve buttons and knee buckles) and a "quantity of visiting cards" presented in the course of business and social calls.[2]

Thomas Finley, a Philadelphia sea captain, died aboard his ship in Charleston, South Carolina, in 1799. The appraisers dutifully itemized his clothing, including two gold watches with chains hung with "trinkets" and silver and gold knee and shoe buckles. Also packed in Finley's trunks were tools of his trade: quadrant, spyglass, and an optimistically labeled "marooning case." Like Richard Brush, Thomas Finley carried other, more ambiguous objects—one-half dozen silver spoons, a basket of crockery, three bottles of claret, anchovies, ketchup (more like modern Worcestershire sauce), and capers.[3]

Charles Willet's estate inventoried out of his trunk in the port of Norfolk offered a similar array of possessions. Well-to-do and dressed to impress, Willet's wardrobe sported "Cassemere" and "Nankeen" breeches, cravats, linen and flannel shirts, handkerchiefs, hose, hats, gold pin and studs, and gold watch and chain. The projection of fashionability and affluence extended to Willet's japanned dressing case and mahogany shaving case; his knowledge of a traveler's perils manifested itself in his mattress and blankets and pocket pistol. What distinguishes Willet's movable estate, though, is the presence of objects, like those of Brush's and Finley's, that stake a personal claim in temporary lodgings. Packed into Willet's two trunks and carefully enumerated and valued were

1 Plated Tea Pot 7$	1 Cream Pot 1.50$
1 Sett Silver Castors 30$	1 Liquor Stand 5$
1 Plated Tea Caddie 5$	1 Silver S Dish 15$
1 Silver Ladle 3$	6 Silver Table Spoons 15$
10 Silver Tea Spoons 7$50	1 Pr Sugar Tongs 1$50

With his luggage unpacked, Charles Willet furnished his surroundings with not only his sartorial self but also his dressing and shaving cases, tea service, and an unidentified miniature portrait. The silver tea service represented dual capital: first, as pawn in the event of financial crisis; second, as social capital for entertainments conducted in his rented apartment. Like Brush with his china and fiddle, Finley and his condiments and wine, and Martin with his calling cards and library, Willet carried a core group of artifacts that enabled him to convert an ephemeral space into his own domain—expressly through objects that enabled the performance of sociability.[4]

Less fashionably equipped travelers abounded. In the Boston suburb of Charlestown, laid waste by the British during the Revolution and now the home of the Boston Navy Yard, mariner and quarter gunner James Barry packed up his kit. A sailor with the crew of the USS *Alligator,* Barry traveled light. Besides his military dress that included pea jacket, muster frock, duck trousers, cap, shirts, and waistcoat, there was scant room for civilian gear. Civilian mariner Lawrence Lindberg, a Swedish crewman aboard the ship *Richmond* out of Baltimore, fell ill at sea and succumbed off the capes of Virginia. Lindberg, "finding that he was about to die, called on James Melcher one of his brother mariners, and desired him to write a will." He desired that his countryman on board, Andrew Wealstrom, "should have all his estate and effects of every sort." Captain Charles Ween, both master and owner of the ship, interceded and forbade Melcher to copy down the dictated will. The captain then sold several articles of Lindberg's estate to the other mariners on the ship: "Besides the articles herein after enumerated there were many brought out in a large Chest which was full: there were also books of account belonging to the decd. who is understood to have been for sometime a publican and to have kept a boarding House in Savannah, on which books of account large sums appeared to be due." Except for his account books, silver watch, and musket, Lindberg sailed with James Barry's material economy. Working clothes, toiletries such as soap, and bedding, including a hammock, made up the remainder of Lindberg's personal estate.[5]

The Atlantic community of the late eighteenth century was a world in motion. Trading house representatives from Glasgow and London took temporary quarters in coffeehouses, inns, and taverns; Santo Domingan refugees rented rooms in Philadelphia town houses; itinerant craftsmen and unmarried artisans occupied garrets and back chambers in the lanes of Southwark and Fells Point; sailors stormed ashore, duffel bags shouldered, and sought the comfort of Charleston and Norfolk boardinghouses. These travelers held no stake in their rented accommodations, but, in a society where outward show counted for much, the need to create and furnish a personal domain, no matter how fleeting, was instrumental to the expression and presentation of self in foreign circumstance. Sense of self and place bound the traveler to the town house worlds of transatlantic trade and society. Owned or rented, town house spaces intrinsically exerted proprietary airs for those who possessed them. How, then, did travelers imprint their temporary residences with their ephemeral mark? The answer lies in the contents of trunks, duffel bags, sea chests, and portmanteaux, for, even as travelers unpacked their luggage, they unpacked themselves. In the merchant family's dining room and parlor, where visitors like Charles Willet or Richard Brush presented themselves, the spheres of trade and sociability blurred, but the proprietorial advantage always remained with the host. To compensate, travelers packed material markers that would convey their identity and rank in society to strangers encountered on the way.[6]

Delayed in Norfolk, Virginia, on business over the 1809 Christmas and New Year holiday season, merchant Robert McKay wrote home to his wife, Eliza Anne, in Savannah, Georgia, commenting on the unpleasantness of the general city environment on one hand, and the pleasures of polite merchant society on the other. "The Town itself," he remarked, "notwithstanding there are many excellent houses in it, appears to be going fast to ruin." But, as he noted elsewhere, "I wish you could see some of the tables here, loaded with the very best of everything." McKay was particularly pleased with his reception in the household of his chief Norfolk trading contact, merchant Robert Maitland: "In Mr. Maitlands family I am very intimate, and have recd. from him the most and unbounded kindness and attention, I dine there almost every other day and generally call every eveng." McKay's letters point up the scrutiny and invidious comparisons a host could be subjected to by a cosmopolitan traveler. Thus, the portmanteau's contents are paralleled by a set of assumptions carried in the traveler's mind by which he or she evaluated people and places.[7]

What we also detect in McKay's letters are a series of nested landscapes of the merchant family's house and the traveler's sojourn. In his correspondence we discern the difference between a coarse world of mud-clogged streets and the evening society of the dinner table and salon: "I think the people appear to be very hospitable, but [Norfolk] is the dirtiest hole I ever saw, the streets have no pavement and are knee deep in mud." The social meanings embedded and communicated in any one of these landscapes depended on its relationships to the others and to the expectations and experience of individuals like McKay and Maitland. The unpaved street led from the wharves to the damask-covered table set with the best Staffordshire china; the conviviality of conversation and the company of card playing gave measure to the competitive world of trade. The particular society of Maitland's household refracts the whole of mannered Norfolk hospitality.

Moreover, the landscape of conversation and negotiation from tea table to counting house in the world of polite behavior and aggressive trade is ultimately and appropriately material. How could McKay claim a domain of his own? And where? The answer lies in the range of accommodations available to travelers and the personal items they carried in their luggage.[8]

Lodgings varied. Well-heeled travelers took the premium rooms in the best taverns and the new hotels that began to appear in the late-eighteenth-century American urban landscape. Sailors slept in shipboard bunks or preferably found their land legs and headed for the inexpensive boarding-houses scattered throughout the waterfront districts of every Atlantic seaport city. On foot, with little cash or credit, the poor claimed fleeting refuge in doorways and cellars or slept at tables in oyster cellars and grogshops. Some of the "strolling poor" availed themselves of the hospitality offered by city almshouses. There was no single brand of traveler, and there was no encompassing category of lodgings for travelers. Like the owners and occupants of town houses, their architectural experiences defined a spectrum of possibilities, some elegant and some wretched. The experience that unified all peripatetic strangers, though, was the fact of travel itself. These were people away from home for a multiplicity of reasons that ranged from trade to criminal flight who carried their personal households on their backs or in their luggage. In their ephemeral accommodations they faced the challenge of somehow defining architectural space as their own.[9]

Luggage also varied. Some sailors carried canvas duffel bags (the tough fabric resistant to tears and water, their soft forms convenient for stuffing into shipboard lockers). Others ported their possessions in wooden sea chests, knocked together with dovetailed or nailed corners, capped with humped or flat lids (often decorated with popular prints pasted on their interior surfaces), and provided with locks to secure the contents (see Figure 7.1). Other travelers shipped their possessions in hide- or leather-covered trunks, ranging from footlockers to small boxes sufficient for a change of clothes and personal valuables. Ephraim Gilman, the maker of an early-nineteenth-century trunk in Alexandria, Virginia, covered the white pine frame with cowhide, lined the interior with the local newspaper, installed a lock, and decorated the exterior with brass tacks (see Figure 7.2). Smaller leather- or hide-covered trunks of sufficient size for a week's worth of shirts and other clothing defined the norm. The Myers family in Norfolk possessed a large, fancy trunk that stood on short, turned legs and had its smooth, dark, leather exterior ornamented with brass tacks arrayed in a suggestion

FIGURE 7.1

Sea Chest, Camphor Wood (early nineteenth century). *19 x 19 x 35 inches, with dovetailed corner joints, cleats for rope handles, and flanged lid. Associated with the Taylor family of Norfolk, Virginia. Private collection*

right:

FIGURE 7.2

Traveler's Chest (early nineteenth century). Attributed to Ephraim Gilman, Alexandria, Virginia. *Courtesy The Winterthur Library, Decorative Arts Photographic Collection*

of neoclassical floral swags—a motif applied in composition ornament to mantels in the family's urban mansion (see Figure 7.3). Other well-to-do travelers invested in portable writing boxes or trunks that opened up as compact dressers and writing desks, luggage designed as much for personal display as convenience. More utilitarian and considerably cheaper were bandboxes covered with marbleized or printed papers and split-oak or willow baskets.

Into trunks, baskets, and bags, travelers packed the belongings that sustained them on the road. Thomas Cooper's late-eighteenth-century epistolary guidance for what genteel male shipboard passengers should pack codified standard practice. Beginning with bedding (feather beds in winter, mattresses in summer) and linen, Cooper itemized clothing and personal items. "In spring," he wrote, "provide yourself with a cloth jacket and trowsers; in summer you should have two or three nankeen or other light jackets, and three or four pair of cotton or linen trowsers." A week's worth of clothing included "two or three shirts, two or three pair of stockings, two or three handkerchiefs, and a towel or two." The well-prepared carried filtering stones or charcoal for purifying water (a basic supplement to medicines targeted for gastrointestinal complaints), "glasses . . . and crockery" to set a table, and "books, and cards, and chess, and draughts" to relieve the tedium of travel and furnish the means for play and conversation. Cooper concluded, "I think the best general rule is to take whatever you can pack up in a box, or a chest, keeping an account of the contents." And, on the basis of their inventories, this is what Richard Brush, James Barry, Lawrence Lindberg, and Charles Willet did.[10]

Every seaport city and inland town possessed its share of rental lodgings to which travelers repaired with luggage in hand, borne on the buckled backs of porters, or piled in rattle-wheeled handcarts. Taverns and inns answered the demand for immediate short-term accommodations where several guests might share a room or even a single bed. Out-of-town sojourners who anticipated longer stays sought residence in boardinghouses, which offered the possibility of a more or less private room and a rising standard of amenity through the early nineteenth century. By 1830, better-off travelers could book a furnished suite of rooms including a bedroom and parlor or sitting room. The boardinghouse environment was experienced by a Connecticut politician residing in the nation's new capital in a house where he shared a room with another lodger. Along with the seven other renters, he enjoyed the use of a parlor that served as both a dining and reception room. Other Washington, D.C., rentiers, like Mrs. Thomson, residing in one of the "Six buildings" that were "nearly in the Style of the London Houses," offered more elaborate lodgings to those with the taste and budget for roomier, more fashionable accommodations (see Figure 7.4). A visitor recounting the quality of his surroundings "rented 'a very respectable parlour with bedroom' on the second and one of the 'two bedrooms and a bed Closet' on the third as a 'business room.'" These lodgings echoed the number and types of rooms individuals like Benjamin Franklin rented in the English metropolis two generations earlier.[11]

Benjamin Franklin occupied a suite of rooms in London in widow Margaret Stephenson's Craven Street house from 1757 to 1762. The widow's dwelling followed a conventional Georgian town house arrangement with an entry opening onto a passage containing the main stair. Two rooms stood to one side of the stair, and a third, much smaller room extended off the back of the main block. The three-story house incorporated a cellar kitchen and servants' hall and a second-floor parlor. Franklin's rental agreement gave him the entire second floor except the entry, which he shared with the widow and her household. Franklin's servant lodged two floors above in a garret chamber. Franklin, who possessed no share in the kitchen, apparently contracted for meals with his landlady (a common practice in cities)

FIGURE 7.3

Sea Chest Associated with Myers Family. Camphor wood, 26 x 24.5 x 41 inches, bound in brass with brass handles, double-flanged lid. The Myers sea chest is particularly elaborate, with equal concern given to making the chest watertight and suitable for display with its brass studded swags and turned feet.
Courtesy The Chrysler Museum, Norfolk

FIGURE 7.4

Plan and Elevation of Town Houses in
Washington, D.C. (late eighteenth century).
By John Nicholson. Similar in form to the "Six
buildings" where Mrs. Thomson rented out
rooms to lodgers. *Courtesy the Philadelphia
Athenaeum, Philadelphia*

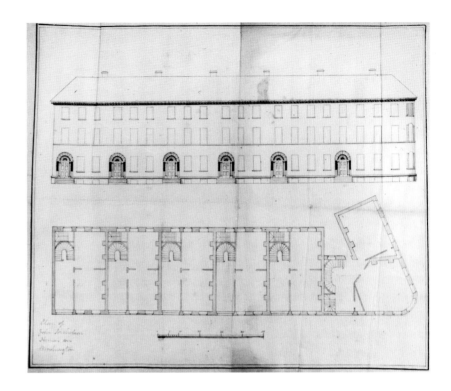

or dined out. Stephenson retained the first- and third-floor rooms and the remaining rooms in the garret and cellar as her own. Placing the inhabitants of the house in motion evokes a sense of the public character implicit in divided houses. Just as Benjamin Franklin and his visitors trooped past the widow's lodgings in her London town house, Stephenson intruded on the business and lodging of her tenant as she made her way to her second-story rooms. But Stephenson's and Franklin's lives were not so segregated as we might imagine. Franklin's informality and Stephenson's hospitality produced a degree of intimacy between the two households residing in the single house. Still, the etiquette of rapping at doors, the temptation for eavesdropping, and the easy familiarity obtained between lodger and landlady is all but lost to modern sensibilities.[12]

Ordinary town houses of varying quality provided the setting; how they were occupied determined their meaning. In the case of Mrs. Thomson's six buildings and Franklin's apartments, the setting conformed to an up-scale row house tradition that included cellar service, ground-floor rooms dedicated to sociability, and upper-story chambers. The key element in the organization of the building lay in the proprietors' claims to their own space. Some established their position, socially and physically, as secondary to their guests by taking the rooms at the back of the house. Other boarding-house operators in Washington and other cities chose the opposite option, claiming the best rooms in the house. The domestic setting of Washington boardinghouses also highlighted notions of passable comfort. Guests slept on "field beds" with curtains, an amenity that may refer more to the protection provided by mosquito netting in the miasmatic morass of Washington's nascent urban landscape and less to a delicate sensibility focused on privacy. Guests also doubled up in rooms and shared a kind of social commons defined by parlor and dining room. Meals in many Washington boardinghouses were served family style and at set times. Finally, boardinghouse keepers furnished their rooms—but only to a limited extent. The number and quality of furnishings might have increased over time and varied with individual circumstance, but they were invariably limited and anonymous. The lodger, whether letting rooms for the long term or just passing though town, carried personal objects that augmented the impersonal furnishings. Colonizing rented spaces with their own furnishings, they achieved some greater measure of psychological and physical comfort.[13]

Although accommodations ranged from a single room shared by several strangers sleeping on cots to a suite of rooms occupying an entire floor in a family's house, boardinghouses held several features in common. They were town houses where travelers could establish themselves away from home. Offering the occasional meal, they held out the possibility of a surrogate family of sorts. In early-nineteenth-century Charleston, Jehu Jones, an African-American tailor and landlord, operated a genteel boardinghouse for travelers in a former town house erected between 1772 and 1774 by a wealthy white merchant. The interior of the frame building, which followed the conventions of the Charleston single house, included an elaborately paneled drawing room with a rococo fireplace wall at one end and a projecting porch alcove lit by a Venetian window (see Figure 7.5). Thomas Hamilton extolled the cosmopolitan virtues of Jones's accommodations:

> Every Englishman who visits Charleston, will, if he be wise, direct his baggage to Jones's hotel. It is a small house, but everything is well managed and the apartments are good. Our party at dinner did not exceed ten, and there was no bolting or scrambling. . . . The pleasure of getting into such a house,—of revisiting the glimpses of clean tablecloths and silver,—of

FIGURE 7.5

Jehu Jones Boardinghouse, Charleston, South Carolina (circa 1774), Best Room Interior. Now installed in the Winterthur Museum as the "Charleston dining room." *Courtesy The Winterthur Library, Winterthur Archives*

exchanging salt pork and greasy corn cakes, for a table furnished with luxuries of all sorts,—was very great.[14]

Hamilton's remarks highlight two elements of his experience: the qualities of Jones's hotel as a house and the improvement over other dining experiences. The general prospect of that meal and its presumed fellowship left something to be desired. A Frenchman visiting Norfolk in 1816 observed:

> One has no suspicion that he has a lodging convenient for a traveler and a decently served table. Dinner lasts about ten minutes; not a word is said during it. Evil-looking ham and boiled corn are the delicacies, and for drink you have water mixed with brandy. The diners get through in a flash. Each one arises and scuttles up the stairs four at a time.[15]

Although after-dinner conversation seems to have been far from the minds of the Norfolk diners, the practice of a shared sitting room or parlor potentially extended the possibilities for the sociability between guest and household. Money also procured the commodity of hospitality in the sense that landlords and especially landladies would contract with their lodgers to help in the entertainment of guests, providing viands and service.

The boardinghouse experience was, of course, never uniformly one of pleasant, comfortable surroundings, happy sociability, and accommodating host families. Englishwoman Ann Ritson moved to Norfolk with her husband in the early 1800s. Arriving in the city, they were compelled to rent rooms as they went about the business of searching for more permanent accommodations. Ritson's poetical critique of their first temporary lodgings began with a description of their rented rooms:

> IN Norfolk meaning to remain,
> We try'd a dwelling to obtain;
> But houses being few for rent,
> We were with lodgings first content;
> And took two rooms near Market-Square,
> Dirty enough indeed they were;
> Five windows in one room were plac'd,
> And three with light the other grac'd,
> Pouring in full the blaze of day,
> Which plainly told—no tax to pay,
> For heav'n's gay sun-shine, or the bright,
> But milder beams, of Luna's light;
> Two days we'ad in our lodging been,
> And thought it tolerably clean.

All too soon, however, a war with the "chintze bugs" that infested their rooms tested the Ritsons' mettle.

> The weather cold, I did desire
> They'd make a brisk and cheerful fire;
> When looking on the white wash'd wall,
> Something, I thought, appeared to crawl;
> But not attending, thoughtful sat,
> Reflecting on my varying fate,
> How distant from my native shore,
> And doubts that I should see it more:
> Caus'd me to heave a pensive sigh,
> The moist'ning drop just fill'd my eye:
> It did not fall, but dim'd the light,
> And threw a cloud across my sight;
> Which drawing with my hand aside,
> I thought I on the wall espy'd
> Innumerable insects move,

And swiftly o'er the white-wash rove;
I look'd, and thought my sight not clear,
So left my seat, approaching near,
They look'd like bugs, but could that be,
Where so much light and air was free;
I must be wrong, for it's allow'd,
Of cleanliness they're very proud;
Surpris'd, I for the mistress call,
Who own'd this live and moving wall,
She at my questions look'd around,
And soon the marching army found.
"O! ma'am, they're chintzes," she did say:
"Chintzes," said I; "pray what are they?"
"They're insects, ma'am," she coolly said,
"Who trouble us sometimes in bed;
This room has not been us'd for years,
As evidently now appears;
The fire you've lit has brought them out,
You'll quickly conquer them no doubt;
Just get some lime, and wash the wall,
'Twill shut them in, their nits and all."
"O! then they're bugs; dear madam, pray,
Do they run always in this way?"
"Not quite," said she, "for spring and fall,
We plaster them within the wall."
So careless down again she went,
When I, determin'd and intent,
My enemies will speed to kill,
Approach'd them with a right good-will;
A bason in one hand I kept,
And with the other gently swept
The fathers, mothers, grandsires, all
The num'rous progeny did fall,
Into the bason, where I'd got
Some water, very scalding hot;
When all the families I'd caught,
There was hundreds, it was thought;
The rooms were clean'd, and seem'd to be

From all the crawling vermin free;
Which, when I first the chintzes view'd,
I thought indeed they never could.[16]

The landlady's engagement with her tenant Ann Ritson over the infestation of chintzes and how they should be vanquished extended only to advice and instruction. Anything more, and the Ritson household was clearly on its own. Ritson's panegyric universalizes the negative experience of temporary lodgings. Rented rooms and their basic furnishings set the stage, but it was the lodgers who, with attention to cleanliness and personal effects, made these fleeting interior landscapes their own. Thus, Ritson's poem speaks to the anonymity of rented rooms and the conflicting values that individuals brought to those spaces.

Lodgings for travelers in taverns, inns, and boardinghouses were a familiar element in the urban landscape. Tavern and inn signs hung from the fronts of buildings like wooden armorial banners and proclaimed the names of premises in both word and image. As part of the urban landscape these signs were a visual conversation between traveler and potential landlord. A generic pictorial vocabulary like the sign of the Hand, Sugar Loaf, Ship and Castle, Pewterplatter, and Horse and Groom reflected standard images, as did signs with European associations such as Prince Frederick, Thirteen Cantons, Prince of Wales, Highlander, and Queen of Hungary. Provincial culture cultivated its own visual cues in regional landscapes like those surrounding Philadelphia and was captured in the signs of the Friends and the Connestogoe Wagon. With a visual lexicon ranging from loaves of sugar to military heroes, signs appropriated the hatchments of "aristocratic" families to proclaim a more plebeian public authority (often suggesting partisan associations) at the street to an audience that easily deciphered the imagery displayed but just as often could neither read nor write. Boardinghouses, usually located in a private dwelling, lacked the signboards that decorated tavern facades. Still, street directories for cities up and down the Atlantic seaboard record the names and addresses of the individuals and families who ran these premises and provide a sense of their numbers and the varied comforts they offered.[17]

Baltimore's Fells Point district contained more than eighty taverns, inns, and boardinghouses in 1804, with one of every four situated on Bond Street. Ranging in quality from John Barnard's imposing brick tavern encompassing well in excess of 1,000 square feet in each of its two stories, to the tight fit offered in Widow Wilson's 18-by-20-foot wood residence, Fells Point visitors found their bed and board in a cross section of the district's town house stock. The three Bond Street boardinghouses identified in the 1798 direct tax conformed to the general residential stock of the larger community. Built of wood, typically frame construction clad with beaded weatherboard, the three buildings ranged in area from 360 to 600 square feet. Only one of the three stood more than a single story tall and was owner occupied. Inferior accommodations placed the lodger in the same room with the family and other renters for eating, sleeping, and domestic socializing. The best situations afforded by these small boardinghouses might have provided a second room, affording a lodger some measure of privacy.[18]

The same range of buildings, each conforming individually to local architectural practice and the sojourner's expectations, defined the traveler's landscape in other early American cities. As an alternative to the large and stylish taverns situated on Philadelphia's main streets, impecunious travelers found a host of more modest accommodations in the city's side streets and alleys. In Southwark, Mary Edgar provided room and board in her rented seventeen-by-thirty-foot, two-story brick house. A piazza containing the main stair and a kitchen wing significantly augmented Edgar's premises. Her boardinghouse belonged to the better class of the city's middling residences. Far more humble, though, were the accommodations Jemimah Dorsey offered in her family's Pewterplatter Alley lodgings. Dorsey's house measured a scant sixteen by twenty-three feet and likely consisted of no more than a single room in each of its two stories, with the kitchen placed in the cellar and additional, possibly unheated lodgings in the garret. In 1810 Dorsey's boardinghouse was home to four men between the ages of twenty-six and forty-five and three women (a young girl and two older women). Boston boardinghouse keepers offered the same range of options defined at one end by the precursors of the hotel and at the other by the legions of rooms set aside in private town houses like Rebecca Kindness's two-story brick dwelling on Fish Street or in lighterman Ezra Gardner's two-story frame house on Cross Street. Essentially town houses with rooms or, more precisely, cots and beds to let, the boardinghouses of Kindness and Gardner, like those of Edgar and Dorsey in Philadelphia, consisted of one or two rooms on a floor and the comfort of living in a household.[19]

But what did taverns and boardinghouses look like, and how were they furnished? Late-eighteenth- and early-nineteenth-century boardinghouses, regardless of quality, were typically town houses divided into rented rooms.

Purpose-built boardinghouses would not become a common fixture in the urban landscape until the mid-1800s. Taverns, however, were often designed with their function in mind. In the most elaborate of these, travelers could expect to find barrooms, assembly halls, and dining rooms. Still, with the exception of a handful of hostelries, travelers found their accommodations in buildings designed around local town house types. The Man Full of Trouble in Philadelphia presented the same two-story brick face to the street as its neighbors (see Figure 7.6). The exteriors of larger, three-story buildings such as the taverns that anchored the Front Street end of Almond Street were indistinguishable from their residential neighbors in all but the signage that advertised their presence. The Pink House in Charleston, the King's Head Tavern in Boston, and similar small-scale establishments in other Atlantic seaboard cities generally followed the precedent of time and place (see Figure 7.7). Furnishing was similarly houselike. Additional beds, cots, and mattresses inventoried for boardinghouse keepers' estates and the archaeological evidence of glassware, ceramics, and foodways posit the domestic face of table and chamber.[20]

Operating a boardinghouse remained one of the more lucrative enterprises open to women, and especially to widows carving out a measure of economic independence. In the English port of Hull, twenty victuallers operated taverns in the city's Humber Ward that defined the working urban waterfront. One-quarter of these establishments, bearing names such as Sailor's Return, Sir John Falstaff, and the Golden Cup, were operated by women, sometimes in concert with their husbands. In London, widowed, unmarried, and married women as well as families managed their town houses, renting a room or even an entire story in their houses to lodgers, typically preferring single men over families to the point of lowering rents or suggesting the common practice that two men double up and share the accommodation of a single bed.[21]

Wills made by husbands and dower laws that specified a widow's life right in the couple's real estate in the early American city held the town house as an asset partaking both of equity and of capital capable of yielding sufficient income. In Boston in 1800 slightly more than one-half of the boardinghouses listed in the city directory were run by women. In the Southwark district of late-eighteenth-century Philadelphia, women oversaw the handful of boardinghouses; in Charleston, women ran two-thirds of the city's listed boardinghouses in 1803. A generation later, in 1823, the proportion of Charleston boardinghouses operated by women stood at 50 percent.

FIGURE 7.6

Man Full of Trouble Tavern, 127 Spruce Street,
Philadelphia (circa 1760s)

A Elevation. *Historic American Buildings Survey,
Library of Congress*

The fact that so many boardinghouses were operated by women, many of them widows, letting rooms and beds in private houses, suggests that those listed in street directories and tax lists represented only a fraction of the accommodations householders offered in their dwellings and used to supplement their incomes. In Portsmouth, New Hampshire, street directories and tax lists explicitly identify only two boardinghouses and three taverns. The scores of women listed only as "widow," however, surely used their houses, whether by legacy or dower, to lodge travelers and supplement their incomes. Still, the numbers of boardinghouses yield little impression about the range and quality of lodgings they contained.[22]

The inventories of three Charleston women, each of whom listed herself as a boardinghouse keeper in the 1803 city directory, reflect the extent of accommodations found in the poorer boardinghouses in early American seaport cities. Jane Hagarthy boarded travelers in her Champney's Alley house as part of an economic collaboration with her husband, owner and captain of the schooner *Two Sisters*. The amenities of Jane Hagarthy's premises were basic. Three cots and mattresses along with an additional bed or two provided her lodgers with a place to bunk, store their gear, and take meals with the household. Mary Hughes offered modest lodgings in the house she owned on leased land. The "4 feather Beds, 6 Bolsters, 8 pillows, 2 Bedsteads, 4 Cots" along with "3 Matrasses, 2 Pavillions, 3 pair Blankets" supplied the basics. Hughes's more astute or better-equipped clientele avoided bedbugs and fleas by rolling out their own mattresses on the owner's cots. All of them would have kept their possessions in their own trunks, chests, and duffels. Jane Boyle addressed herself to the needs of a different custom. Keeper of a ladies' boardinghouse, she equipped her house with three feather beds (one apparently reserved for her own use) as well as an extensive supply of bedding, including sheets, blankets, bedcovers, and bed gowns. Boyle expected her ladies to supply their own pillows. Besides beds and linens, Boyle also provided an environment that included chests and trunks for storage and chairs and tables for dining and conversation.[23]

Far from sumptuous, especially by Charleston's cosmopolitan standards, these three boardinghouses were distinguished further by the absence of slaves. In a city defined by its African-American majority, the boardinghouses of Boyle, Hughes, and Hagarthy were all operated by Irish-American women apparently without the aid of servants. They were all contained in the smaller, less elaborate town houses occupied by the city's less-affluent residents, one- and two-room dwellings now largely vanished from the Charleston landscape but still represented in the maritime neighborhoods

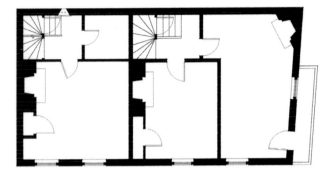

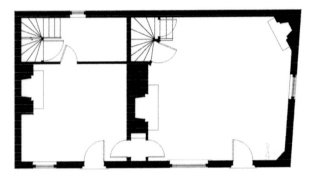

B First (bottom)- and Second (top)-Floor Plans. After *Historic American Buildings Survey*, *Library of Congress*. Drawn by *Jeff Klee*

FIGURE 7.7
Pink House, 17 Chalmers Street,
Charleston (circa 1712, with multiple
changes). Photo: *Historic American
Buildings Survey, Library of Congress*

of Philadelphia and Baltimore, Hull and Bristol. Their clientele expected only a modest level of convenience and little of the fashionable affectations that marked the accommodations and society of Charleston's bigger hostelries.

The luxury of a rented room and the cost for an evening of genteel entertainment exceeded the means and desires of the majority of travelers. Taverns, typically town houses with their interiors furnished as drinking and lodging rooms, met the needs and expectations of those who socialized in more modest ways. James Bickerton, a Philadelphia ship joiner, kept a tavern in his two-story brick house located in a largely undeveloped section of the city's southern suburb, Southwark. The house, standing amid vacant lots and new construction, contained two rooms on each floor and a wash-house in the backyard. The furnishings of the public front room inspired little confidence in visitors seeking a higher measure of civility and comfort. A broken cast-iron, ten-plate stove seeped smoke into a room crowded with five cheap pine tables and "four boxes with seats" for a clientele that likely found it more reassuring to stand. One end of the room contained the bar, a framed grillwork cage for storing and dispensing liquor, where Bickerton kept his spirits, "suppos'd to be 9 gal," and half a barrel of beer, pewter mugs, some decanters, and "china and Glassware." The kitchen behind the taproom and bar offered relative comfort with two tables surrounded by seven chairs. Low-grade crockery and cheap china graced a table that stood a few feet from the hearth, where the clatter of cooking and the stinging smell of grease and smoke gave the room a particularly homey feel.

The best room in the Bickertons' hostelry occupied the second floor looking out over the ragged landscape of a Philadelphia very much a work in progress. Also heated with a ten-plate stove and arrayed with three tables (one of walnut), nearly a dozen chairs, a settee, and the luxury of curtains for the windows, the second-floor room exuded the quality of a best apartment reserved for company and special occasions. For overnight accommodations, paying guests climbed the winder stair that corkscrewed up through the house to the garret filled with beds of varying quality, ranging from the deluxe, two feather beds, to the budget, one "cattale" bed. Also packed into the garret, a room sweat-drenching hot in the summer and bone-cracking cold in the winter, was household surplus, including sundry clothing and the Bickertons' "sign" that had broken free of its moorings outside their establishment.

As for the Bickertons, they appear to have lived in comparative luxury crammed into the "Back Room up Stairs." The elegance of their mahogany furniture, including four chairs, stand, and dining table, distinguished this space as the family's private parlor; the presence of the best feather bed, bureau, and a chest full of clothing stated the function of family chamber and dressing room. Seen in the overall scheme of the house, the Bickertons' upper-story chamber located above the kitchen describes a particularized use of a standard urban house type that lined the streets of eighteenth-century Philadelphia's middling neighborhoods. With its tavern and boardinghouse functions packed into the first- and second-story front rooms and the garret and spilling over into the kitchen, the Bickertons' town house left little room for the householder's personal use. Only the second-floor back room with its collapsed functions of dining room, sitting room, and chamber remained their exclusive domain. Like many working households where food preparation composed part of the family's business, the Bickertons' kitchen doubled in its functions of providing for both household and guests.[24]

Inventories record similar situations in other cities. René Godard, a Charleston innkeeper, ran a business that combined a dramshop with modest lodgings. Although the plan of the house remains uncertain, the number of rooms and their furnishings suggest a building not unlike the Bickertons'. The first room listed contained a pine table covered with a green woolen cloth and eight "very common" chairs, and the second room and its closet held only a pine chest and a keyless trunk filled with odds and ends of clothing. The spare, rough furnishings placed in these two rooms announced a pattern that ran through the house. A pine table and canopy bed were the sum contents of one room, a bedstead and two mattresses furnished another. Lacking a designated bar, Godard lubricated his customers with gin and "very common Liquors" dispensed from a storeroom seemingly attached to the house. Godard served meals prepared in the separate kitchen standing in the yard on a selection of "Several Pieces of Dutch Ware as Plates, Dishes etc." Godard lacked even the comfort and refinement the Bickertons managed to compress into a single room. Both Godard's and the Bickertons' taverns represented one alternative on an open-ended scale of amenities. Town houses routinely found use as boardinghouses, with the proprietors occupying one or two rooms and renting the rest to a clientele whose stays ranged from overnight to longer sojourns that sometimes stretched into weeks or even months.[25]

Insurance surveys for several of Norfolk's fifty boardinghouse and tavern operators yield a refined picture of the range of temporary urban lodgings. Smaller premises like those operated by the Bickertons abounded. Samuel Higgins owned one of several lodging houses and taverns along Woodsides Lane, a side street that ran from the city waterfront up to Main Street. His two-story frame building likely contained two rooms on a floor, with one used as a taproom furnished with an enclosed bar. Down the street, William Baldry rented rooms to travelers in his three-story wooden building that looked out over the corner of Maxwell's Lane. In both these situations landlords provided a room that served as little more than a sleeping chamber where overnight guests often shared their beds.[26]

Prosperous travelers with a taste for exclusivity, privacy, and the replication of a more refined home environment could find suitable accommodations in the best taverns or in rented rooms in fashionable houses. An extended sojourn might have led travelers to choose a boardinghouse or rented rooms over a tavern, but the satisfaction of their social expectations and self-perceived status was paramount. Jane Patterson let rooms in her three-story frame premises on Norfolk's Main Street. The forty-by-twenty-eight-foot structure with its cellar kitchen was sufficiently large to contain four rooms and a passage on each floor. With service in the cellar and dining room and parlors on the ground floor, Mrs. Patterson rented rooms in the upper stories, where she also maintained her own quarters. The largest and most elegant of the Norfolk establishments, though, was the Eagle Tavern operated by Martha Street in the large building that she rented on the corner of Market Street and Kelly Lane in the city center. In 1796, Martha Street published a notice proclaiming her "sincere thanks to her friends and the Public in general" and concluded by advertising that her enterprise was "now furnished with the best of Liquors and good attendants for those who please to favor her with their custom." An insurance survey made at the same time recorded a three-story wooden Tavern" measuring thirty by fifty feet along with a separate billiard house, kitchen, barbershop, and back tenement.[27]

The rooms within the Eagle Tavern were furnished to meet the needs and desires of the better sort of traveler. Twenty-five beds, an assortment of mahogany tables and looking glasses, and window curtains equipped the upstairs chambers. The absence of all but a single mahogany chest of drawers suggests that guests lived out of their luggage—a practice that enabled them to secure their possessions in rooms shared with fellow lodgers. The ground floor of the Eagle Tavern presented the material culture of sociability found in the town houses of Norfolk merchant families—card and backgammon tables, extensive dining service, and teaware. At least one of the ground-floor rooms served the familiar functions of a barroom furnished with windsor chairs and six small pine tables. A seventeen-by-twenty-four-foot billard room and a similarly sized kitchen, both built of wood and standing behind the premises, supported the pleasures of Martha Street's establishment. The scale of cooking and dining at the Eagle Tavern was reflected not only in the furniture within the building but also in the contents of the kitchen with its multiple dutch ovens, roasting spits and racks, gridirons, pots, kettles, and pudding dishes. Slaves Nancy, Dinah, Polly, and William composed the staff of "good attendants," and Martha Street provided each servant with a lantern for lighting the nocturnal paths between the kitchen where they worked and lived and the house that they served.[28]

Akin to Martha Street's Eagle Tavern was Edward McCrady's Charleston tavern and its associated "long room" on East Bay Street and Unity Alley and facing the Cooper River wharves (see Figure 7.8). Like the Eagle Tavern, McCrady's establishment was a compound of multiple structures. The main building facing East Bay Street consisted of a center-passage-plan town house; the main stair was tucked into an ell placed at right angles to the entry, partially sheltered under a piazza and an adjoining arcade, that ran through the building and effectively connected the public street to a private courtyard. The main floor of the East Bay Street building presented an arrangement of three heated rooms with a fourth unheated space located behind the stairwell in an arrangement seen in the city's mid-eighteenth-century merchant houses where counting rooms and offices stood in close association with parlors and dining rooms. Behind the East Bay Street town house stretched a range of buildings designed around entertainment and service. Immediately to the rear of the house stood a strategically placed storehouse and pantry that abutted a two-story, *L*-shaped building with ground-floor kitchens served by two chimneys, an open arcade with two privies shoved into the back corner, and a broad stair running up to a "long spacious room." The long room was an architectural feature associated with the best establishments. Designed as a space for public and private assemblies, McCrady's long room and others like it in cities on both sides of the Atlantic provided a stage for the public sociability of both locals and strangers.[29]

Beef, mutton, and a variety of dishes concocted from local seafood and game (including venison, turtle, oysters, crabs, wildfowl, and fish like red and black drum and sheepshead) were the mainstays of McCrady's menu.

Diners availed themselves of McCrady's stock of beer, wines, and liquors that ranged from generic ales to fine clarets from Bordeaux. Guests drank McCrady's best from hand-blown stemware and tumblers. Creamware and pearlware plates, bowls, and soup dishes linked the topography of the tavern table to the same dining landscape that mapped the social experience of the merchant family house. Gaming pieces and white, kaolin-clay tobacco pipes similarly reflect a shared culture of sociability where the art of conversation and competition linked tavern life to countinghouse and parlor. McCrady's long room answered the needs of more elaborate social functions such as balls, private galas, club meetings, and performances. As such, McCrady's long room, a comparatively rare architectural feature associated only with the best inns and taverns, offered a stage that surpassed the intimacy of the parlor.[30]

References to city taverns with grand assembly halls, tap- and barrooms, dining rooms, and lodging chambers crop up with notable frequency in eighteenth-century cities. In Philadelphia the renowned Indian Queen, located in Fourth Street just off Market, sought new management in 1776, lauding the establishment's many attractions: "built for the purpose of an Inn, five large rooms on the first floor, to entertain companies, two large kitchens, cellars under the whole, 16 lodging rooms on the second and third stories, besides four large garret rooms for servants; four rooms in the house can be made into two, which will entertain from 80 to 100 gentlemen." Stables, carriage sheds, granaries, and laundry facilities rounded out the features of the Indian Queen.[31]

Among the most impressive Philadelphia establishments, though, was the newly built City Tavern. Located on Second Street between Walnut and Chestnut, City Tavern was constructed in 1773 through a private subscription that was directed to the city's elite community. An early-nineteenth-century view of City Tavern illustrates a three-story building with a pedimented and slightly projecting central pavilion (see Figure 7.9). On the interior the building contained two coffee rooms for business and conversation. An adjacent long room provided space for banquets, balls, and fetes. Fashionability, however, was hard to sustain, and, by the end of the eighteenth century other Philadelphia establishments eclipsed the City Tavern's popularity.[32]

In the 1790s, Oeller's Hotel located in Chestnut Street four blocks west of the City Tavern became the place to drink, dine, game, and be seen. The sixty-foot-square open hall with its "handsome music gallery at one end

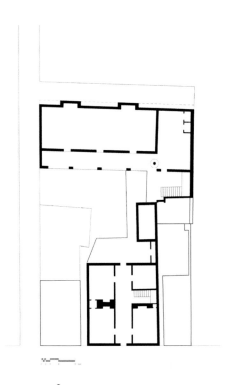

FIGURE 7.8
Edward McCrady's Tavern and "Long Room," 62–64 East Bay Street and Unity Alley, Charleston (circa 1769, plat circa 1808). *Charleston County Deed Book C-7, p. 387, Charleston County Register of Mesne and Conveyances. Drawn by Jeff Klee*

City Tavern, Second Street between Walnut
and Chestnut Streets, Philadelphia (circa 1773).
*Detail from William Birch, "Bank of Pennsylvania,
South Second Street[,] Philadelphia" (1800).
Courtesy The Winterthur Library: Joseph Downs
Collection of Manuscripts and Printed Ephemera*

[and] papered after the French taste, with the Pantheon figures in compart-
ments, imitating festoons, pillars, and groups of antique drawings, in the
same style as lately introduced in the most elegant houses in London" was
immense and ornate even by the standards of neoclassical Philadelphia. The
destruction of Oeller's Hotel by fire in 1799 only exacerbated the dismal loss
of the city's preeminence as the national capital at the same time. Taverns
with assembly and club rooms remained a fixture in urban landscapes on
both sides of the Atlantic. The impressive brick fronts and internal amenities of institutions like Fraunces Tavern in New York and Gadsby's Tavern in
Alexandria, Virginia, provided an architectural and social cohesion familiar

and accessible to both traveler and local resident. Clientele with the financial means to purchase hospitality and the social savvy to project themselves into it enjoyed access to a world of exclusivity that publicly proclaimed their status.[33]

Purpose-built structures for entertainment and lodging included coffeehouses from the beginning of the eighteenth and into the early nineteenth centuries. With its cross-gabled roof, arched windows, and decorative brickwork, Philadelphia's London Coffee House dominated the intersection of High and Front Streets. Charleston also possessed its coffeehouses. Sited on State Street at the foot of the entry to Chalmers Street, the three-story stuccoed brick building was built as a rental property around 1821 by widow Eleanor Cook (see Figure 7.10). The original plan of the building, consisting of a main nineteen-by-thirty-eight-foot block with an eleven-foot-square ell off the back, distinguishes it from more common Charleston town house types. On the interior, the first and second floors each contained two equal-size rooms, each heated with a fireplace centered on the side wall. An ell housed the stair that wound up against the rear elevation. The placement of the stair in an extension facilitated separate and segregated access between the stories. The broad ground-floor shop–front entry facing onto State Street admitted clientele directly into the coffeehouse's most public rooms. The staircase in the ell enabled the proprietor to set aside the second story as a more formal space, finished with tripartite window, balcony, and folding doors that could be thrown open, converting the space into an open reception hall for private entertainments such as club meetings, theatrical performances, or musical recitations. The third floor conformed to an arrangement more closely tied to dwellings and likely provided limited but convenient lodgings for guests whose caffeine intake did not preclude a restful night. A separate building in the backyard housed a kitchen, washhouse, and servants' quarters in the typical pattern of Charleston town houses.[34]

The degree to which coffeehouses with their club rooms and grand taverns with their assembly halls served as places of concourse for locals and strangers brings us back to the artifacts carried in the genteel traveler's portmanteau. The silver tea service, the chafing dish, and the set of china all stand out as objects for personal display and rituals of sociability. In this regard, their meanings were simultaneously private in the context of town house parlors and public in the enactment of sociable behaviors. The traveler's constellation of objects associated with sociability and gentility extended to dress, the most movable of all artifacts. Personal display was at

its most public in assembly halls. In such settings, silver buckles, gold studs, bejeweled watches, and cashmere and silk clothing established personal space in the socially fluid surroundings of quasi-public events and even the street.[35]

Travelers' experiences were defined by an audience of strangers. Their ability to occupy urban space—in town house lodgings, at quayside, and in assembly halls and parlors—proved instrumental in colonizing ephemeral situations as their own. Private dinner parties and teas and public extravaganzas presented situations in a transatlantic society preoccupied with rites of display that claimed space and projected self into the urban landscape. Richard Brush's fiddle was an object that captured space in particular ways. The musical strains Brush sawed on his instrument varied with situation and audience. Alone in his rented rooms, Brush might have played for an audience of one, where his melodies might have offered comfort and remembrance in the same way that other travelers cupped miniature portraits in their hands or penned letters home. With guests to entertain, Brush would have served up different airs that answered the moment, sometimes reels and folk tunes, sometimes the freshest scores published by European composers.[36]

Other travelers used objects both as keepsakes and touchstones for conversation. Printer James Stenson "formerly of Derby . . . but late of Charleston" packed "a curious Piece of Petrification from the Mineral Mines of Derbyshire" in his luggage, along with a more predictable array of clothing, scientific instruments, mahogany tea chest, and books, including "Several entertaining Miscellaneous Pamphlets." Keepsake and oddity, Stenson's mineral specimen represented a kind of souvenir of home—one that connected its owner with his origins and, at the same time, spoke to a display of the exotic that pervaded late-eighteenth-century Atlantic culture.[37]

Finally, the collection, transformation, and exhibition of natural and native curiosities enabled resident individuals to assume the role of travelers in their own society in the sense that they could capture and introduce alien objects into domestic settings. In a reversal of roles, householders became vicarious travelers who sought to establish themselves in fleeting circumstances. Exotic and curious artifacts gave them the ability to inject the foreign into familiar space, often with the potential for communicating powerful associations, as in the instance of Charleston merchant Joseph Moore's cowrie shell snuffbox (see Figure 7.11).[38]

The cowrie shell possesses a remarkable cultural history tied to the slave trade and to traditional African belief systems, ranging from the symbolism of fertility to acts of divination. As jewelry or a sacred object related to divination, the appearance of cowrie shells in African-American settings documents the maintenance of African traditions and their outward expression through a small but symbolically charged artifact (see Figure 7.12). As the primary currency of the Atlantic slave trade in the seventeenth and

FIGURE 7.11

Joseph Moore's Cowrie Shell Snuffbox (early nineteenth century). *Photo by Rick Rhodes.*
Courtesy The Charleston Museum, Charleston, South Carolina

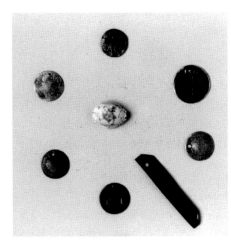

FIGURE 7.12

Cowrie Shell and Pierced Coins. Recovered from African-American archaeological contexts in Charleston. *Photo by Rick Rhodes. Courtesy The Charleston Museum, Charleston, South Carolina*

eighteenth centuries, cowries were also invested with strong negative associations. Harvested and processed off the south coast of India, the shells were shipped first to Europe for further processing and packaging and then exported to the west coast of Africa to be traded for enslaved labor and commodities. Except for limited local purchases, the cowries, once in African circulation, did not find their way back into a European market. As money they colonized Africa in two ways—cowries purchased slave workers and controlled native currency.[39]

The cowrie shells of the slave trade are small, averaging less than an inch in length and under one-half inch in height and width. The cowrie used for Moore's monogrammed snuffbox, however, was considerably larger, measuring roughly three by two by two inches and set in a silver mount, chased with a scroll design, stamped with a floral pattern, and gilded with gold wash. Likely harvested from the Caribbean or off the northern coast of South America, the snuffbox cowrie was not of the type directly related to either African belief systems or American slavery, but it was a cowrie, and it was made visible and public through the genteel act of storing and taking snuff from a culturally transformed natural object. In settings such as parlor or countinghouse where white and black experience intersected, the cowrie shell as an artifact of display and performance textured the relationships between actors and audience in subtle ways. Although the cowrie mounted for the snuffbox came from a different species, it still evoked a chain of associations that reinforced the cultural tensions that defined Charleston society. For Moore, the cowrie shell snuffbox spoke to the possession of the exotic and its conversion to Western social uses; it affirmed perceptions of European and American economic and cultural dominion in the Atlantic rim. For Charleston African-Americans, slave and free, the same object symbolized both an instrument of slavery and the often clandestine preservation of African belief. The oversized cowrie of the *wrong* species crystallized the lack of subtlety that rendered white perceptions of power vulnerable.

The cowrie made into a snuffbox, worn in a strand of waist beads, or cast in divination possessed the potential for claimed space in many dimensions, but it was not unique. Portsmouth merchant Thomas Manning placed a coconut transformed into a silver-edged cup in the formal dining room he furnished with his wife Margaret; sea captain Thomas Mendenhall, of Wilmington, Delaware, brought home a colono pot (most likely from one of his voyages to Brazil or the Caribbean) and kept it until the family moved out of their three-story town house in the 1820s and dumped the globular vessel into the privy, along with ceramics, glass, and other household debris (see Figure 7.13). Mariners from Salem, Massachusetts, brought home Asian exotica, including furniture, paintings, and ceramics. Carved whale teeth and walrus tusks, coconut gunpowder flasks, and talking parrots and brightly plumed tropical birds, along with natural plant and animal specimens, filled the luggage of homeward-bound travelers who displayed these souvenirs in their town houses. The act of display exoticized the domestic just as it civilized the exotic in an endless round of cultural affirmation and conflict. The roles keepsake and souvenir played in town house settings jelled around their use as social capital and touchstones for conversation and the presentation of self. The difference between Joseph Moore's cowrie shell snuffbox, Manning's silver-mounted coconut cup or Mendenhall's colono pot, Richard Brush's fiddle, Charles Willet's tea service, and James Stenson's Derbyshire "petrification" was the direction of the voyage. Moore, Manning, and Mendenhall freighted the exotic into the realm of the familiar; Brush, Willet, and Stenson imported the familiar into the foreign domain of temporary lodgings. For these travelers and their many contemporaries, the contents of their portmanteaux armed them with objects to domesticate alien spaces or make exotic the comforts of home.[40]

FIGURE 7.13
Colono Pot. Recovered from the Thomas Mendenhall House (circa 1790, demolished), Front and Walnut Streets, Wilmington, Delaware. The archaeological context for the pot dates circa 1822. *Photo courtesy Delaware Bureau of Museums*

A POETICAL CITY

The event unfolded at the intersection of Lombard and Third Streets in Philadelphia (see Figure 8.1).

A young girl clasps her hands to her head in a paroxysm of dismay. A breeze ruffles her long white skirt and carries her cries of distress to her unseen neighbors' ears. The objects of her misery, an eathernware pie dish and its contents, lie shattered at her feet. Chimney sweeps in tattered clothes and the black face of their occupation scamper in antic dance, laughing and pointing at the ruined pie. Streetwise dogs yap at her hem and charge the savory remains:

> The pye from Bake-house she had brought
> But let it fall for want of thought
> And laughing Sweeps collect around
> The pye that's scatter'd on the ground.

Just behind and to either side of the central figures engrossed in the demise of the pie, two young women move through the street—one carries a steaming pie past a three-story brick town house; the other carries a babe in arms passing a one-story wooden building, its front in shadow. A citizen of the town trudges through the dappled shadows cast by saplings across the sidewalk. One side of the street gleams in morning sunlight; the other retreats into shade. Lombard Street stretches into the distance toward New Market, its shambles and shops visible in the distance.

Events take place. Place matters. The substance of experience matters. The story of urban houses begins in the spaces between buildings and how people designed, occupied, and viewed their houses and those of others. That space, however, is not simply the material reflection of everyday life—it is also where the commonplace achieves the currency of symbolic language. Elizabeth Myers's spun-sugar desserts, Angus and Jane Grant's tea tray, and Richard Brush's fiddle comprised actions and objects that enlivened household spaces and gave them particular, situational meanings. Their actions enacted everyday objects.

The material world of early American space constitutes what might be best thought of as the poetical city. "I have the idea," writes Edward Hirsch, "that a certain kind of exemplary poem teaches you how to read it. It carries its own encoded instructions, enacting its subject, pointing to its own operation. It enacts what it is about—a made thing that indicates the nature of its own making." Poems also possess the capacity to communicate their sense before they are fully understood on a rationalized, self-conscious level. Urban space, it seems, is a poem, and a poetics of urban space provides a means for domesticating the expressive licentiousness of everyday city life. The poetical city possesses two key aesthetic attributes: ambiguity and lyricism.[1]

Ambiguity addresses two problems in reading the poetical city through its material culture. First, because history remains text-dependent in such literal ways, there is a tendency to distrust the voice of the object because of its perceived inexactness. The artifact—house, spun-sugar globe, or cowrie shell—simply does not state the meanings it superintends. Instead, the study of material culture lends itself to acts of inscription that invite the writing of significances onto its surfaces. As critical graffiti, acts of interpretation tag territory and effect a kind of substitution that can mask the nature of the things we study. The connotative quality of objects, their semiotic ambiguity, is what makes their ability to convey sense and significance at once situational, provisional, and performative. Interpretations carry meaning to the world of things; acts of interpretation in the world of the everyday are constant and slippery. Second, ambiguity admits that there are multiple, simultaneous, often conflicted constructions of meaning that depend on the perceptions of audience and actors in shared contexts. Accordingly, ambi-

The pye from Bake-house she had brought / But let it fall for want of thought | The ACCIDENT in LOMBARD-STREET / PHILAD. 1787 *designed & engraved by C.W. Peale* | And laughing Sweeps collet around / The pye that's scattere on the groune N.

FIGURE 8.1

Charles Willson Peale, *The Accident in Lombard Street* (1787). *Courtesy The Winterthur Library: Joseph Downs Collection of Manuscripts and Printed Ephemera*

guity makes it possible to admit and reconcile difference in a single critical gesture.[2]

Lyricism functions in the poetical city by incorporating subjectivity, sensuousness, and cadence. Lyricism speaks to the fact that any understanding of urban space is at some fundamental level personal and physical. Striving to write and speak about the experience of urban space is how we begin to construct and communicate an order of things. Lyricism also implies an aesthetics of urban experience. The use of aesthetics here departs from what constitutes a philosophy of the beautiful and concentrates instead on the idea that aesthetics are a vital aspect in the practice of everyday life. Aesthetic process is located in the worlds of act and expression that describe the balances (and imbalances) between people and the worlds they make, inhabit, communicate, and render symbolically coherent. Aesthetics are not intrinsic to the physical appearance of objects but are grounded instead in the circumstances of individual and group expression and reception. Lyricism, as an aestheticized form of writing, depends on the measured use of language. Urban space, however, is lyrical in the sense that it can be thought of as privileging voice over text. It is literally the shout in the street and the breathed word performed. What is lyrical ceases to be fossilized in written word and is energized through performance of place.[3]

Ambiguity and lyricism in a poetics of urban space embrace the idea of "affecting presence," the emotional response to the material world. Affecting "objects and happenings in any given culture are accepted by those native to that culture as being purposefully concerned with potency, emotions, values, and states of being or experience—all, in a clear sense, *powers*." Three key attributes define affect: it is about feeling, it is presentation or enactment, and it is material, either as artifact or the recorded event. The core idea lurking within the concept of affect recognizes that aesthetic and critical thought is not necessarily objective. Although the intended use of the concept of affect tends to privilege the ascription of purpose and intent, we can enlarge the idea to comprehend a concept of tradition as the cultural process of making situational, strategic, and continuing sense of the world around us. Tradition enables us to read purpose and intent into objects as well as out of them; it is about making and enacting a sense of the world. As with ambiguity and lyricism, affect and tradition invite sensuousness into the poetical city.[4]

The Accident in Lombard Street, designed and engraved by Charles Willson Peale as a moral and didactic commentary on urban life in Philadelphia, ostensibly offers a cautionary tale about virtue. The young girl at the center of the composition has dropped the pie. The comical cavorting of the chimney sweeps and two small dogs refract and amplify her horror. The sweeps are the individuals who literally occupy the interstices of the city's architectural fabric. With ropes, buckets, and brushes, they plumbed town house flues, literally boring into the world of the hearth. Their age similarly places them in a liminal position within urban society. As boys, they are youthful and undisciplined, a quality underscored by the dogs that romp at their feet. The sweeps transgress the city's most intimate margins; their mocking gestures celebrate the young woman's misfortune. But what is the cause and nature of her circumstance?

"For want of thought," the young woman has dropped her pie. Virtue lies shattered through inattention. The circumstance of lost virtue is the substance of Peale's engraving. At the most immediate level, attention to work has been compromised. The trip to and from the bakehouse was a common chore in everyday city life. Bakeshops like the Southers' in Portsmouth, New Hampshire, regularly catered to a clientele who relied on the convenience of early American "take out." John Gwer's (also Geyer) premises fronted Lombard Street only three doors away from the Peales' residence. But Peale's young woman has also been inattentive to moral virtue. In the immediate background two young women pass through the scene. To one side in the sunlight and screened behind the gang of sweeps, one of the young women parades her pie intact. Behind her and around the corner a solitary male figure walks carrying a long, bowlike device. A second young woman at the opposite end of the picture, and nearer the figure at the center of the action, steps from the sidewalk with an infant in her arms. The ways in which these figures physically relate to each other underscore Peale's second message, which focuses on feminine virtue. Inattention to virtue has left the central figure trapped between the mocking sweeps and the young mother and child. The attentive woman carrying her pie safely home, however, is not secure. The man in Lombard Street traces her footsteps, a plodding artisan Apollo in pursuit of his Daphne, an allusion made more apparent by the sole absence of a young sapling by the bollard she passes in that moment. Virtue, it seems, is always threatened, and vigilance is always required.

In the background, Lombard Street asymmetrically stretches away to New Market in Second Street. To the right where the young girl with pie intact passes by, a two-story brick house stands in the light; to the left mother and daughter descend into the street from the deep shadows cast by a single-story wooden building. Saplings flourish on the sunny side of Lombard Street. Only irregularly spaced bollards, some bent, line the shadowed curb across the way. The two-story brick house is neatly shuttered, and the hint of a firemark, indicating that the premises are insured (literally a mark of the well-ordered city), occupies a space beneath the uppermost attic window. A brick wall screens a garden or dooryard to the far side of the brick house. The gable of the wooden building is featureless in the shadows, but the cellar doors are askew, suggesting neglect and disrepair. Far in the distance the view is closed off by a pair of three-story brick houses that overlook the market stalls and, in Peale's composition, echo the brick house and the virtuous woman. Like the merchant family's house, the competitive, conversational world of trade resonates within domestic spaces; like the artisan family's household, social knowledge enacted in the material world creates critical space for both emulation and ridicule. At this level Peale's attentions focus on civic virtue measured out in the fabric of city houses. The tension between the old and new evokes the architectural dialogue between the houses of Boston's North Square. The narrative of *The Accident in Lombard Street* mediates the tension between domestic service and domestic virtue. The extraordinary medium of the print makes the world of the transparent visible just as Billy Robinson counted on his architectural defense to prove his innocence.

Charles Willson Peale (1741–1827), painter, inventor, scientist, and impresario, engraved from life. The house behind the virtuous woman was Peale's own residence; the brick wall screened access from the street to his private picture gallery. The engraving allegedly reflected an incident in the Peale family household. The bakeshop identified as the premises of "J Gwer Baker" in Peale's engraving was indeed the business of Peale's neighbor. At the time the engraving was produced, the occupational profile of the neighborhood was largely artisan. A baker, blacksmith, soap boiler, tinplate worker, instrument maker, two house carpenters, and three tailors all listed their addresses in Lombard Street. Households headed by a schoolmistress, gentlemen and gentlewomen, a sea captain, and innkeeper rounded out the population of the Peales' immediate neighborhood.[5]

Peale appropriates the world of the ordinary into a realistic, didactic work that draws on the very essence of the poetical city. His strategy owed its origins to nearly a century of British printmakers, including William Hogarth. Peale's actions were unique only in the particulars of *The Accident in Lombard Street*. What makes Peale's allegory succeed, however, is its fundamental, unspoken understanding of individuals' placement of themselves in relation to the worlds of people and objects around them—their sense of comportment. The sense of circumstance and presence of place made visible and explicit in Peale's engraving was the stuff of everyday life. The genius of his work and that of his viewers lay in its collective meditation on the symbolic richness of the urban material world.

Notes

CHAPTER ONE

1 Works on early American cities include Billy G. Smith, *The "Lower Sort": Philadelphia's Laboring People, 1750–1800* (Ithaca, N.Y., 1990); Peter A. Coclannis, "The Sociology of Architecture in Colonial Charleston: Pattern and Process in an Eighteenth-Century Southern City," *Journal of Social History,* XVIII (1984–1985), 607–623; Elizabeth Blackmar, *Manhattan for Rent, 1785–1850* (Ithaca, N.Y., 1989); Stuart M. Blumin, *The Emergence of the Middle Class: Social Experience in the American City, 1760–1900* (Cambridge, 1989); Thomas M. Doerflinger, *A Vigorous Spirit of Enterprise: Merchants and Economic Development in Revolutionary Philadelphia* (Chapel Hill, N.C., 1986); Peter Borsay, *The English Urban Renaissance: Culture and Society in the Provincial Town, 1660–1770* (Oxford, 1989); John W. Reps, *The Making of Urban America: A History of City Planning in the United States* (Princeton, N.J., 1965); Dietrich Denecke, "Social Status and Place of Residence in Preindustrial German Towns: Recent Studies in Social Topography," in Denecke and Gareth Shaw, eds., *Urban Historical Geography: Recent Progress in Britain and Germany* (Cambridge, 1988), 125–140, 368–374.

Ruth-E. Mohrmann offers an overview of everyday material life that emphasizes *Wohnkultur* ("art of living") in "Everyday Culture in Early Modern Times," *New Literary History,* XXIV (1993), 75–86. See also Henry Glassie, "Tradition," *Journal of American Folklore,* CVIII (1995), 395–412; Peter Jukes, *A Shout in the Street: An Excursion into the Modern City* (Berkeley, Calif., 1991); Susan Stewart, *On Longing: Narratives of the Miniature, the Gigantic, the Souvenir, the Collection* (1984; Durham, N.C., 1993), 78–86; Michel de Certeau, *The Practice of Everyday Life,* trans. Steven Rendall (Berkeley, Calif., 1984), 99–110.

2 Dell Upton, "The City as Material Culture," in Anne Elizabeth Yentsch and Mary C. Beaudry, eds., *The Art and Mystery of Historical Archaeology: Essays in Honor of James Deetz* (Boca Raton, Fla., 1992), 52–53. See also Robert Blair St. George's discussion on the "poetics of implication" in *Conversing by Signs: Poetics of Implication in Colonial New England Culture* (Chapel Hill, N.C., 1998), 2–13. The perspectives offered by Upton and St. George emphasize expressive relations and their symbolic connections and the placement of those relationships within systematically constructed contexts.

3 William Drayton, "Journal of a Tour from Charleston to New

York, 1786," #34/631/1, South Carolina Historical Society, Charleston. Delores Hayden, in *The Power of Place: Urban Landscapes as Public History* (Cambridge, Mass., 1995), argues persuasively for the instrumentality of place in the construction of evolving social identities in history and memory. See also David Lowenthal, *The Past Is a Foreign Country* (Cambridge, 1985), 185–259.

4 Edward Hooker, Journals, 1805–1807, Connecticut Historical Society, Hartford; information cited here courtesy of Jonathan Poston, Historic Charleston Foundation.

5 Dell Upton provides a compelling interpretation of intersecting, competing landscapes and their moral force in "Another City: The Urban Cultural Landscape in the Early Republic," in Catherine E. Hutchins, ed., *Everyday Life in the Early Republic* (Winterthur, Del., 1994), 63–65. Of particular note is Upton's interpretation of systematic, competitive, and shadow landscapes. For the ways in which urban civic order was represented and contested, see the literature on parades and processions, particularly Susan G. Davis, *Parades and Power: Street Theatre in Nineteenth-Century Philadelphia* (Philadelphia, 1986); Mary Ryan, "The American Parade: Representations of the Nineteenth-Century Social Order," in Lynn Hunt, ed., *The New Cultural History* (Berkeley, Calif., 1989), 131–153; Robert Darnton, *The Great Cat Massacre and Other Episodes in French Cultural History* (New York, 1984), 107–143. For riots in English towns, see Mark Harrison, *Crowds and History: Mass Phenomena in English Towns, 1790–1835* (Cambridge, 1988), 268–314. For period examples of ordered urban landscapes and society, see Edward Hazen, *The Panorama of Professions and Trades; or, Every Man's Book* (Philadelphia, 1836), as an idealized model for the sociology of work in the urban landscape; Free Library of Philadelphia, *Birch's Views of Philadelphia: A Reduced Facsimile of the City of Philadelphia—as It Appeared in the Year 1800* . . . (Philadelphia, 1983).

6 For a parallel discussion of comportment as a strategy for the interpretation of material culture, see Bernard L. Herman, *The Stolen House* (Charlottesville, Va., 1992), 9–10, 54–55. The idea of comportment draws on an extended discussion of context in material culture. See Ian Hodder, *Reading the Past: Current Approaches to Interpretation in Archaeology*, 2d ed. (Cambridge, 1991), 121–155; Henry Glassie, "Studying Material Culture Today," in Gerald L. Pocius, ed., *Living in a Material World: Canadian and American Approaches to Material Culture* (St. John's, Newfoundland, 1991), 253–266; Lu Ann De Cunzo, "Introduction: People, Material Culture, Context, and Culture in Historical Archaeolgy," in De Cunzo and Bernard L. Herman, eds., *Historical Archaeology and the Study of American Culture* (Winterthur, Del., Knoxville, Tenn., 1996), 1–17.

7 Nathaniel B. Shurtleff, *A Topographical and Historical Description of Boston* (Boston, 1871), 124–157; Walter Muir Whitehill, *Boston: A Topographical History,* 2d ed. (Cambridge, Mass., 1968), 1–94. For information on residential patterns in late-eighteenth-century Boston, I am indebted to Len Travers of the Massachusetts Historical Society, Boston, for access to the Boston Directory Database, 1789–1809, created under his direction. Samuel Clough, an early-nineteenth-century Boston historian, began plotting the returns of the 1798 direct tax onto a detailed map of the city. Never completed, the project was named "Clough's 1799 Atlas of the Town of Boston, Property Owners." The manuscript atlas is now held by the Massachusetts Historical Society. Clough's materials are contained in several collections at the society, including Samuel C. Clough, "Papers, 1630–1798" and "Maps of Early Boston and Vicinity." My thanks to Claire Dempsey and Michael Steinitz for bringing Clough's work to my attention.

8 Boston, Record Commissioners, Twenty-second Report, *A Report of the Record Commissioners of the City of Boston, Containing the Statistics of the United States' Direct Tax of 1798, as Assessed on Boston; and the Names of the Inhabitants of Boston in 1790 as Collected for the First National Census* (Boston, 1890), 162–225.

On fire, see Jane H. Pease and William H. Pease, "The Blood-Thirsty Tiger: Charleston and the Psychology of Fire," *South Carolina Historical Magazine,* LXXIX (1978), 281–293; Richard M. Candee, "Social Conflict and Urban Rebuilding: The Portsmouth, New Hampshire, Brick Act of 1814," *Winterthur Porfolio,* XXXII (1997), 119–146; Anthony N. B. Garvan, Cynthia Koch, Donald Arbuckle, and Deborah Hart, *The Architectural Surveys,1784–1794,* I, *The Mutual Assurance Company Papers* (Philadelphia, 1976), xi–xii; Nicholas B. Wainwright, "Philadelphia's Eighteenth-Century Fire Insurance Companies," in *Historic Philadelphia: From the Founding until the*

Early Nineteenth Century, American Philosophical Society, *Transactions,* XLIII, pt. 3 (1953), 249.

9 Abbott Lowell Cummings, *The Framed Houses of Massachusetts Bay, 1625–1725* (Cambridge, Mass., 1979), 38–39, 150, 152; Cummings, "Summary Abstracts of the Structural History of a Significant Sampling of First Period Houses at Massachusetts Bay," in *Architecture of Colonial Massachusetts,* Colonial Society of Massachusetts, *Publications,* LV (Charlottesville, Va., 1979), 130; Norman M. Isham and Albert F. Brown, *Early Connecticut Houses: An Historical and Architectural Study* (1900; rpt. New York, 1965); J. Frederick Kelly, *The Early Domestic Architecture of Connecticut* (1924; rpt. New York, 1963); Robert Blair St. George, "Afterthoughts on *Material Life in America, 1600–1860:* Household Space in Boston, 1670–1730," *Winterthur Portfolio,* XXXII (1997), 1–38.

10 In northern New England's seaport towns, buildings of this type are particularly well documented in Portsmouth, N.H. See Richard M. Candee, *Building Portsmouth: The Neighborhoods and Architecture of New Hampshire's Oldest City* (Portsmouth, N.H., 1992), 51–73; also Bernard L. Herman, "The Architectural and Social Topography of Early-Nineteenth-Century Portsmouth, New Hampshire," in Elizabeth Collins Cromley and Carter L. Hudgins, eds., *Gender, Class, and Shelter,* Perspectives in Vernacular Architecture, V (Knoxville, Tenn., 1995), 225–242.

11 Abbott Lowell Cummings, "The Beginnings of Provincial Renaissance Architecture in Boston, 1690–1725," *Journal of the Society of Architectural Historians,* XLII (1983), 45–53; St. George, "Afterthoughts on *Material Life in America, 1600–1860,*" *Winterthur Portfolio,* XXXII (1997), 26–37.

12 P. J. Corfield, *The Impact of English Towns, 1700–1800* (Oxford, 1982), 124–145; Borsay, *The English Urban Renaissance,* 232–241.

13 Elizabeth McKellar, *The Birth of Modern London: Development and Design of the City, 1660–1720* (Manchester, 1999), 155–187; Peter Guillery and Bernard Herman, "Deptford Houses: 1650–1800," *Vernacular Architecture,* XXX (1999), 58–84; John Summerson, *Georgian London* (New York, 1946), 28–35. See also Dan Cruickshank and Neil Burton, *Life in the Georgian City* (London, 1990), 51–73.

14 R. Meischke, H. J. Zantkuijl, W. Raue, and P. T. E. E. Rosen-berg, *Huizen in Nederland: Amsterdam, architectuurhistorische verkenningen aan de hand van het bezit van de Vereniging Hendrick de Keyser* (Amsterdam, 1995), 211–214; Henk J. Zantkuyl, "The Netherlands Town House: How and Why It Works," in *New World Dutch Studies: Dutch Arts and Culture in Colonial America, 1609–1776* (Albany, N.Y., 1987), 147–149.

15 Joseph Moxon, *Mechanick Exercises; or, The Doctrine of Handy Works* (1703; rpt. Scarsdale, N.Y., 1979), facing 265–facing 266; City Lands and Bridge House Properties (ca. 1680–1720), 2 vols., London Record Office, London.

16 Mary Ellen Hayward, "Urban Vernacular Architecture in Nineteenth-Century Baltimore," *Winterthur Portfolio,* XVI (1981), 33–63; William John Murtagh, "The Philadelphia Row House," *Journal of the Society of Architectural Historians,* XVI, no. 4 (December 1957), 8–13.

17 A. F. Kelsall, "The London House Plan in the Later Seventeenth Century," *Post-Medieval Archaeology,* VIII (1974), 80–91; Neil Burton, Peter Guillery, and Bernard L. Herman, *Another Georgian London* (London, 1999), drawings 27, 28, 29, 34, 37, plans 25, 44, 46.

18 Julienne Hanson, *Decoding Homes and Houses* (Cambridge, 1998), 1–79.

19 Cummings, "The Beginnings of Provincial Renaissance Architecture in Boston," *Journal of the Society of Architectural Historians,* XLII (1983), 45–53; St. George, *Conversing by Signs,* 288–293; Mark Girouard, *The English Town: A History of Urban Life* (New Haven, Conn., 1990), 109–112; Borsay, *The English Urban Renaissance,* 41–59. See the inventory of historic properties within the "Walled City," in Jonathan H. Poston, *The Buildings of Charleston: A Guide to the City's Architecture* (Columbia, S.C., 1997), 47–153.

20 Annie Haven Thwing, *The Crooked and Narrow Streets of the Town of Boston, 1630–1822* (Boston, 1920), 49–50.

21 Cummings, *The Framed Houses of Massachusetts Bay,* 202–209; Cummings, "The Beginnings of Provincial Renaissance Architecture in Boston," *Journal of the Society of Architectural Historians,* XLII (1983), 45–53.

22 Henry Glassie, *Folk Housing in Middle Virginia: A Structural Analysis of Historic Artifacts* (Knoxville, Tenn., 1975), 66–113; Dell Upton, *Holy Things and Profane: Anglican Parish Churches in Colonial Virginia* (New York, 1986), 206–218.

23 Harold Donaldson Eberlein and Cortlandt V. D. Hubbard, *Historic Houses and Buildings of Delaware* (Dover, Del., 1962), 173–175; George Fletcher Bennett, *Early Architecture of Delaware* (Wilmington, Del., 1932), 95–98, 188–191; Bernard L. Herman, "Kensey Johns and His Carpenters," in J. Ritchie Garrison, Bernard L. Herman, and Barbara McLean Ward, eds., *After Ratification: Material Life in Delaware, 1789–1820* (Newark, Del., 1988), 65–77.

24 "Articles of Agreement" between Kensey Johns, George Vansandt, and Joseph Baldin (June 16, 1788), Kensey Johns House File, Historical Society of Delware, Wilmington.

25 The Amstel House, also standing in New Castle and Buena Vista outside the town of Smyrna, is an example of an early Georgian plantation house of the Delaware elite. The John and Mary Dickinson House located near Dover also possessed a pedimented front elevation that was lost in a subsequent fire. Eberlein and Hubbard, *Historic Houses and Buildings of Delaware,* 73–77, 168–169.

26 Carolyn Elizabeth "Eliza" (Burgwin) Clitherall (1784–1863), *Diary and Reminiscences, 1795–1860* (University of North Carolina, Southern Historical Collection, American Women's Diaries, Southern Series, microfilm, reel 12), II, 17–24 (I am deeply indebted to Nancy Packer for sharing Caroline Burgwin's story); Walter Ison, *The Georgian Buildings of Bristol* (1952; rpt. Bath, 1978), 173–177, advertisement quoted 174.

27 Upton, "The City as Material Culture," in Yentsch and Beaudry, eds., *The Art and Mystery of Historical Archaeology,* 52–53; Mohrmann, "Everyday Culture in Early Modern Times," *New Literary History,* XXIV (1993), 76–77.

CHAPTER TWO

1 Excerpt from "Observations on Making Decorations for a Table," from Elizabeth Raffald, *The Experienced English House-Keeper, for the Use and Ease of Ladies, House-Keepers, Cooks, etc. . . .* , 10th ed. (Dublin, 1789), 159–160.

2 Myers Family Household Accounts, October 1824–July 1826, Collections of the Moses Myers House, Chrysler Museum of Art, Norfolk, Va.

3 Sidney W. Mintz, *Sweetness and Power: The Place of Sugar in Modern History* (New York, 1985), 87–96; Reay Tannahill, *Food in History* (New York, 1973), 223–224; Margaret Visser, *The Rituals of Dinner: The Origins, Evolutions, Eccentricities, and Meaning of Table Manners* (New York, 1991), 161–163.

4 Cary Carson, "The Consumer Revolution in Colonial British America: Why Demand?" in Cary Carson, Ronald Hoffman, and Peter J. Albert, eds., *Of Consuming Interests: The Style of Life in the Eighteenth Century* (Charlottesville, Va., 1994), 587–608.

5 George E. Marcus, ed., *Elites: Ethnographic Issues* (Albuquerque, N.Mex., 1983), 11 (for a full discussion of elites in complex modern societies, see 9–12). See also Dell Upton's model of mode and style applied to the interpretation of eighteenth-century Anglican parish churches in Virginia: *Holy Things and Profane: Anglican Parish Churches in Colonial Virginia* (New York, 1986), 101–102.

6 Marcus, ed., *Elites,* 12; Ann Smart Martin, "Makers, Buyers, and Users: Consumerism as a Material Culture Framework," *Winterthur Portfolio,* XXVIII (1993), 141–157; Richard L. Bushman, *The Refinement of America: Persons, Houses, Cities* (New York, 1992), 231–234; Cary Carson, "The Consumer Revolution," in Carson, Hoffman, and Albert, eds., *Of Consuming Interests,* 589–592; Rhys Isaac, *The Transformation of Virginia, 1740–1790* (Chapel Hill, N.C., 1982), 77–78; David S. Shields, *Civil Tongues and Polite Letters in British America* (Chapel Hill, N.C., 1997), 99–140; Martha A. Zierden, "A Trans-Atlantic Merchant's House in Charleston: Archaeological Exploration of Refinement and Subsistence in an Urban Setting," *Historical Archaeology,* XXXIII, no. 3 (1999), 73–87; Peter Borsay, "'All the Town's a Stage': Urban Ritual and Ceremony, 1600–1800," in Peter Clark, ed., *The Transformation of English Provincial Towns, 1600–1800* (London, 1984), 232–233.

7 [George Tucker], trans., *Letters from Virginia* (Baltimore, 1816), 21.

8 Gordon Jackson, *Hull in the Eighteenth Century: A Study in Economic and Social History* (London, 1972), 277; Thomas M. Doerflinger, *A Vigorous Spirit of Enterprise: Merchants and Economic Development in Revolutionary Philadelphia* (Chapel Hill, N.C., 1986), 38; Thomas Costa and Peter Stewart, "The Life and Legacy of Moses Myers: Merchant of Norfolk, Virginia," MS report for the Moses Myers House, Chrysler Museum, n.d. (rev. 2000), 163.

9 Robert J. Gough, "The Philadelphia Economic Elite at the End of the Eighteenth Century," in Catherine E. Hutchins,

ed., *Shaping a National Culture: The Philadelphia Experience, 1750–1800* (Winterthur, Del., 1994), 15–43; Jackson, *Hull in the Eighteenth Century,* 262–288; John Bold, "The Design of a House for a Merchant, 1724," *Architectural History,* XXXIII (1990), 75–82; Leonore Davidoff and Catherine Hall, *Family Fortunes: Men and Women of the English Middle Class, 1780–1850* (Chicago, 1987), 357–400; Upton, *Holy Things and Profane,* 101–102.

10 James R. Melchor and Mark R. Wenger, "Myers House Architectural Investigations, 3–5 October 2000," Myers House, Chrysler Museum.

11 Form of the Declaration of Assurance, Virginia Mutual Assurance Society (hereafter VMAS Declarations), VII, no. 226 (1797), LXXXVIII, no. 6452 resurvey (1829), CVI, no. 11890 resurvey (1843), Virginia State Library, Richmond; "A Plan . . . of the Intersection of Free Mason and Catherine Streets with a Ground Plan of the Buildings thereon . . . Property of Moses Myers" (ca. 1816), Myers House, Chrysler Museum. The physical history of the Myers House was investigated with Mark R. Wenger and Willie Graham, Colonial Williamsburg Foundation.

12 Camille Wells, "The Planter's Prospect: Houses, Outbuildings, and Rural Landscapes in Eighteenth-Century Virginia," *Winterthur Portfolio,* XXVIII (1993), 1–31.

13 *Virginia Chronicle and, Norfolk and Portsmouth General Advertiser,* Oct. 6, 1792; VMAS Declarations, VI, no. 107 (1796).

14 VMAS Declarations, XXIX, no. 2044 (1803), LXIV, no. 712 resurvey (1806); George Holbert Tucker, "Old Norfolk Lives Yet within Whittle House," *Virginian-Pilot,* Feb. 5, 1950.

15 *Virginia Chronicle,* Dec. 15, 1792, Sept. 14, 1793.

16 Anne Ritson, *A Poetical Picture of America, Being Observations Made, during Several Years at Alexandria, and Norfolk, in Virginia . . .* (London, 1809), 96–98.

17 John B. Boles, ed., *The Microfilm Edition of the William Wirt Papers, 1786–1873* (Baltimore, 1971), roll 1, letters for Nov. 30, Dec. 6, 1803, Jan. 16, 1804. For a detailed discussion of Elizabeth Wirt's architectural endeavors, see Jill Haley, "'I Can Live No Longer Here': Elizabeth Wirt's Decision to Buy a New House" (master's thesis, University of Delaware, 1995); Dan Cruickshank, *Mawson's Row, 110–118 Chiswick Lane: An Architectural and Historical Assessment* (London, 1992), 11, 22; Cruickshank and Neil Burton, *Life in the Georgian City* (London, 1990), 79–89.

18 Edward C. Carter II et al., eds., *The Virginia Journals of Benjamin Henry Latrobe, 1795–1798* (New Haven, Conn., 1977), I, 79–80; Jeffrey A. Cohen and Charles E. Brownell, eds., *The Architectural Drawings of Benjamin Henry Latrobe* (New Haven, Conn., 1994), part 1, 82–90; John C. Van Horne et al., eds., *The Correspondence and Miscellaneous Papers of Benjamin Henry Latrobe,* I (New Haven, Conn., 1984), 147–150.

19 Van Horne et al., eds., *The Correspondence and Miscellaneous Papers of Latrobe,* I, 147–149.

20 Cohen and Brownell, eds., *The Architectural Drawings of Latrobe,* part 1, 82–90; Carter et al., eds., *The Virginia Journals of Latrobe,* I, 79–80.

21 An overview of Norfolk women property holders and their occupations was compiled from Norfolk Borough Land Book and Personal Property, 1800, Virginia State Library, and Charles H. Simmons, *Simmons's Norfolk Directory, Containing the Names, Occupations, and Places of Abode of the Inhabitants . . .* (Norfolk, Va., 1801); VMAS Declarations, VI, no. 56 (1796). For a range of housing types standing in Norfolk in the early 1830s, see Description of Real Estate Held by the [Virginia Bank], c. 1833–1856, unaccessioned manuscript, Sergeant Memorial Room, Kirn Memorial Library, Norfolk, Va. Norfolk database constructed from Simmons, *Simmons's Norfolk Directory;* Norfolk Borough Land Book and Personal Property, 1800; VMAS Policies and Revaluations, 1796–1803.

22 VMAS Declarations, VI, no. 6 (1796).

23 Dell Upton, "White and Black Landscapes in Eighteenth-Century Virginia," in Robert Blair St. George, ed., *Material Life in America, 1600–1860* (Boston, 1988), 357–369; Susan G. Davis, *Parades and Power: Street Theatre in Nineteenth-Century Philadelphia* (Philadelphia, 1986), 23–48; [Tucker], trans., *Letters from Virginia,* 18–19; Thomas J. Wertenbaker, *Norfolk: Historic Southern Port* (Durham, N.C., 1931), 141–143; Anne Royall, *The Black Book; or, A Continuation of Travels, in the United States* (Washington, D.C., 1828), I, 254.

24 Indenture between Moses Myers and Lamb & Co. Trust, Borough of Norfolk, Deed Book 16 (1820), 9–16. The indenture includes a room-by-room listing of the contents of the house. Myers House report.

25 Isaac, *The Transformation of Virginia,* 77–78. The difficulty of pinning down distinctively Jewish artifacts in household inventories is reflected in Judith Marla Guston, "The Almanacs of Michael Gratz: Time, Community, and Jewish Identity in Eighteenth-Century Philadelphia" (master's thesis, University of Delaware, 1999). See also James William Hagy, *This Happy Land: The Jews of Colonial and Antebellum Charleston* (Tuscaloosa, Ala., 1993), 167–169.

26 Inventory for Conway Whittle (May 26, 1818), Borough of Norfolk, Will Book 3, 369–374.

27 Inventory for Phineas Dana (May 3, 1808), Borough of Norfolk, Will Book 2, 456–461; VMAS Declarations, VIII, no. 358 (1802).

28 Inventory for James Maxwell (1795, filed 1798), Borough of Norfolk, Will Book 1, esp. 178; inventory for Robert Hayes (1796), Will Book 1, 134–135.

29 Mark Girouard, *The English Town: A History of Urban Life* (New Haven, Conn., 1990), 101–126; Peter Borsay, *The English Urban Renaissance: Culture and Society in the Provincial Town, 1660–1770* (Oxford, 1989), 41–59, Peter Brown, *Fairfax House: An Illustrated History and a Guide* (York, 1989).

30 L. W., "Wren's House and Pallant House, Chichester," *Country Life,* XXXI (1912), 614–619; John Belcher and Mervyn E. Macartney, eds., *Later Renaissance Architecture in England: A Series of Examples of the Domestic Buildings Erected Subsequent to the Elizabethan Period* (London, 1901), I, part 3, plate 56; Borsay, *The English Urban Renaissance,* 208.

31 For the Blaydes House, see Ivan Hall and Elisabeth Hall, *A New Picture of Georgian Hull* (York, 1979), 29–31, 39. I am indebted to Robin Thornes, formerly of the Royal Commission for the Historic Monuments of England, for sharing information on the house in Grape Lane. For a general sense of the Georgian town house, see also Dan Cruickshank and Peter Wyld, *London: The Art of Georgian Building* (London, 1975).

32 Upton, "White and Black Landscapes," in St. George, ed., *Material Life in America,* 357–369; Robert Blair St. George, *Conversing by Signs: Poetics of Implication in Colonial New England Culture* (Chapel Hill, N.C., 1998), 302–306; Gillian Rose, *Feminism and Geography: The Limits of Geographical Knowledge* (Minneapolis, Minn., 1993), 86–112.

33 For detailed accounts of Portsmouth's eighteenth-century houses, see Richard M. Candee, *Building Portsmouth: The Neighborhoods and Architecture of New Hampshire's Oldest City* (Portsmouth, N.H., 1992); John Mead Howells, *The Architectural Heritage of the Piscataqua: Houses and Gardens of the Portsmouth District of Maine and New Hampshire* (New York, 1937).

34 Inventory for Thomas Manning, Rockingham County, N.H., Wills and Administrations, Docket 9908 o.s. (Apr. 8, 1819). Photographs of the Manning House prior to its demolition are in the collections of the Strawbery Banke Museum Library, Portsmouth, N.H.

35 For a general survey of Charleston's architecture, see Jonathan H. Poston, *The Buildings of Charleston: A Guide to the City's Architecture* (Columbia, S.C., 1997); Alice R. Huger Smith and D. E. Huger Smith, *The Dwelling Houses of Charleston, South Carolina* (1917; rpt. New York, 1974).

36 Bernard L. Herman, "The Embedded Landscapes of the Charleston Single House, 1780–1820," in Annmarie Adams and Sally McMurry, eds., *Exploring Everyday Landscapes,* Perspectives in Vernacular Architecture, VII (Knoxville, Tenn., 1997), 41–57; Martha A. Zierden and Bernard L. Herman, "Charleston Townhouses: Archaeology, Architecture, and the Urban Landscape, 1750–1850," in Rebecca Yamin and Karen Bescherer Metheny, eds., *Landscape Archaeology: Reading and Interpreting the American Historical Landscape* (Knoxville, Tenn., 1996), 193–227.

37 Edward Chappell, "Looking at Buildings," *Fresh Advices* (November 1984), Research Supplement to Colonial Williiamsburg, *Interpreter* (November 1984), i–vi; Orlando Ridout V, *Building the Octagon* (Washington, D.C., 1989), 117–122.

38 Mark Reinberger, *Utility and Beauty: Robert Wellford and Composition Ornament in America* (Newark, Del., 2003); Damie Stillman, *English Neo-classical Architecture,* I (London, 1988), 195–214.

39 Inventory for Francis Simmonds (1815), Charleston County Inventories, Book E, 259–261, and inventory for Angus Bethune (1815), 288; Benjamin A. Hewitt, Patricia E. Kane, and Gerald W. R. Ward, *The Work of Many Hands: Card Tables in Federal America, 1790–1820* (New Haven, Conn., 1982), 15–38.

40 Inventory for Joseph Spear (Oct. 27, 1810), Baltimore County, Md., Inventories (1809–1811), 474–475, Maryland Hall of

Records, Annapolis; inventory for Stephen Collins (1794), Philadelphia Wills (1794), no. 140, Philadelphia City Archives; probate inventory for Michael Gundacker (1815), Lancaster County Court House Archives, Lancaster, Pa.

41 Carson, *Ambitious Appetites,* 110–118; David S. Shields, *Civil Tongues and Polite Letters in British America* (Chapel Hill, N.C., 1997), 301–303.

42 Hewitt, Kane, and Ward, eds., *The Work of Many Hands,* 16–21.

43 Shields, *Civil Tongues and Polite Letters,* 104–126; Ann Smart Martin, "Frontier Boys and Country Cousins: The Context for Choice in Eighteenth-Century Consumerism," in Lu Ann De Cunzo and Bernard L. Herman, eds., *Historical Archaeology and the Study of American Culture* (Winterthur, Del., Knoxville, Tenn., 1996), 78–80.

44 Hewitt, Kane, and Ward, eds., *The Work of Many Hands,* 29–35; Shields, *Civil Tongues and Polite Letters,* 112–114; Carson, *Ambitious Appetites,* 130–135.

45 Upton, "The City as Material Culture," in Anne Elizabeth Yentsch and Mary C. Beaudry, eds., *The Art and Mystery of Historical Archaeology: Essays in Honor of James Deetz* (Boca Raton, Fla., 1992), 52–53; Myers Family Household Accounts, October 1824–July 1826. For examples of archaeologically recovered ceramic and glass ware from the house lots of wealthy Charlestonians, see Zierden, "A Trans-Atlantic Merchant's House in Charleston," *Historical Archaeology,* XXXIII (1999), 73–87.

CHAPTER THREE

1 Entry for Carl Reisinger, 1798 Federal Direct Tax Census, National Archives, Washington, D.C.; entry for Charles Reisinger, 1815 Federal Direct Tax Census, Lancaster County Historical Society (LCHS), Lancaster, Pa.; Charles Reisinger, Will, Lancaster County Will Book, vol. P, 414–416, Lancaster County Recorder of Wills, Lancaster, Pa.

2 1798 Federal Direct Tax Census; 1815 Federal Direct Tax Census.

3 On the regional identity of architecture in urban contexts, see Kenneth Severens, *Charleston Antebellum Architecture and Civic Destiny* (Knoxville, Tenn., 1988), 19–24.

4 James H. Mast, ed., "John Pearson's Description of Lancaster and Columbia in 1801," *Journal of the Lancaster County Histori-cal Society,* LXI, no. 3 (July 1957), 49–61; Edward C. Carter II et al., eds., *The Journals of Benjamin Henry Latrobe, 1799–1820,* III, *From Philadelphia to New Orleans* (New Haven, Conn., 1980), plate 3. Unfortunately, his preoccupation in verbally recording a colleague's death by typhoid fever distracted Latrobe from writing a descriptive narrative of the city he recorded in his September 1801 watercolor. Jerome H. Wood, Jr., sketches the broad history of the Borough of Lancaster in *Conestoga Crossroads: Lancaster, Pennsylvania, 1730–1790* (Harrisburg, Pa., 1979), 23–89.

5 Mast, ed., "John Pearson's Description," *Journal of the Lancaster County Historical Society,* LXI, no. 3 (July 1957), 51–52. Pearson's conflicted reading of Pennsylvania-German buildings was shared by his Anglo-Pennsylvanian contemporaries, including Benjamin Rush and international observers such as Johann David Schoepf, both of whom commented on the rural landscape. See Gabrielle Milan Lanier, "A Region of Regions: Local and Regional Culture in the Delaware Valley" (Ph.D. diss., University of Delaware, 1998), 44–46, 49–52.

6 Lanier, "A Region of Regions," 50–52; Stuart M. Blumin, *The Emergence of the Middle Class: Social Experience in the American City, 1760–1900* (Cambridge, 1989), 42–46; Horst Ossenberg, *Das Bürgerhaus in Baden* (Tübingen, 1986), 46–49.

7 In Charleston, the eighteenth-century core was roughly triangular, with its base stretching along East Bay Street and its pinnacle defined by Civic Square. By the mid-nineteenth century, however, the core shifted its axis from Broad Street to the commercial thoroughfare of King Street running northward from Civic Square. See Jeanne A. Calhoun and Martha A. Zierden, *Charleston's Commercial Landscape, 1803–1860,* Charleston Museum, Archaeological Contributions, no. 7 (Charleston, S.C., 1984), 59–60.

For a brief discussion of the topographical nature of Joseph Breintnall's 1729 poem on Philadelphia's High (now Market) Street, see Bernard L. Herman, "The Pennsylvania Gazette—CD-ROM Technology and Historical Research," *Research and Exploration,* VIII (1992), 262–263; Pamela J. Cressey et al., "The Core-Periphery Relationship and the Archaeological Record in Alexandria, Virginia," in Roy S. Dickens, Jr., ed., *Archaeology of Urban America: The Search for Pattern and Process* (New York, 1982), 144–146.

8 Henry C. Mercer, *The Bible in Iron; or, Pictured Stoves and Stove Plates of the Pennsylvania Germans* (Doylestown, Pa., 1941), 35–36; Scott T. Swank, "Proxemic Patterns," in Catherine E. Hutchins, ed., *Arts of the Pennsylvania Germans* (New York, 1983), 54–55.

 The observations on Mussertown in the Borough of Lancaster are based on the 1798 Direct Tax Census (National Archives) and the 1815 Direct Tax Census (LCHS). Supplementary materials include the Borough of Lancaster Tax List for 1800 (LCHS).

9 On the Pennsylvania-German house: William Woys Weaver, "The Pennsylvania German House: European Antecedents and New World Forms," *Winterthur Portfolio,* XXI (1986), 243–264; Edward A. Chappell, "Acculturation in the Shenandoah Valley: Rhenish Houses of the Massanutten Settlement," American Philosophical Society, *Proceedings,* CXXIV (1980), 55–89; Charles Lang Bergengren, "The Cycle of Transformations in the Houses of Schaefferstown, Pennsylvania" (Ph.D. diss., University of Pennsylvania, 1988), 1–62; Robert C. Bucher, "The Continental Log House," *Pennsylvania Folklife,* XII, no. 4 (Summer 1962), 14–19; Henry Glassie, "Eighteenth-Century Cultural Process in Delaware Valley Folk Building," *Winterthur Portfolio,* VII (1972), 41–44, Philip E. Pendleton, *Oley Valley Heritage: The Colonial Years, 1700–1775* (Birdsboro, Pa., 1994), 55–84, 167–175.

10 Susannah Dietrich House, 125 Howard Avenue, Lancaster, Pa., Historic Preservation Trust of Lancaster County.

11 Dellow-Mellinger House, 519 Church Street, Lancaster, Pa., Historic Preservation Trust of Lancaster County. These arguments have been advanced for rural Pennsylvania-German building traditions. See Chappell, "Acculturation in the Shenandoah Valley," APS, *Proceedings,* CXXIV (1980), 55–89; Glassie, "Eighteenth-Century Cultural Process," *Winterthur Portfolio,* VII (1972), 41–44.

12 Ossenberg, *Das Bürgerhaus in Baden.*

13 Ibid., 46–48, plates 38, 40, 67, 86, 88, 217; Ernst Stephan, *Das Bürgerhaus in Mainz* (Tübingen, 1974), 61, 98–99.

14 Jeffrey E. Klee, "An English House in the Germanic City: The Case of the William Montgomery House," MS, 1997.

15 Ellicott-Sehner House, 123 North Prince Street, Lancaster, Pa., Historic Preservation Trust of Lancaster County; probate inventory for Michael Gundacker (1815), Lancaster County Court House Archives, Lancaster, Pa.; see also Michael Gundacker's property assessments in the 1815 Federal Direct Tax Census (LCHS).

16 Blumin, *The Emergence of the Middle Class,* 177–179.

17 Lanier, "A Region of Regions," 84–86; Bernard L. Herman, "Town Houses: Dwellings in American Cities at the End of the Eighteenth Century," in Michael S. Steinitz, ed., *Landscapes Lost and Found: Architecture and Place in a New Nation* (Knoxville, Tenn., forthcoming).

18 Dell Upton, "The City as Material Culture," in Anne Elizabeth Yentsch and Mary C. Beaudry, eds., *The Art and Mystery of Historical Archaeology: Essays in Honor of James Deetz* (Boca Raton, Fla, 1992), 52–53; Gabrielle M. Lanier, "Ethnic Perceptions, Ethnic Landscapes: Material and Cultural Identity in a Region of Regions," in Steinitz, ed., *Landscapes Lost and Found;* Swank, "The Germanic Fragment," in Hutchins, ed., *Arts of the Pennsylvania Germans,* 4–5.

19 Severens, *Charleston Antebellum Architecture and Civic Destiny,* 8–19; Louis Perry Nelson, "The Material Word: Anglican Visual Culture in Colonial South Carolina" (Ph.D. diss., University of Delaware, 2000), 162–248; Carl Lounsbury, "The Dynamics of Architectural Design in Eighteenth-Century Charleston and the Lowcountry," in Annmarie Adams and Sally McMurry, eds., *Exploring Everyday Landscapes,* Perspectives in Vernacular Architecture, VII (Knoxville, Tenn., 1997), 58–65; Jeanne A. Calhoun, Elizabeth J. Reitz, Michael B. Trinkley, and Martha A. Zierden, *Meat in Due Season: Preliminary Investigations of Marketing Practices in Colonial Charleston,* Charleston Museum, Archaeological Contributions, no. 9 (Charleston, S.C., 1984).

 The characteristics of the Charleston single house have generated a great deal of comment. See, for example, Gene Waddell, "The Charleston Single House: An Architectural Survey," *Preservation Progress,* XXII, no. 2 (March 1977), 4–8; Harriet P. Simons and Albert Simons, "The William Burrows House of Charleston," *Winterthur Portfolio,* III (1967), 172–203; Bernard L. Herman, "The Embedded Landscapes of the Charleston Single House, 1780–1820," in Adams and McMurry, eds., *Exploring Everyday Landscapes,* 41–57.

20 Cressey et al., "The Core-Periphery Relationship and the Ar-

chaeological Record in Alexandria, Virginia," in Dickens, ed., *Archaeology of Urban America,* 143–173.

21 James Gregorie, McCrady Plat Collection, #503 (1797), Charleston, S.C., City Archives.

22 Benjamin Smith, McCrady Plat Collection, #557 (n.d.), Charleston, S.C., City Archives; plat of the property of Roger Smith, Charleston County Deed Book X-6 (February 1799), following 122; McCrady Plat Collection, #485 (1837); *Charleston Courier,* Feb. 20, 1816.

23 *Charleston Courier,* Feb. 20, 1816; McCrady Plat Collection, #485 (1837).

24 Edward A. Pearson, *Designs against Charleston: The Trial Record of the Denmark Vesey Slave Conspiracy of 1822* (Chapel Hill, N.C., 1999), 152–154; Gina Haney, "In Complete Order: Social Control and Architectural Organization in the Charleston Back Lot" (master's thesis, University of Virginia, 1997).

25 Blake tenements: Jonathan H. Poston, *The Buildings of Charleston: A Guide to the City's Architecture* (Charleston, S.C., 1997), 180–181.

26 Peter A. Coclanis, "The Sociology of Architecture in Colonial Charleston: Pattern and Process in an Eighteenth-Century Southern City," *Journal of Social History,* XVIII (1984–1985), 607–623; Richard C. Wade, *Slavery in the Cities: The South, 1820–1860* (New York, 1964), 55–79; Herman, "The Embedded Landscapes of the Charleston Single House, 1780–1820," in Adams and McMurry, eds., *Exploring Everyday Houses,* 41–57; Simons and Simons, "The William Burrows House of Charleston," *Winterthur Portfolio,* III (1967), 182–183, 191–200.

27 Information on Petersburg's early-nineteenth-century commercial buildings courtesy of Willie Graham, Colonial Williamsburg Foundation. Databases for Northern Liberties West, 1798 Federal Direct Tax Census (National Archives) compiled by Gabrielle M. Lanier, www.math.udel.edu/~rstevens/datasets/nlibe_98.dbf; Cornelius William Stafford, *The Philadelphia Directory, for 1801* . . . (Philadelphia, 1801); James Robinson, *The Philadelphia Directory for 1806* . . . (Philadelphia, 1806); *Census Directory for 1811* . . . (Philadelphia, 1811); Dan Cruickshank, "Analyses of Beauty," *Renovation: A Supplement Published by the Architects' Journal* (October 1989), 16–25; Peter Guillery and Bernard L. Herman, *Deptford Houses: 1650–1800: A Report Based on Field Survey in Deptford, London,*

SE8 (London, 1998); Sylvia Collier and Sarah Pearson, *Whitehaven, 1660–1800: A New Town of the Late Seventeenth Century: A Study of Its Buildings and Urban Development* (London, 1991), 87, 105–106.

28 John Bold, "The Design of a House for a Merchant, 1724," *Architectural History,* XXXIII (1990), 77–79.

29 Nicholas B. Wainwright, *Colonial Grandeur in Philadelphia: The House and Furniture of General John Cadwalader* (Philadelphia, 1964), 8–9.

30 Richard M. Candee, "Social Conflict and Urban Rebuilding: The Portsmouth, New Hampshire, Brick Act of 1814," *Winterthur Portfolio,* XXXII (1997), 119–146.

31 Richard M. Candee, *Building Portsmouth: The Neighborhoods and Architecture of New Hampshire's Oldest City* (Portsmouth, N.H., 1992), 99, 111–113.

32 Ibid., 90–91; Joseph S. Wood and Michael P. Steinitz, *The New England Village* (Baltimore, 1997), 74.

33 A common form in seaport towns north of Boston, dwellings placed with their gables to the street date from the early eighteenth century through the early nineteenth. The siting strategy was especially favored in Charlestown and Salem.

34 Bernard L. Herman, "Southern City, National Ambition: Washington's Early Town Houses," in Howard Gillette, Jr., ed., *Southern City, National Ambition: The Growth of Early Washington, D.C., 1800–1860* (Washington D.C., 1995), 38–39; Ethelyn Cox, *Historic Alexandria, Virginia, Street by Street: A Survey of Existing Early Buildings* (Alexandria, Va., 1976); Christopher Martin, "'Hope Deferred': The Origin and Development of Alexandria's Flounder House," in Camille Wells, ed., *Perspectives in Vernacular Architecture,* II (Columbia, Mo., 1986), 111–119; Gary Stanton, "'Alarmed by the Cry of Fire': How Fire Changed Fredericksburg, Virginia," in Carter L. Hudgins and Elizabeth Collins Cromley, eds., *Shaping Communities,* Perspectives in Vernacular Architecture, VI (Knoxville, Tenn., 1997), 128–129.

35 Henry Glassie, "Eighteenth-Century Cultural Process," *Winterthur Portfolio,* VII (1972), 41–44; Robert F. Ensminger, *The Pennsylvania Barn: Its Origin, Evolution, and Distribution in North America* (Baltimore, 1992), 107–146.

CHAPTER FOUR

1 The trial transcripts for Billy Robinson as well as other conspirators brought before the Charleston court are found in Edward A. Pearson, *Designs against Charleston: The Trial Record of the Denmark Vesey Slave Conspiracy of 1822* (Chapel Hill, N.C., 1999), 253–257, 306. Because Pearson's transcription and editing of the Denmark Vesey trial transcripts have been subject to extensive criticism, I quote from Oliver Killens, ed., *The Trial Record of Denmark Vesey* (Boston, 1970), whenever possible, in this case 125–126, 147.

2 Dell Upton, "White and Black Landscapes in Eighteenth-Century Virginia," in Robert Blair St. George, ed., *Material Life in America, 1600–1860* (Boston, 1988), 357–369; Mechal Sobel, *The World They Made Together: Black and White Values in Eighteenth-Century Virginia* (Princeton, N.J., 1987), 100–153; Martha A. Zierden and Bernard L. Herman, "Charleston Townhouses: Archaeology, Architecture, and the Urban Landscape, 1750–1850," in Rebecca Yamin and Karen Bescherer Metheny, eds., *Landscape Archaeology: Reading and Interpreting the American Historical Landscape* (Knoxville, Tenn., 1996), 193–227; Herman, "The Embedded Landscapes of the Charleston Single House, 1780–1820," in Annmarie Adams and Sally McMurry, eds., *Exploring Everyday Landscapes,* Perspectives in Vernacular Architecture, VII (Knoxville, Tenn., 1997), 41–57; Richard C. Wade, *Slavery in the Cities: The South, 1820–1860* (New York, 1964), 55–79.

3 Lionel Chalmers, "A Sketch of the Climate, Water, and Soil in South Carolina," in *American Museum; or, Repository of Ancient and Modern Fugitive Pieces, etc. Prose and Poetical,* III (1788), 333.

The occupational profile of Elliott Street was derived from James R. Schenck, *The Directory and Stranger's Guide for the City of Charleston; also a Directory for Charleston Neck . . . for the Year 1822* (Charleston, S.C., 1822).

4 David A. Smith, "Dependent Urbanization in Colonial America: The Case of Charleston, South Carolina," *Social Forces,* LXVI (1987–1988), 1–28. The overall pattern of Elliott Street's occupational mix is based on databases developed from local street directories. See Schenk, *The Directory and Stranger's Guide;* Eleazer Elizer, *A Directory, for 1803; Containing, the Names of All House-Keepers and Traders in the City of Charleston . . .* (Charleston, S.C., [1803]).

5 McCrady Plat Collection, #3385 (1851); see also plat #3371.

6 Jonathan H. Poston, *The Buildings of Charleston: A Guide to the City's Architecture* (Columbia, S.C., 1997), 77–79, 80–81; Gina Haney, "In Complete Order: Social Control and Architectural Organization in the Charleston Back Lot" (master's thesis, University of Virginia, 1997).

7 Susan Buck, "Paint Discoveries in the Aiken-Rhett House Outbuildings," paper presented to the Vernacular Architecture Forum, Newport, R.I., 2001.

8 Field information on the Bocquet-Simons House was compiled in the course of an environmental assessment leading to the construction of a new judicial center. See Preservation Consultants, *Phase One Cultural Resource Assessment, Hollings Judicial Center Annex* (Charleston, S.C., 1996), entries for 93 Broad Street (Bocquet-Simons House); Michael Trinkley and Debi Hacker, *Life on Broad Street: Archaeological Survey of the Hollings Judicial Center Annex, Charleston, South Carolina,* Chicora Research Contribution no. 192 (Columbia, S.C., 1996).

9 McCrady Plat Collection, #464 (1797), #536 (1799), #172 (n.d., late eighteenth century), #178 (1798), #3334 (n.d., early nineteenth century), #562 (1801).

10 Joseph W. Barnwell, ed., "Diary of Timothy Ford, 1785–1786," *South Carolina Historical and Genealogical Magazine,* XIII (1912), 142–143.

11 Bristol (England) Municipal Charities documentation of Orchard Street properties, courtesy Roger Leech, Royal Commission for the Historic Monuments of England; Mark Girouard, *The English Town: A History of Urban Life* (New Haven, Conn., 1990), 121; Sylvia Collier and Sara Pearson, *Whitehaven, 1660–1800: A New Town of the Late Seventeenth Century: A Study of Its Buildings and Urban Development* (London, 1991), 108–109.

12 Virginia Mutual Assurance Surveys (VMAS), James Dyson, VI, #55 (1796), William Plume, VI, #99 (1796), Virginia State Archives, Richmond.

13 Collier and Pearson, *Whitehaven,* 108–109, 115, 117, 121–122.

14 Dan Cruickshank and Neil Burton, *Life in the Georgian City* (London, 1990), 52–53, 87, 237–254. Comments on unhealth-

ful cellar kitchens are found in Collier and Pearson, *White-haven*, 108–109.

15 Walter Ison, *The Georgian Buildings of Bristol* (1952; rpt. Bath, 1978), 204–209.

16 Cruickshank and Burton, *Life in the Georgian City*, 58–59.

17 Inventory for Penelope Iremonger, circa 1827, 12 Bolton Row, London, Downs Collection, Winterthur Museum and Library. The motive behind Penelope Iremonger's inventory appears to be an estate settlement. Although the document details the contents of her house, room by room, and provides a total valuation, it does not assign monetary values to individual objects. Moreover, such listings related to estate settlements are rare in early-nineteenth-century England.

18 Adam Menuge and Robert Hook, *The Crescent, Buxton, Derbyshire: Historic Building Report* (Swindon, 1996).

19 James Fenimore Cooper quoted in Montgomery Schuyler, "The Small City House in New York," *Architectural Record*, VIII (1898–1899), 357.

20 VMAS Declarations, VII, no. 226 (1797); "A Plan . . . of the Intersection of Free Mason and Catherine Streets with a Ground Plan of the Buildings thereon . . . Property of Moses Myers" (n.d., est. ca. 1816), Collections of the Moses Myers House, Chrysler Museum of Art, Norfolk, Va.; Anna Vemer Andrzejewski, "Architecture and the Ideology of Surveillance in Modern America, 1850–1950" (Ph.D. diss., University of Delaware, 2000), 138–204.

Fire insurance surveys for 1796 list 176 houses. Of the 112 kitchens identified in these surveys, 68 (nearly two-thirds) were separate buildings, and 26 (just fewer than one-quarter) were found in cellars. Kitchen ells were more unusual (15 cases). Of all the properties surveyed, 64 (just more than one-third) had no specified kitchen, an indication that these domestic work spaces were incorporated within the main floor of the house.

21 An overview of garret and cellar spaces in Philadelphia town houses is provided in John M. Bacon, *Cellars, Garrets, and Related Spaces in Philadelphia Houses, 1750–1850* (Philadelphia, 1991). Similar arrangements also existed in New York City. See Shane White, *Somewhat More Independent: The End of Slavery in New York City, 1770–1810* (Athens, Ga., 1991), 92.

22 612 Spruce Street (Summers House) research file, Philadelphia Historical Commission; "Estimate for Mr. Proll[?] for Alterations at his House in Race Street abov[e] 7th St.," Thomas Somerville Stewart, Ledger, 1829–mid-nineteenth century, 18; Cruickshank and Burton, *Life in the Georgian City*, 52, 118, 130 (of particular note is the case study of 4–13 Queen Anne's Gate, Westminster, 236–254); Pancoast-Lewis-Wharton House, Historic American Buildings Survey, Pennsylvania #1083, Library of Congress; Pancoast-Lewis-Wharton House research file, Philadelphia Historical Commission; George B. Tatum, *Philadelphia Georgian: The City House of Samuel Powel and Some of Its Eighteenth-Century Neighbors* (Middletown, Conn., 1976), 55–61.

23 Karie Diethorn, *Domestic Servants in Philadelphia, 1780–1830* (Philadelphia, 1986), 101–102 (punctuation corrected). Diethorn's monograph, available only as a technical report, remains the single best work on Philadelphia service spaces and servant quarters.

24 Annik Pardailhé-Galabrun, *The Birth of Intimacy: Privacy and Domestic Life in Early Modern Paris* (Philadelphia, 1991), 37–39, 51–58; Daniel Roche, *The People of Paris: An Essay in Popular Culture in the Eighteenth Century* (Berkeley, Calif., 1987), 105–106.

25 Simon Schama, *The Embarrassment of Riches: An Interpretation of Dutch Culture in the Golden Age* (Berkeley, Calif., 1988), 460; Mariet Westermann, "'Costly and Curious, Full of Pleasure and Home Contentment': Making Home in the Dutch Republic," in Mariet Westermann, ed., *Art and Home: Dutch Interiors in the Age of Rembrandt* (Zwolle, Neth., 2001), 62–63; H. Perry Chapman, Wouter Th. Kloek, and Arthur K. Wheelock, Jr., *Jan Steen: Painter and Storyteller*, ed. Guido M. C. Jansen (Washington, D.C., 1996), 168; Peter Stallybrass and Allon White, *The Poetics and Politics of Transgression* (Ithaca, N.Y., 1986), 1–26; Susan Stewart, *On Longing: Narratives of the Miniature, the Gigantic, the Souvenir, the Collection* (Durham, N.C.,1993), 118–119; Robert Darnton, *The Great Cat Massacre and Other Episodes in French Cultural History* (New York, 1984), 75–104.

26 McCrady Plat Collection, #569 (1789); Zierden and Herman, "Charleston Townhouses," in Yamin and Metheny, *Landscape Archaeology*, 213–218. Mills Lane offers a discussion of the

house plan without consideration for the ways in which it functioned in the overall lot ensemble in *Architecture of the Old South: South Carolina* (New York, 1989), 74–75.

27 Barnwell, ed., "Diary of Timothy Ford," *South Carolina Historical and Genealogical Magazine*, XIII (1912), 142–143.

28 James Sidbury, "Gabriel's World: Race Relations in Richmond, Virginia, 1750–1810" (Ph.D. diss., Johns Hopkins University, 1991), 138 (the account of Sally's experience in the Boyce household does not appear in Sidbury's *Ploughshares into Swords: Race, Rebellion, and Identity in Gabriel's Virginia, 1730–1810* [Cambridge, 1997]).

29 Martha Zierden, "Excavations at the Miles Brewton House, 1988–1990," notes on file, Charleston Museum, Charleston, S.C.

30 *Charleston Courier*, Mar. 25, 1816. Transcriptions of real estate advertisements published in early-nineteenth-century Charleston are in the collections of the McKissick Museum, University of South Carolina, Columbia. I am indebted to Gary Stanton for access to this material.

31 Inventory for Martha Godin (1786), Charleston Inventories, Inventory Book B, 22–23; inventory for Matthew William Cross (1811), Inventory Book E (1811), 43–44.

32 Inventory for George Ingliss (1755), Charleston County Inventories, Inventory Book A, 452–455; inventory for Alexander Ingliss (1791), Inventory Book B, 369–376.

33 Colonoware and creamware: Martha A. Zierden, *Excavations at 14 Legare Street, Charleston, South Carolina,* Charleston Museum, Archaeological Contributions, no. 28 (Charleston, S.C., 2001), 8-16-8-20; Leland Ferguson, *Uncommon Ground: Archaeology and Early African America, 1650–1800* (Washington, D.C., 1992), 18–32, 82–107, 110–116; Theresa A. Singleton, "The Archaeology of Slave Life," in Edward D. C. Campbell, Jr., and Kym S. Rice, eds., *Before Freedom Came: African-American Life in the Antebellum South* (Charlottesville, Va., 1991), 159–161.

Sweetgrass baskets: Dale Rosengarten, *Row upon Row: Sea Grass Baskets of the South Carolina Lowcountry* (Columbia, S.C., 1986).

Body adornments: Martha Zierden, Archaeological Collections of the Charleston Museum. The permanent collections of the Charleston Museum include the archaeological materials recovered from numerous sites within both the city and the surrounding lowcountry. The specifics of these sites appear in an excellent series of reports published by the Charleston Museum.

Servant possessions: excavations in Annapolis, personal communication from Anne Yentsch; Michael Blakey, "The New York African Burial Ground: Bio-Cultural and Engaged," Delaware Seminar in American Art, History, and Material Culture, University of Delaware, Newark, Nov. 7, 1996.

Foods: Singleton, "The Archaeology of Slave Life," in Campbell and Rice, eds., *Before Freedom Came,* 171–172; Ferguson, *Uncommon Ground,* 96–100. Clear evidence of provisions purchased expressly for segregated diets appears in the Myers family household account books in Norfolk, Va., during the 1820s. The notation "kitchen" indicates items intended for the family's servants. Myers Family Papers, Chrysler Museum.

34 Pearson, *Designs against Charleston,* 182, 199, 255; Killens, *The Trial Record of Denmark Vesey,* 53, 107, 127.

CHAPTER FIVE

1 I extend heartfelt thanks to Richard M. Candee, Holly Mitchell, Gerald and Barbara Ward, Joanna McBrien, Jane and Richard Nylander, and Michael Steinitz for all their help with fieldwork and documentary research in Portsmouth. Thanks are also extended to the staff of Strawbery Banke for their collegiality and kindnesses. Information on Samuel and Hannah Rand comes from a variety of sources, including city street directories, probate court dockets, and the registry of deeds for Rockingham County, N.H. See Samuel Rand, Docket #10442 (1821) Rockingham County, N.H., Probate Records.

2 The dower division for Hannah Rand is contained in Samuel Rand Estate, Docket #10442 (1822), Rockingham County Probate Records.

3 Marylynn Salmon, *Women and the Law of Property in Early America* (Chapel Hill, N.C., 1986), esp. 141–184; Jane C. Nylander, *Our Own Snug Fireside: Images of the New England Home, 1760–1860* (New York, 1993), 62–65. See also Suzanne Lebsock, *The Free Women of Petersburg: Status and Culture in a Southern Town, 1784–1860* (New York, 1985), esp. chaps. 2, 5; Christine Stansell, *City of Women: Sex and Class in New York, 1789–1860* (Urbana, Ill., 1987), 11–30. Laurel Thatcher Ulrich

discusses widows and their maintenance only in passing; see *Good Wives: Image and Reality in the Lives of Women in Northern New England, 1650–1750* (New York, 1982). For an English perspective, see Leonore Davidoff and Catherine Hall, *Family Fortunes: Men and Women of the English Middle Class, 1780–1850* (New York, 1987), 275–279. Davidoff and Hall's assessment of widows' possessions springs from a larger reading of patterns of concepts of dependence and patterns of control reflected in women's property. For changing notions of widows' dower rights in colonial Connecticut, see Cornelia Hughes Dayton, *Women before the Bar: Gender, Law, and Society in Connecticut, 1639–1789* (Chapel Hill, N.C., 1995), 40–44.

4 The concept of competency and its social dimensions is fully explored in Daniel Vickers, "Competency and Competition: Economic Culture in Early America," *William and Mary Quarterly*, 3d Ser., XLVII (1990), 3–29, and in Vickers, *Farmers and Fishermen: Two Centuries of Work in Essex County, Massachusetts, 1630–1850* (Chapel Hill, N.C., 1994), 14–23. An excellent overview of the concept of competency and its relationship to the landscapes of the early New England village appears in Joseph S. Wood and Michael P. Steinitz, *The New England Village* (Baltimore, 1997), 20, 38–39.

For definitions of competency, see William L. Barney: "Competency [was] the comfortable existence of independence and self-sufficiency that an individual could achieve with a sufficient amount of income-producing property" (*The Passage of the Republic: An Interdisciplinary History of Nineteenth-Century America* [Lexington, Mass., 1987], 23). Drew R. McCoy uses the term "independence" as a synonym for competency in *The Elusive Republic: Political Economy in Jeffersonian America* (Chapel Hill, N.C., 1980), 67–70.

5 Holly Bentley Mitchell, "'Power of Thirds': The Material Lives of Widows, Portsmouth, New Hampshire, 1816–1826" (master's thesis, University of Delaware, 1991), 23–35.

6 Abbott Lowell Cummings, *Framed Houses of Massachusetts Bay, 1625–1725* (Cambridge, Mass., 1979), 22–39; Henry Glassie, *Pattern in the Material Folk Culture of the Eastern United States* (Philadelphia, 1968), 125–127. For a fuller discussion of Portsmouth housing forms, see Richard M. Candee, *Building Portsmouth: The Neighborhoods and Architecture of New Hampshire's Oldest City* (Portsmouth, N.H., 1992); James Leo Garvin, "Academic Architecture and the Building Trades in the Piscataqua Region of New Hampshire and Maine, 1715–1815" (Ph.D. diss., Boston University, 1983).

7 Comparative information on occupations and community identity is based on a collection of databases constructed from city street directories compiled between 1795 and 1830. Among those cited here are Wibird Penhallow, *The Portsmouth Directory, Containing Names of the Inhabitants, Their Occupations, Places of Business and Dwelling Houses* (Portsmouth, N.H., 1822); "Invoice of Polls and Taxable Property on which the Taxes for the Town of Portsmouth are assessed for the Year 1823," Portsmouth Public Library; Eleazer Elizer, *A Directory for 1803; Containing, the Names of All House-Keepers and Traders in the City of Charleston . . .* (Charleston, S.C., [1803]); James R. Schenk, *The Directory and Stranger's Guide for the City of Charleston; also a Directory for Charleston Neck . . . for the Year 1822* (Charleston, S.C., 1822); Charles H. Simmons, *Simmons Norfolk Directory, Containing the Names, Occupations, and Places of Abode of the Inhabitants, Arranged in Alphabetical Order* (Norfolk, Va., 1801); database for the Southwark district of Philadelphia, 1798–1800 (http//www.math.udel.edu/~rstevens/datasets.html; *Census Directory for 1811 . . .* (Philadelphia, 1811); Robert Desilver, *Desilver's Philadelphia Directory, and Stranger's Guide, for 1828* (Philadelphia, 1828). Also cited are returns from the street directory database project of Massachusetts Historical Society, Boston. I am indebted to Len Travers for his kindness in answering multiple requests.

For the hazards and conditions of life at sea in the first half of the eighteenth century, see Marcus Rediker, *Between the Devil and the Deep Blue Sea: Merchant Seamen, Pirates, and the Anglo-American Maritime World, 1700–1750* (New York, 1987).

8 Tax databases have been developed for a number of cities. Those using the 1798 Federal Direct Tax Census were supported through the National Endowment for the Humanities and include Boston, Providence, Philadelphia, Lancaster, and Baltimore. Tax list databases using local assessments have been compiled for Philadelphia (1798–1799), Portsmouth (1821), Lancaster (1800), and Norfolk (1800). All databases are on file at the Center for Historic Architecture and Design, University of Delaware, Newark.

9 Candee, *Building Portsmouth*, 73.

10 Inventory for Samuel Rand, Docket #10442 (1822), Rockingham County, N.H., Probate Records.

11 Samuel Rand Estate Papers, Docket #10442 (1822), Rockingham County, N.H., Probate Court.

12 Mark R. Wenger, "The Central Passage in Virginia: Evolution of an Eighteenth-Century Living Space," in Camille Wells, ed., *Perspectives in Vernacular Architecture*, II (Columbia, Mo., 1986), 137–149; Wenger, "The Dining Room in Early Virginia," in Thomas Carter and Bernard L. Herman, eds., *Perspectives in Vernacular Architecture*, III (Columbia, Mo., 1989), 149–159; Richard L. Bushman, *The Refinement of America: Persons, Houses, Cities* (New York, 1992), 242–267.

13 James Hill Dower Division, Docket #8809 (1814), Rockingham County, N.H., Probate Records.

14 Inventory for James Hill, ibid. For the idea of a recipe, see Scott T. Swank, "Proxemic Patterns," in Catherine E. Hutchins, ed., *Arts of the Pennsylvania Germans* (New York, 1983), 40–43; Nylander, *Our Own Snug Fireside*, 59–63; Laurel Thatcher Ulrich, *A Midwife's Tale: The Life of Martha Ballard, Based on Her Diary, 1785–1812* (New York, 1990), 142–143.

15 Samuel Beck Dower Division, Docket #9878 (1819), George Hill Dower Division, Docket #10200 (1821), Rockingham County, N.H., Probate Records.

16 Salmon suggests this approach to creating dowers in *Women and the Law of Property*, 141, 168.

17 Nathaniel Souther Dower Division, Docket #10766 (1824), Rockingham County, N.H., Probate Court.

18 Inventory for John Eberth (1786), Book I, 175, Philadelphia Wills and Administrations; Annik Pardailhé-Galabrun, *The Birth Of Intimacy: Privacy and Domestic Life in Early Modern Paris* (1988), trans. Jocelyn Phelps (Philadelphia, 1991), 112–113. Chain of title and residential listings for 423 Vine Street provided courtesy of Miriam and Rick Camitta and on file at the Philadelphia Historical Commission.

19 Joseph Amazeen Dower Division, Docket #10845 (1824), Rockingham County, N.H., Probate Records; Mitchell, "'Power of Thirds,'" 34–35, 66. The Amazeen dwelling survives as a museum house at Strawbery Banke Museum, Portsmouth, N.H. The Mary Ryder Wood House is also open to visitors in the same museum complex.

20 Salmon, *Women and the Law of Property*, 142–160; Carole Shammas, Marylynn Salmon, and Michel Dahlin, *Inheritance in America from Colonial Times to the Present* (New Brunswick, N.J., 1987), 67–69; Dayton, *Women before the Bar*, 40–44.

21 Inventory for Thomas Manning, Docket #9908 o.s. (1819), Dower of Margaret Manning widow of Thomas, Docket #9908 (1819), Rockingham County, N.H., Probate Records.

22 Alexander Petrie, Will (1768), Charleston County, S.C., Will Book, XI, 307; inventory for Elizabeth Petrie (ca. 1808), Orange Street Research File, Historic Charleston Foundation, Charleston, S.C.; Salmon, *Women and the Law of Property*, 156–160.

23 Barbara G. Carson, *Ambitious Appetites: Dining, Behavior, and Patterns of Consumption in Federal Washington* (Washington, D.C., 1990), 103–135.

24 Marylynn Salmon, *Women and the Law of Property*, 156–160; Salmon, "Women and Property in South Carolina: The Evidence from Marriage Settlements, 1730–1830," in Robert Blair St. George, ed., *Material Life in America, 1600–1860* (Boston, 1988), 295–296; will and inventory for Latitia Lavergne (1802), Philadelphia County, Wills, N, 37. For an excellent introduction to servants and service in eighteenth-century Philadelphia town houses, see Karie Diethorn, *Domestic Servants in Philadelphia, 1780–1830* (Philadelphia, 1986).

25 Orange Street Research File, Historic Charleston Foundation.

26 Elias B. Bull, "Tobias Cambridge House (c. 1789), 12 Orange Street," 16–18, MS report (1988), Orange Street Research File, Historic Charleston Foundation.

27 Inventory for Elizabeth Greenleaf (1804), Suffolk County, Mass., Probate Records, CII, 127–128; inventory for Sarah Doubt, XCVII, 402–403; inventory for Johanna Conner (ca. 1799), XCVIII, 187–188; Boston, Record Commissioners, Twenty-second Report, *A Report of the Record Commissioners of the City of Boston, Containing the Statistics of the United States' Direct Tax of 1798, as Assessed on Boston; and the Names of the Inhabitants of Boston in 1790 as Collected for the First National Census* (Boston, 1890), 163. For information on residential patterns in late-eighteenth-century Boston, I am again indebted to Len Travers of the Massachusetts Historical Society, Boston, for access to the Boston Directory Database, 1789–1809, created under his direction (see above, Chapter 1, n. 7).

28 Inventory for Mary Harper (1801), Philadelphia County, Will Book, W-61. Additional information on Mary Harper is drawn from the 1798 Federal Direct Tax Census and city directories for 1798–1801.

29 Will and inventory for David Duncan (1800), Philadelphia County, Will Book, W-41. Additional information on Phebe Duncan is drawn from the 1798 Federal Direct Tax Census and city directories for 1798–1801. Deed transactions for Phebe Duncan's house and lot include John Broomwick to Phebe Duncan, "his sister" (1801), EF 6 216; Phebe Duncan to John Broomwick (1811), IC 14 621, Philadelphia Recorder of Deeds. I am indebted to Ann Kirschner for her kindness in providing the title trace for Phebe Duncan's real property.

30 Inventory for Elizabeth Lawrence (1801), Philadelphia County, Will Book, Y, 552; will and inventory for Isabella Caldwell (1803), I, 136; Billy G. Smith, *The "Lower Sort": Philadelphia's Laboring People, 1750–1800* (Ithaca, N.Y., 1990), 127, 168–170; Elizabeth Blackmar, *Manhattan for Rent, 1785–1850* (Ithaca, N.Y., 1989), 170–171.

31 Scotland Hill's estate papers are located in the New Castle County, Del., Wills, Inventories, and Administrations, Delaware State Archives, Dover. The Delaware State Archives also holds the tax assessment books for the city of Wilmington and Christiana Hundred. See also R. Porter, *A Directory and Register for the Year 1814 . . . of the City of Wilmington and Brandywine* (Wilmington, 1814), esp. 48 (also typescript, n.d., Historical Society of Delaware, Wilmington). An earlier version of the story of the Hills appeared as Bernard L. Herman, "The *Bricoleur* Revisited," in Ann Smart Martin and J. Ritchie Garrison, eds., *American Material Culture: The Shape of the Field* (Knoxville, Tenn., 1997), 37–63.

32 John Knapp Dower (1814), Essex County, Mass., Probate Court, CCCLXXXV, 522; inventory for John Knapp (1814), CCCLXXXV, 490; inventory for Mary Knapp (1814), CCCLXXXVII, 314–315.

33 Fieldwork on the Mary Knapp House was supported by the Massachusetts Historical Commission in the course of evaluating the historic resources of Newburyport in 1998.

34 Julie Hardwick, "Widowhood and Patriarchy in Seventeenth-Century France," *Journal of Social History,* XXVI (1992–1993), 134–135.

35 Ibid., 133–148; Joan R. Gundersen, "Independence, Citizenship, and the American Revolution," *Signs: Journal of Women in Culture and Society,* XIII (1987–1988), 59–77.

36 Hannah Rand to Ebenezer Pike (July 3, 1823), Deed Book 236, p. 452, Rockingham County Recorder of Deeds, and John Locke to Hannah Rand (Mar. 22, 1824), Deed Book 237, p. 340.

CHAPTER SIX

1 Inventory for Angus Grant (Jan. 7, 1800), Baltimore County Wills (1799–1800), WK 1063, no. 20, 369–370, Maryland State Archives, Annapolis; 1798 Federal Direct Tax Census, Fells Point, Maryland Historical Society, Baltimore; John Mullin, *The Baltimore Directory, for 1799, Containing the Names, Occupations, and Places of Abode of the Citizens . . .* (Baltimore, 1799).

2 See Paul E. Buchanan, "The Eighteenth-Century Frame Houses of Tidewater Virginia," in Charles E. Peterson, ed., *Building Early America: Contributions toward the History of a Great Industry* (Radnor, Pa., 1976), 54–73; Dell Upton, "Traditional Timber Framing," in Brooke Hindle, ed., *Material Culture of the Wooden Age* (Tarrytown, N.Y., 1981), 51–61.

3 Elizabeth Blackmar, *Manhattan for Rent, 1785–1850* (Ithaca, N.Y., 1989), 60–68. The residences of Elizabeth Claxton and her neighbors along with their uses are described in the Federal Direct Tax Census, Northern Liberties West, Philadelphia, National Archives, Washington, D.C.; James Robinson, *The Philadelphia Directory, for 1808 . . .* (Philadelphia, 1808); 306 Lawrence Street File, Philadelphia Historical Commission, Philadelphia. The building files at the Philadelphia Historical Commission contain ownership histories and copies of early-nineteenth-century insurance surveys.

4 Billy G. Smith, *The "Lower Sort": Philadelphia's Laboring People, 1750–1800* (Ithaca, N.Y., 1990), 4–6; Stuart M. Blumin, *The Emergence of the Middle Class: Social Experience in the American City, 1760–1900* (Cambridge, 1989), 26–38; Richard M. Candee, *Building Portsmouth: The Neighborhoods and Architecture of New Hampshire's Oldest City* (Portsmouth, N.H., 1992), 114; Bernard L. Herman, "The Architectural and Social Topography of Early-Nineteenth-Century Portsmouth, New Hampshire," in Elizabeth Collins Cromley and Carter L. Hudgins,

eds., *Gender, Class, and Shelter,* Perspectives in Vernacular Architecture, V (Knoxville, Tenn., 1995), 227, 235–236.

5 Herman, "The Architectural and Social Topography of Early-Nineteenth-Century Portsmouth, New Hampshire," in Cromley and Hudgins, eds., *Gender, Class, and Shelter,* 225–242; Candee, *Building Portsmouth,* 68–73.

6 Blumin, *Emergence of the Middle Class,* 38–65; Smith, *The "Lower Sort,"* 197–200; Susan Stewart, *On Longing: Narratives of the Miniature, the Gigantic, the Souvenir, the Collection* (Durham, N.C., 1993), 134–139. For the material culture of the consumer revolutions, see Cary Carson, "The Consumer Revolution in Colonial British America: Why Demand?" in Carson, Ronald Hoffman, and Peter J. Albert, eds., *Of Consuming Interests: The Style of Life in the Eighteenth Century* (Charlottesville, Va., 1994), 483–495; Ann Smart Martin, "Makers, Buyers, and Users: Consumerism as a Material Culture Framework," *Winterthur Portfolio,* XXVIII (1993), 141–157.

7 For a failure in the ability to enact the rituals of sociability and its consequence, see Rhys Isaac, *The Transformation of Virginia, 1740–1790* (Chapel Hill, N.C., 1982), 77–78.

8 Stewart, *On Longing,* 106; Peter Stallybrass and Allon White, *The Politics and Poetics of Transgression* (Ithaca, N.Y., 1986), 13, 25–26; Robert Mugerauer, *Interpreting Environments: Tradition, Deconstruction, Hermeneutics* (Austin, Tex., 1995), 30–56; Robert Darnton, *The Great Cat Massacre and Other Episodes in French Cultural History* (New York, 1985), 75–104.

9 David Bindman, *Hogarth and His Times: Serious Comedy* (London, 1997), plates 10, 45; Jenny Uglow, *Hogarth: A Life and a World* (New York, 1997), 196–208.

10 John Gay, "The Tea-Table: A Town Ecologue," in Vinton A. Dearing, ed., *John Gay: Poetry and Prose* (Oxford, 1974), I, 234–237; Uglow, *Hogarth: A Life and a World;* John Brewer, *The Pleasures of the Imagination: English Culture in the Eighteenth Century* (New York, 1997), 263–264.

11 Pattern in the architectural fabric of Fells Point drawn from a database linking the 1798 Federal Direct Tax Census for Fells Point (Maryland Historical Society) and Mullin, *The Baltimore Directory, for 1799.* See also Richard M. Bernard, "A Portrait of Baltimore in 1800: Economic and Occupational Patterns in an Early American City," *Maryland Historical Magazine,* LXIX (1974), 341–360.

12 Margaret B. Tinkcom, "Southwark, a River Community: Its Shape and Substance," American Philosophical Society, *Proceedings,* CXIV (1970), 327–342. The profile of housing in Southwark is based on linking the Southwark East List of Rateables for 1799 (Philadelphia City Archives) with the Phladelphia street directories for 1798, 1799, and 1800 and the 1798 Federal Direct Tax Census, Southwark East (National Archives). Cornelius William Stafford, *The Philadelphia Directory, for 1798* . . . (Philadelphia, 1798); Stafford, *The Philadelphia Directory, for 1799* . . . (Philadelphia, 1799); James Robinson, *Robinson's Philadelphia Register and City Directory, for 1799* . . . (Philadelphia, 1799); Stafford, *The Philadelphia Directory, for 1800* . . . (Philadelphia, 1800).

Becks and Parhams Alleys: database for Southwark East, 1798–1800: http://www.math.udel.edu/˜rstevens/datasets.html.

13 Jennifer Barrett, "A Profile of Almond Street, 1800–1840," Southwark, Philadelphia, MS, 2001.

14 The plans and elevations for the Jackson Court tenements are represented in an agreement between Michael Pepper and George J. Ewing (May 18, 1829) illustrated and discussed in Donna J. Rilling, *Making Houses, Crafting Capitalism: Builders in Philadelphia, 1790–1850* (Philadelphia, 2001), 79–80, 84; Survey no. 510 (June 5, 1832), Franklin Fire Insurance Company of Philadelphia Papers, Historical Society of Pennsylvania, Philadelphia.

15 Inventory for Matthew Johns, City of Philadelphia Wills and Adminstrations (1800), no. 120.

16 Southwark East List of Rateables for 1799; 1798 Federal Direct Tax Census, Southwark East; Stafford, *The Philadelphia Directory, for 1798; The Philadelphia Directory, for 1799; The Philadelphia Directory, for 1800;* Robinson, *Robinson's Philadelphia Register and City Directory, for 1799.*

17 Database for Southwark East, 1798–1800. Information on caulkers developed from database for Southwark East, 1798–1800.

18 Database for Southwark East, 1798–1800; Wharton-Stewart House (survey number HABS PA-1185), 27 Christian St., Philadelphia, Philadelphia County, recorded 1966, demolished 1967, Historic American Buildings Survey, Library of Congress, Washington, D.C., http://memory.loc.gov/ammem/hhhtml/hhhome.html; Drinkers Court File, Delancey Street,

Philadelphia Historical Commission. For a definition of "neat" in the eighteenth century, see Carl R. Lounsbury, ed., *An Illustrated Glossary of Early Southern Architecture and Landscape* (New York, 1994), 240: "Frequently joined with plain in 18th-century usage, this term connoted a substantial, workmanlike quality, a simple sufficiency, an absence of extraneous ornament."

19 Pamela Herrick, "Reconstructing the Social and Architectural Landscape of Southwark, Philadelphia, 1795–1800" (master's thesis, University of Delaware, 1991); Tinkcom, "Southwark, a River Community: Its Shape and Substance," APS, *Proceedings,* CXIV (1970), 327–342; Herrick, "Mead Alley: Philadelphia: Urbanization in the Early Nineteenth-Century City," MS, 1989.

20 Dell Upton, *Holy Things and Profane: Anglican Parish Churches in Colonial Virginia* (New York, 1986), 101–102. I am indebted to Robin Thornes, formerly of the Royal Commission on Historical Monuments of England, for sharing his research and insights into Whitby's vernacular buildings.

21 Roger Leech, *Early Industrial Housing: The Trinity Area of Frome* (London, 1981); M. W. Beresford, *East End, West End: The Face of Leeds during Urbanisation, 1684–1842* (Leeds, 1988), 180–202; Ivan Hall and Elizabeth Hall, *A New View of Georgian Hull* (York, 1979), 13, 17; Andrew White, *The Buildings of Georgian Lancaster* (Lancaster, 1992), 33.

22 Inventory for Joseph Hambury (1804), Suffolk County, Mass., Probate Court, CII, 394–395.

23 Inventory for William Moore (1801), ibid., XCIX, 546–547.

24 Inventory for Samuel Aves (1800), ibid., XCVIII, 29–30, inventory for Jeremiah Smallage (1803), CI, 686–688.

25 Inventory for Samuel Baker (1807), Inventories and Sales, United States District Court for the District of Columbia, entry 119, HCN1 (July 27, 1805–Nov. 2, 1823), 19; inventory for Jeremiah Hemworth (1821), 43.

26 Richard Walsh, *Charleston's Sons of Liberty: A Study of the Artisans, 1763–1789* (Columbia, S.C., 1959), 3–26. For distortions in the distribution of wealth, see David A. Smith, "Dependent Urbanization in Colonial America: The Case of Charleston, South Carolina," *Social Forces,* LXVI (1987–1988), 1–29. For information on the Saylor House, see Jonathan H. Poston, *The Buildings of Charleston: A Guide to the City's Architecture* (Charleston, S.C., 1997), 116–117. See also Saylor House Research File, Historic Charleston Foundation, Charleston, S.C.

27 Poston, *The Buildings of Charleston,* 130–131.

28 Inventory for John Douglas (1805), Charleston County Inventories, Book D (1800–1810), 373–374.

29 Inventory for Aaron Fairchild (1809), ibid., 522, inventory for John Eddy (1805), 328–329.

30 Blumin, *The Emergence of the Middle Class,* 67–68; inventory for Thomas Baas (1809), Charleston County Inventories, Book D (1800–1810), 520–521; inventory for Jean Desbeaux (1801), 289–290.

31 John T. Kirk, *American Furniture: Understanding Styles, Construction, and Quality* (New York, 2000), 79. For slaveholding patterns in Norfolk, see Thomas C. Parramore, Peter C. Stewart, and Tommy L. Bogger, *Norfolk: The First Four Centuries* (Charlottesville, Va., 1994), 119–131. Inventory for Richard Lewelling Inventory (July 27, 1802), Borough of Norfolk, Will Book 2, 129; inventory for John Mitchell (Feb. 26, 1802), 102–104.

32 Inventory for Finlay Ferguson (Aug. 26, 1812), Will Book 3, 72–73. A number of individuals have addressed the fluid and hierarchical nature of eighteenth- and early-nineteenth-century artisan society. See Christine Daniels, "'Wanted: A Blacksmith Who Understands Plantation Work': Artisans in Maryland, 1700–1810," *William and Mary Quarterly,* 3d Ser., L (1993), 743–767; Lisa B. Lubow, "From Carpenter to Capitalist: The Business of Building in Postrevolutionary Boston," in Conrad Edick White and Katheryn P. Viens, eds., *Entrepreneurs: The Boston Business Community, 1700–1850* (Boston, 1997), 180–209; Blumin, *The Emergence of the Middle Class,* 138–191.

33 Inventory for William Palmer, City of Philadelphia Wills, Administration no. 235 (Sept. 20, 1815), City Hall Archives, Philadelphia.

34 M. Elizabeth Appleby, "Thomas Rimer of Number 10 Carter's Alley: A Philadelphia Shoemaker and Proposed Furnishing Plan for His Residence," MS, 1994. Appleby links a variety of disparate primary sources into a provocative reconstruction of Thomas Rimer's material world.

35 Candee, *Building Portsmouth,* 114–115; James Leo Garvin, "Academic Architecture and the Building Trades in the Piscataqua Region of New Hampshire and Maine, 1715–1815"

(Ph.D. diss., Boston University, 1983), 435–437; database linking Wibird Penhallow, *The Portsmouth Directory, Containing Names of the Inhabitants, Their Occupations, Places of Business, and Dwelling Houses* (Portsmouth, N.H., 1822) and "Invoice of Polls and Taxable Property on which the Taxes for the Town of Portsmouth are assessed for the Year 1823," Portsmouth Public Library.

36 Wayne Craven, *Colonial American Portraiture: The Economic, Religious, Social, Cultural, Philosophical, Scientific, and Aesthetic Foundations* (Cambridge, 1986), 334–336; Gary B. Nash, *The Urban Crucible: Social Change, Political Consciousness, and the Origins of the American Revolution* (Cambridge, Mass., 1979), xii, 374–375; Sean Wilentz, *Chants Democratic: New York City and the Rise of the American Working Class, 1788–1850* (New York, 1984), 23–60.

37 Portsmouth, N.H., inventories: for Joseph Walker (January 1824), Rockingham County Wills and Inventories, Docket 8817 o.s., Exeter, N.H.; for Robert Harold (January 1792), Docket 5743 o.s.

38 Inventory for William Butler (1822), United States District Court for the District of Columbia, entry 119, Inventories and Sales, HCN1 (July 27, 1805–Nov. 2, 1823), 236.

CHAPTER SEVEN

1 Richard Brush (Nov. 12, 1804), Suffolk County, Mass., Wills and Inventories, CII, 488.

2 Inventory for Joshua Martin (1794), PTR III, 252A, Rockingham County, N.H., Probate Records.

3 Inventory for Thomas Finley (1799), Charleston County, S.C., Inventories, Book C, 392–393.

4 Inventory for Charles Willet (Oct. 7, 1807), Norfolk, Va., Will Book 2, 369, Norfolk, Va., Probate Court.

5 Inventory for James Barry (1821), Middlesex County, Mass., Wills and Inventories, Docket #1325; inventory for Lawrence Lindberg (Dec. 23, 1805), mariner, Borough of Norfolk, Will Book 2, 300–301.

6 Erving Goffman, *The Presentation of Self in Everyday Life* (Garden City, N.Y., 1959), 106–109.

7 Walter Charlton Hartridge, ed., *The Letters of Robert Mackay to His Wife: Written from Ports in America and England, 1795–1816* (Athens, Ga., 1949), 197, 201.

8 Bernard L. Herman, "The Embedded Landscapes of the Charleston Single House, 1780–1820," in Annmarie Adams and Sally McMurry, eds., *Experiencing Everyday Landscapes, Perspectives in Vernacular Architecture, VII* (Knoxville, Tenn., 1997), 43; Hartridge, ed., *The Letters of Robert Mackay*, 194.

9 For almshouse lodgings, see David J. Rothman, *The Discovery of the Asylum: Social Order and Disorder in the New Republic* (Glenview, Ill., 1971), 180–205; Monique C.-E. Bourque, "Virtue, Industry, and Independence: Almshouses and Labor in the Philadelphia Region, 1791–1860" (Ph.D. diss., University of Delaware, 1995), 120–123. For itinerant accommodations, see Billy G. Smith, *The "Lower Sort": Philadelphia's Laboring People, 1750–1800* (Ithaca, N.Y., 1990), 167–168.

10 Thomas Cooper, *Some Information respecting America* (London, 1794), 80–84.

11 Barbara G. Carson, *Ambitious Appetites: Dining, Behavior, and Patterns of Consumption in Federal Washington* (Washington, D.C., 1990), 138, 140; Orlando Ridout V, *Building the Octagon* (Washington, D.C., 1989), 24–29; Bernard L. Herman, "Franklin's Houses," in Carla Mulford and David S. Shields, eds., *Finding Colonial Americas: Essays Honoring J. A. Leo Lemay* (Newark, Del., 2001), 250–254.

12 The documentation for Margaret Stephenson's Craven Street house, recorded by the Greater London Council, resides in the National Monuments Record, Swindon. I am indebted to Anna-Marie Pagano and Leo Lemay for access to and information on Franklin's lodgings. Herman, "Franklin's Houses," in Mulford and Shields, eds., *Finding Colonial America*, 249–260.

13 Carson, *Ambitious Appetites*, 138.

14 Harriet P. Simons and Albert Simons, "The William Burrows House of Charleston," *Winterthur Portfolio*, III, 181–186; Thomas Hamilton (1832) quoted, 187.

15 L. G. Moffatt and J. M. Carrière, eds., "A Frenchman Visits Norfolk, Fredericksburg, and Orange County, 1816, Part 1," *Virginia Magazine of History and Biography*, LIII (1945), 111.

16 Anne Ritson, *A Poetical Picture of America, Being Observations Made during Several Years at Alexandria and Norfolk, in Virginia* (London, 1809), 69–73.

17 Tavern names were gleaned from John Nagy, ed. and comp., *The Pennsylvania Gazette, 1728–1800*, fols. I–IV (1991–), www.accessible.com.

18 The statistics for Fells Point are compiled from the 1798 Federal Direct Tax Census for Baltimore (Maryland Historical Society, Baltimore), various street directories compiled between 1798 and 1810, and insurance surveys in the collection of the Equitable Insurance Company (still operating in Baltimore).

19 Boston information was compiled from the 1798 Federal Direct Tax Census transcribed and printed in Boston, Record Commissioners, Twenty-second Report, *A Report of the Record Commissioners of the City of Boston, Containing the Statistics of the United States' Direct Tax of 1798, as Assessed on Boston; and the Names of the Inhabitants of Boston in 1790 as Collected for the First National Census* (Boston, 1890), and from the Boston Directory Database, 1789–1809, developed by the Massachusetts Historical Society, Boston. Philadelphia evidence came from the 1798 Federal Direct Tax Census for Philadelphia's High Street Ward, National Archives, Washington, D.C.; Manuscript Federal Census Returns from 1800 and 1810, National Archives; and street directories published from 1798 through 1810.

20 Robert F. Looney, *Old Philadelphia in Early Photographs, 1839–1914: 215 Prints from the Collection of the Free Library of Philadelphia* (New York, 1976), 21; Jonathan H. Poston, *Buildings of Charleston: A Guide to the City's Architecture* (Columbia, S.C., 1997), 65–66; Philip Bergen, *Old Boston in Early Photographs, 1850–1918: 174 Prints from the Collection of the Bostonian Society* (New York, 1990), 27, 44.

21 David W. Conroy, *In Public Houses: Drink and the Revolution of Authority in Colonial Massachusetts* (Chapel Hill, N.C., 1995), 111–113; Peter Thompson, *Rum Punch and Revolution: Taverngoing and Public Life in Eighteenth-Century Philadelphia* (Philadelphia, 1999), 56–60; Patricia Cleary, "'She Will Be in the Shop': Women's Sphere of Trade in Eighteenth-Century Philadelphia and New York," *Pennsylvania Magazine of History and Biography,* CXIX (1995), 183–202; Karin Wulf, *Not All Wives: Women of Colonial Philadelphia* (Ithaca, N.Y., 2000), 101–102; M. Dorothy George, *London Life in the Eighteenth Century* (1925; London, 1966), 100–101. Information on Humber Ward tavernkeepers in R. G. Battle, *Battle's Original Hull Directory, for the Year 1803, Containing . . . the Names, Together with the Residences of the Gentlemen, Merchants, and Tradesmen, in Hull* (Hull, 1803).

22 See directory databases for Charleston (1822), Portsmouth (1821–1823), Southwark East, Philadelphia (1798–1800), Norfolk (1800–1801). See also Battle, *Battle's Original Hull Directory, for the Year 1803.* For additional information on the development of Humber Ward, see C. W. Chalklin, *The Provincial Towns of Georgian England: A Study of the Building Process, 1740–1820* (Montreal, 1974), 213–216.

23 Inventory for Mary Hughes (1803), Charleston County Inventories, Book D, 205; inventory for Jane Boyle (1803), 206; inventory for Dennis Hagarthy (1802), 143.

24 Inventory for James Bickerton (1803), Book 1, 79, City of Philadelphia. The description of Bickerton's house comes from the 1798 Federal Direct Tax Census, National Archives, and the 1799 local property assessments for Southwark East and West, Philadelphia Archives.

25 Inventory for René Godard (1785), Charleston County Inventories, Book A, 400–401.

26 Virginia Mutual Assurance Surveys (VMAS), VI, no. 139 (1796), VII, no. 246 (1798), VIII, no. 335 (1802), no. 337 (1802), Virginia State Library, Richmond.

27 *American Gazette* (Norfolk), May 6, 1796; VMAS Declarations, VI, no. 15 (1796). Martha Street apparently assumed management of the Eagle Tavern in 1793 when the former operator, James Dickenson, vacated the premises. *Virginia Chronicle and, Norfolk and Portsmouth General Advertiser,* Feb. 2, 1793.

28 Inventory for Benjamin Street (1797), Borough of Norfolk, Will Book 1, 150–151.

29 "A Plan of a Lot of Land . . . Belonging to John McCrady Esq.," Charleston County, S.C., Deed Book C-7, 386–[387]; Martha A. Zierden, Elizabeth Reitz, Michael Trinkley, and Elizabeth Paysinger, *Archaeological Excavations at McCrady's Longroom,* Charleston Museum, Archaeological Contributions, no. 3 (Charleston, S.C., 1982), 5–10; Mark Girouard, *The English Town: A History of Urban Life* (New Haven, Conn., 1990), 127–144; David S. Shields, *Civil Tongues and Polite Letters in British America* (Chapel Hill, N.C., 1997), 141–174.

30 Zierden, Reitz, Trinkley, and Paysinger, *Archaeological Excavations at McCrady's Longroom,* 11–20, 43–44, 63–70, 78–82.

31 *Pennsylvania Gazette,* Jan. 3, 1776, *The Pennsylvania Gazette, 1728–1800,* fols. I–IV (1991–), www.accessible.com.

32 Robert Earle Graham, "The Taverns of Colonial Philadelphia,"

in *Historic Philadelphia: From the Founding until the Early Nineteenth Century,* American Philosophical Society, *Transactions,* XLIII, part 1 (1953), 323. An advertisement in the *Pennsylvania Gazette,* Apr. 7, 1773, describes newly built premises, apparently the city tavern, in some detail: "Intended to be kept as a genteel tavern; it contains several large club rooms, two of which being thrown into one make a spacious room of near fifty feet in length, for public entertainment: There are likewise several commodious lodging rooms, for the accommodation of strangers, two large kitchens, and every other conveniency for the purpose."

33 Graham, "The Taverns of Colonial Philadelphia," in *Historic Philadelphia,* APS, *Transactions,* XLIII, part 1 (1953), 324; Kym S. Rice, *Early American Taverns: For the Entertainment of Friends and Strangers* (Chicago, 1983), 31–42; Ethelyn Cox, *Historic Alexandria, Virginia, Street by Street: A Survey of Existing Buildings* (Alexandria, Va., 1976), 152–153.

34 Kenneth Finkel, *Nineteenth-Century Photography in Philadelphia: 250 Historic Prints from the Library Company of Philadelphia* (New York, 1980), 73; Poston, *The Buildings of Charleston,* 129.

35 Dell Upton, "Another City: Urban Cultural Landscape in the Early Republic," in Catherine E. Hutchins, ed., *Everyday Life in the Early Republic* (Winterthur, Del., 1994), 103.

36 For the ways in which a formal ceremony could be appropriated to unsanctioned uses, see John Wood, *A Description of the Exchange of Bristol: Wherein the Ceremony of Laying the First Stone of That Structure, Together with That of Opening the Building for Publick Use Is Particularly Recited* (Bath, 1745), 35–36. For Rush's text on the dauphin's birthday party and its significance to the rites of socialbility, see Shields, *Civil Tongues and Polite Letters,* 1–10. Key works on processional culture include Susan G. Davis, *Parades and Power: Street Theatre in Nineteenth-Century Philadelphia* (Philadelphia, 1986); Dell Upton, "White and Black Landscapes in Eighteenth-Century Virginia," in Robert Blair St. George, ed., *Material Life in America, 1600–1800* (Boston, 1988), 357–369; Mary Ryan, "The American Parade: Representations of the Nineteenth-Century Social Order," in Lynn Hunt, ed., *The New Cultural History* (Berkeley, Calif., 1989), 131–153.

The best works on this arena of material behavior in the antebellum period, especially related to dress and the transgression of social authority, remain Upton, "Another City," in Hutchins, ed., *Everyday Life in the Early Republic;* Christine Stansell, *City of Women: Sex and Class in New York, 1789–1860* (Urbana, Ill., 1987), 91–95.

37 Inventory of James Stenson (1784), Charleston County Inventories, Book A, 262–263; Stewart, *On Longing,* 148–150. See also Mark Antliff and Patricia Leighten, "Primitive," in Robert S. Nelson and Richard Shiff, eds., *Critical Terms for Art History* (Chicago, 1996), 170–184; Frances S. Connelly, *The Sleep of Reason: Primitivism in Modern European Art and Aesthetics, 1725–1907* (University Park, Pa., 1995), 120–121.

38 Joseph Moore's cowrie shell snuffbox is located in the Charleston Museum, acc. no. 1926.60 (2385). Little is known about Joseph Moore other than his death date of 1813 and his occupation gleaned from the city street directories. The snuffbox is inscribed "J. Moore" on the lid and bears a maker's mark inside the lid of "P" boxed within a square.

39 Theresa A. Singleton, "The Archaeology of Slave Life," in Edward D. C. Campbell, Jr., and Kym S. Rice, eds., *Before Freedom Came: African-American Life in the Antebellum South* (Richmond, Va., 1991), 157–158; Jan Hogendorn and Marion Johnson, *The Shell Money of the Slave Trade* (Cambridge, 1986), 2–3, 109–113.

40 Inventory for Thomas Manning (1819), Rockingham County, N.H., Probate Court, Docket 9908 o.s., Exeter, N.H. The Mendenhall site colono pot is in the archaeological collections of the Delaware Bureau of Museums, Dover; the ceramic history of the site is discussed in Bernard L. Herman, "Multiple Materials, Multiple Meanings: The Fortunes of Thomas Mendenhall," *Winterthur Portfolio,* XIX (1984), 73–83. See also Stewart, *On Longing,* 151–154.

CHAPTER EIGHT

1 Edward Hirsch, *How to Read a Poem: And Fall in Love with Poetry* (New York, 1999), 31.

2 Dell Upton, "Ethnicity, Authenticity, and Invented Traditions," *Historical Archaeology,* XXX, no. 2 (1996), 1–7.

3 Michel de Certeau, *The Practice of Everyday Life,* trans. Steven

Rendall (Berkeley, Calif., 1984); Erving Goffman, *The Presentation of Self in Everyday Life* (Garden City, N.Y., 1959).

4 Robert Plant Armstrong, *The Affecting Presence: An Essay in Humanistic Anthropology* (Urbana, Ill., 1971), 4. For debates on this relationship, see Michael Owen Jones, *The Hand Made Object and Its Maker* (Berkeley, Calif., 1975), 202–242; Henry Glassie, *Material Culture* (Bloomington, Ind., 1999), 184–186.

5 Edgar P. Richardson, Brooke Hindle, and Lillian B. Miller, *Charles Willson Peale and His World* (New York, 1983), 73–79.

Index

Folios for illustrations are in italics.

Hillis, Samuel, 187–188
Hirsch, Edward, 262
Hogarth, William, 202, *204–205*
Holmes, Benjamin, Jr., 112, 155
Holmes, Benjamin, house (Portsmouth, N.H.), 112–113, *112–113*
Holmes, James, 162
Holmes, James, house (Portsmouth, N.H.), 162, *162*
Holmes, Mary, 162
Hooker, Edward, 3
Hospitality toward travelers, 234, 238, 240, 251–252, 255
Hotels, 235, 253–254. *See also* Boardinghouses; Lodgings
Houses: design of, 21–24, 26–28; advertisements for, 47, 150–151; and separation of commercial and domestic spaces, 47, 65, 88, 99, 103, 105–106, 108, 123, 173–174, 219, 221; shoddy construction of, 53; dower divisions of, 155–161, 164–167, 169–171, 172–174, 176–178, 183–184, 188–191
Howe, Mr. (grocer), 119–120
Hughes, Mary, 247
Hughes boardinghouse (Charleston, S.C.), 247
Hull, Eng., 61–62, 69, 211, 245

Indian Queen Inn (Philadelphia), 253
Ingliss, George, 152
Inns, 237, 253. *See also* Taverns
Inn signs, 243
Insured houses, 45, 265
Ipswich, Mass., 8
Iremonger, Penelope, 140, 277n. 17
Iremonger house (London), 140–142

Jackson Court houses (Philadelphia), 205, 207

Johns, Kensey, 6, 23–24, 26–28
Johns, Kensey, house (New Castle, Del.), 6, *22–25, 23–28*
Johns, Mary, 207
Johns, Matthew, 207
Johns, Matthew, house (Philadelphia), 207–208
Johnson-Poinsett house (Charleston, S.C.), 221
Jones, Jehu, 239
Jones boardinghouse (Charleston, S.C.), 239–240
Justice house (Philadelphia), *197*
Justis, Peter, 23

Kindness, Rebecca, 244
Kindness boardinghouse (Boston), 244
King, Nicholas, 116
King's Head Tavern (Boston), 245
Kitchens, 137, 143, 147, 151, 185, 208, 277n. 20; in outbuildings, 43–44, 57, 140; with quarters, 121, 123–135, 143, 149–150; in cellars, 137, 140, 143, 207, 223–224; and dowers, 167, 170, 174, 177–178
Kitchen yards, 150, *151*, 152
Knapp, John, 189
Knapp, Mary, 189–190
Knapp house (Newburyport, Mass.), 189, *189*

Lamparter house (Lancaster, Pa.), 85, *86*
Lancaster, Pa.: houses in, 70–71, 77–97; Center Square, 80, *82*; courthouse in, 80–82; cityscape of, 80–85, *81*, 95, 98; Mussertown, 84–85, 95; Adamstown, 95
Langdon mansion (Portsmouth, N.H.), 161, *161*
Langley, Edward, 117

Langley house (Washington, D.C.), *116*, 117
Lathrop, John, 7
Lathrop house (Boston), 20
Latrobe, Benjamin Henry, 51–53, 81–82, *82*, 273n. 4
Lavergne, Latitia, 182
Lawrence, Elizabeth, 186
Lawrence house (Philadelphia), 186
Leeds, Eng., 211
Legare house (Charleston, S.C.), 65–67, *67–68*, 125
Leighton, John, 197–198
Leighton house (Portsmouth, N.H.), 108, 197–198, *199*
Lewelling, Richard, 223
Lewelling house (Norfolk, Va.), 223
Limehouse estate (Charleston, S.C.), *125*
Lindberg, Lawrence, 233
Livingston, Ann, 54
Livingston houses (Norfolk, Va.), 54
Lock, John, 166
Locke, James, Jr., 191
Lodgings, 50–51, 232–235, 237–256; accounts of, 47–49, 239–243; and women, 188, 195, 197, 237–238, 244–247; personalization of, 232–235, 239; drinking rooms in, 249–252
London, Eng.: houses in, 10, 12, 14–15, *14–15*, 69, 140–142; lodgings in, 237–238, 245
London Coffee House (Philadelphia), 255
Long rooms, 252–253
Loyall, Paul, 54
Loyall houses (Norfolk, Va.), 54–55
Lyricism of urban space, 262–264

McCrady, Edward, 252
McCrady's Tavern (Charleston, S.C.), 252–253, *253*
McKay, Eliza Anne, 234